Dounia

Revue d'intelligence stratégique

et des relations internationales

Kinshasa, Bruxelles, Paris

Juillet 2016

Une publication du Centre d'Intelligence Stratégique

et des Relations Internationales

 5-7, rue de l'École-Polytechnique, 75 005 Paris. ISBN : 978-2-343-10542-0

La transition de la R. D. Congo vers l'émergence économique

The D. R. of Congo transition towards an emerging economy

Numéro coordonné

par Jean-Marc Kilolo et André Nyembwe

Qualité des auteurs

Biographical notes

Bertrand ATEBA ☞ Titulaire d'un Ph.D. de l'Université de Pékin en Science Politique option Etudes Internationales, il est actuellement Chargé de Cours au Département de Science Politique de l'Université de Douala au Cameroun où il occupe par ailleurs les fonctions de Chef de Service des programmes d'enseignement à la Direction des Affaires Académiques et de la Coopération.

Thaddée BADIBANGA ☞ Postdoctoral at IFPRI fellow and Coordinator of IFPRI's DRC Strategy Support Program since 2011. He worked as Adjunct Professor at the College of Saint Benedict and Saint John University and at Hamline University (Minnesota). He received his Ph.D. in Applied Economics from the University of Minnesota. He is involved in research and policy advisory on sectoral policy and strategy issues related to the implementation of the Comprehensive Africa Agricultural Development Program.

Auguy BOLANDA MENGA ☞ Coordonnateur de la Cellule d'Appui aux Zones Economiques Spéciales (CAZES) en République démocratique du Congo.

Andrianasy DJISTERA ☞ Maitre de conférences en sciences économiques à l'université de Toamasina, à Madagascar.

Jean-Marc KILOLO MALAMBWE ☞ Docteur en sciences économiques de l'École Polytechnique, Paris et MBA de l'UQÀM, il est chercheur affilié à l'Université Pédagogique National en RDC.

Eliane MANYONGA MAJAMBO ☞ Assistante d'enseignement à la Faculté des sciences économiques et de gestion de l'Université de Kinshasa.

André NYEMBWE MUSUNGAIE ☞ Docteur en sciences économiques de l'Université catholique de Louvain, il est professeur de macroéconomie à l'Université de Kinshasa et professeur invité de politique macroéconomique à l'Université catholique de Louvain.

Serge SONGOLO ARUNA ☞ Assistant à la Faculté des sciences économiques et de gestion de l'Université de Goma.

Claude SUMATA ☞ Docteur en Sciences Economiques l'Université de Paris X-Nanterre, est Professeur d'Economie à l'Université Catholique du Congo et également Professeur visiteur à l'Université de Toulouse 1 Capitole/Toulouse, France. Il exerce aussi les fonctions de Consultant International en Macroéconomie. Il a enseigné aux Universités de Paris X-Nanterre, Paris II, Cergy-Pontoise, Maine/Le Mans, Lille II, Bikbeck College et SOAS (Université de Londres) et à l'Université de Surrey. Ses récents travaux sur la politique macroéconomique de la RD. Congo concernent la dynamique de la croissance et la réduction de la pauvreté.

John ULIMWENGU ☞ holds PhD in agricultural economics from Ohio State University. Research Fellow at the International Food Policy Research Institute, he is involved in research and policy advisory work on sector policy and strategy issues related to the implementation of the AU/NEPAD's Comprehensive Africa Agricultural Development Program (CAADP). He is currently advising the Prime Minister of the Democratic Republic of Congo in Agricultural and Rural Development.

Sommaire

Contents

La transition de la RDC vers le statut de pays émergent : le défi

Jean-Marc Kilolo & André Nyembwe

La croissance économique soutenue du Brésil, de la Russie, de l'Inde et de la Chine (membres du BRIC, sigle fait des premières lettres de leurs noms) retient l'attention de nombreux observateurs et fait l'objet d'une abondante littérature sur le sujet. Jadis connus pour leurs régimes communismes ou dictatoriaux ainsi pour des violations des droits humains (sauf pour l'Inde), ces pays sont aujourd'hui les porte-étendards du groupe des économies émergentes, considérées comme économiquement plus viables que le reste des pays en développement. Les dirigeants des pays du BRIC ont su jouer un rôle stratégique à travers des réformes et des politiques économiques qui ont permis le relèvement du niveau de vie moyen de leurs populations, même si d'une part, des disparités substantielles internes demeurent, et d'autre part, ce niveau de vie reste très en retrait par rapport au niveau moyen des pays dits développés. Ce « succès » inspire les décideurs de nombreux pays en développement, dont ceux la République démocratique du Congo (RDC), et suscite la définition de certains objectifs économiques pour assurer la transition vers le statut de pays emergent. Aux yeux des décideurs de la RDC, il semble possible de transformer une économie très peu diversifiée et fortement dépendante des exportations de matières premières en une économie émergente à l'horizon 2030[1].

Ce statut de pays émergent appelle à être circonscrit tant il est vrai que plu-

1. Le Président de la République Démocratique du Congo, Joseph Kabila, a dans son discours prononcé le 30 juin 2015 à Kinshasa réitéré cet objectif d'émergence pour 2030.

sieurs acceptions sont proposées par différents auteurs. Ces pays sont désignés comme « pays émergents », « marchés émergents » ou « économies émergentes ». La diversité des pays inclus dans cette catégorie ajoute également une certaine complexité rendant utile une précision sémantique.

La paternité du concept est attribuée à l'économiste néerlandais Antoine van Agtmael de la Société Financière Internationale (Banque Mondiale). Il a en 1981 évoqué l'expression « marchés émergents » pour désigner les pays en développement qui offrent des opportunités pour les investisseurs. Ainsi, la première acception de l'« émergence » se rapporte à l'existence des marchés financiers. Dans cette perspective, un pays dit émergent se caractérise par une croissance rapide et par la présence de marchés financiers capables d'absorber les investissements étrangers.

La compréhension qui découle aisément des diverses utilisations du concept suggère que les « pays émergents » affichent un PIB par habitant supérieur à ceux des autres pays en développement, mais inférieur à celui des pays développés. Ils connaissent une croissance économique rapide qui facilite la convergence de leur niveau de vie ainsi que les structures économiques vers ceux des pays développés.

La transformation des structures économiques suppose une diversification de l'activité économique et un basculement vers une participation différente de l'économie concernée dans la division internationale du travail. Ceci peut être réalisé à la suite des changements structurels, en l'occurrence des politiques publiques pluriannuelles axées sur des résultats, des réformes juridiques et institutionnelles, telle que l'ouverture au marché mondial des produits et services et aux flux internationaux de capitaux. Ces changements répondent aux exigences de compétitivité et d'attractivité pour saisir les opportunités qu'offrent les échanges mondiaux de biens et services d'une part, et de la valorisation financière, d'autre part.

Cavusgil (2012) propose une schématisation de l'évolution tendancielle des pays émergents au cours de la décennie 2000 d'un point du point de vue des affaires.

À partir du tableau ci-après, on peut se faire une idée des changements qu'un pays désireux d'intégrer la catégorie des économies émergentes devrait apporter à son environnement des affaires, et de l'impact de ce dernier sur la perception qu'ont les firmes, les investisseurs et les analystes du pays.

Il semble donc que le chemin à parcourir par la RDC sera pour le moins comparable à un défi énorme. S'il est vrai que ce pays manque encore des capacités technologiques de base, lesquelles sont à l'origine des mutations économiques profondes observées dans les pays dits émergents, la RDC partage les mêmes atouts que les pays du BRIC, en l'occurrence un important réservoir de main-d'œuvre ainsi que la richesse du sol et du sous-sol. Le point de départ en termes de dotations de ressources naturelles et humaines est donc encourageant.

Toutefois, l'histoire économique récente montre que la transition vers l'émergence est un processus qui se passe sur plusieurs décennies.[1] En effet, deve-

1. Nicet-Chenaf (2014) note que l'émergence de la Chine a démarré avec la politique « de la porte ouverte » initiée en 1978, tandis que celle de l'Inde, du Brésil ou du Chili est associée au délaissement des politiques de substitu-

TABLEAU 1

Transformations tendancielles dans les marchés émergents

PAYS EN DÉVELOPPEMENT AVANT 2000	MARCHÉS ÉMERGENTS (DÉCENNIE 2000 ET AU-DELÀ)
Risques élevés pour les affaires	Risques progressivement maîtrisés
Économiquement et technologiquement retardés	Technologiquement compétitifs
Faible pouvoir d'achat des consommateurs	Accroissement du pouvoir d'achat parmi les consommateurs
Peu d'opportunités d'affaires	Plusieurs opportunités d'affaire avec de larges marchés inexploités ainsi que des sources d'approvisionnement (inputs) à faible coût et de qualité.
Trajectoire de la croissance difficile à prédire	Croissance de revenu supérieure à celle des pays développés

Source : Cavusgil et al. (2012). Traduction par les auteurs.

nir une économie émergente requiert un « traitement de choc » basé sur une stratégie de développement à moyen et long terme. Une telle stratégie devrait se décliner en plusieurs politiques sectorielles ayant une trame commune. Des politiques macroéconomiques, industrielles, commerciales, etc. sont censées être accompagnées d'un approfondissement du secteur financier, condition sine qua non pour favoriser les investissements nécessaires à la transformation industrielle. Du reste, selon J. Sgard (2008 : 52-53), l'échec « des pays qui n'émergent pas du tout » - localisés pour la plupart en Afrique s'explique par les faillites multiples de l'État : financière, institutionnelle et politique. Il faudrait en conclure que les faiblesses financières, institutionnelles et l'instabilité politique sont de sérieux obstacles sur la route de l'émergence.

Les décideurs de la République démocratique du Congo posent les jalons d'une transformation économique, ne fut-ce qu'en termes d'intentions. Tout d'abord, le gouvernement s'est attelé à stabiliser le cadre macroéconomique afin d'envoyer des signaux positifs aux agents économiques, lesquels sont compatibles avec son but de favoriser une croissance durable. Par ailleurs, cette volonté d'industrialiser l'économie congolaise est aussi clairement exprimée à travers les réformes économiques et structurelles, notamment la création de zones économiques spéciales pour attirer les investissements étrangers ou encore la création de parcs agro-industriels. Ces deux mesures sont le prototype d'instruments visant à développer des pôles de compétitivité et de croissance afin de saisir les opportunités offertes par l'économie mondiale et

tions aux importations dans les années 1980 et une plus forte extraversion de l'économie.

nationale. Par ailleurs, la RDC endosse la stratégie d'intégration régionale pour un co-développement plus volontariste notamment dans la région des Grands Lacs (appartenance à la Communauté des Pays des Grands Lacs), l'Afrique centrale (appartenance à la Communauté Economique des Etats d'Afrique Centrale) ou l'Afrique australe (Appartenance à la Communauté des Etats d'Afrique Australe). Toutes ces initiatives s'inscrivent dans cette stratégie de transition vers le statut de pays émergent.

Pourtant, compte tenu des pesanteurs institutionnelles multiples sur l'économie congolaise comme le suggèrent les mauvais classements de la République démocratique du Congo (Doing Business, Transparency International, CPIA, indice de développement etc.), la route vers l'émergence est loin d'être simple. En effet, le mauvais état des infrastructures, la faiblesse du système financier, le dysfonctionnement de l'administration, la détérioration du système éducatif et, ce faisant, la dépréciation du capital humain, posent de sérieux défis. Il s'avère nécessaire de mener une analyse approfondie de la situation de la RDC et des politiques envisagées afin de s'assurer de la cohérence, la pertinence et l'efficience dans l'allocation des ressources consécutive à la stratégie d'émergence qui se dessine. Le contenu des contributions des auteurs proposées dans la suite contribue à ce processus nécessaire d'analyse. À travers un prisme multidisciplinaire, il met à la disposition des décideurs de la RDC une grille de lecture pouvant leur permettre de poursuivre, rectifier les politiques mises en place ou innover afin de maximiser les chances d'aboutissement de la transition vers le statut de pays émergent.

Ce huitième numéro de Dounia, revue internationale d'intelligence stratégique et des relations internationales, est donc consacré à la transition de la R.D. Congo vers le statut d'économie émergente. Son objectif spécifique est de rendre compte des préalables structurels et des politiques concrètes à mettre ou mises sur pied par le gouvernement congolais en vue d'assurer une croissance économique soutenue. Il présente des diagnostics sectoriels et des propositions inspirées de l'expérience internationale.

La première question abordée dans ce volume est celle des déterminants de la transformation structurelle de l'économie congolaise. En effet, dans le premier article de ce volume intutilé *Determinants of Structural Transformation of the Congolese Economy*, Thaddee Badibanga et John M. Ulimwengu montrent que la diversification et la sophistication (spécialisation) de la production ou des exportations d'un pays sont facteurs conjoints de succès d'un processus de transformation économique sain. Selon ces auteurs, la faible performance économique de la RDC sur la période 1962-2008 s'explique par une spécialisation dans des produits à faible valeur marchande. Ils recommandent aux décideurs congolais de suivre l'exemple des pays comme l'Indonésie, la Malaisie et la Thaïlande qui n'ont pas tout de suite visé la diversification à travers la productions des biens très élaborés avec des avantages comparatifs substantiels, mais on plutôt opté pour une évolution par étape. Ils ont d'abord lancé la production de biens moins élaborés avant d'investir plus tard dans le développement des produits et la recherche et développement pour créer des avantages comparatifs au fil du temps. Pour atteindre leurs performances spectaculaires, ces pays ont eu pour stratégie d'attirer des firmes étrangères qui développent les biens de transition dans des zones économiques spéciales créées à cette fin. Par effet d'entraînement, ces firmes ont développé des marchés locaux d'approvisionnement en intrants. Le développement de l'échange d'information et de technologies entre les firmes étrangères et des centres de recherche locaux a complété le dispositif stratégique.

Après l'étude des déterminants, Andrianasy Djistera souligne l'importance du capital humain dans le processus d'accumulation des richesses. Dans son étude, *Le capital humain et la trajectoire économique de la République Démocratique du Congo*, il montre, chiffres à l'appui, le faible niveau d'instruction de la population active congolaise ; ce qui s'explique notamment par le manque de financement des investissements éducatifs et par l'instabilité macroéconomique liée à la guerre. Il tire la conclusion selon laquelle l'insuffisance du capital humain en RDC limite le potentiel de croissance et de développement du pays. De son analyse, il ressort donc que sans une politique de formation professionnelle et technique adéquate ni un investissement plus conséquent et qualitatif dans l'éducation en général, le décollage vers l'émergence sera compromis.

Sur un autre plan du volet « facteur humain », Claude Sumata analyse l'apport des migrants congolais à l'économie congolaise. Son article, *La contribution de la diaspora* à *l'émergence de la RD Congo : la promotion de l'investissement dans le secteur privé*, montre que les investissements de la diaspora congolaise au profit de leur pays d'origine peuvent être des canaux de transmission de la croissance et du développement économique, à travers la création d'entreprises génératrices d'emplois. Toutefois, conclut-il, il est nécessaire de mettre sur pied des mesures incitatives en faveur de la diaspora pour mieux canaliser leurs ressources dans l'optique de la création d'une classe moyenne d'entrepreneurs.

Dans sa contribution *Les défis de la transformation économique de la RD Congo*, Jean-Marc Kilolo Malambwe discute des facteurs de succès des politiques industrielles. Il en identifie trois, à savoir le positionnement dans la chaîne des valeurs, la localisation des activités économiques ainsi que la qualification de la main-d'œuvre. Selon l'auteur, il convient de progresser dans la chaîne des valeurs dans le secteur des mines et dans l'agriculture, notamment en raffinant des minerais à l'intérieur du pays au lieu d'exporter les produits bruts. À l'image des pays du BRIC, le succès de la stratégie d'industrialisation du gouvernement devrait s'appuyer sur une main-d'œuvre suffisante et adéquatement qualifiée, mais aussi sur des entrepreneurs locaux.

Dans leur article conjoint, *Les zones économiques spéciales en République* Démocratique *du Congo*, Serge Songolo, Auguy Bolanda et Eliane Manyonga présentent les avantages de la politique de ZES, s'inspirant de l'expérience internationale, notamment de la Chine et de l'Inde. Cet article présente également les 4 grands axes de développement tels que défini par le gouvernement ainsi que les activités économiques qui y seront menées. Les auteurs identifient également quelques obstacles potentiels au succès; il s'agit des contraintes institutionnelles ainsi que le mauvais état des infrastructures. En raison des avantages qu'ils offrent aux opérateurs économiques, les ZES devraient servir d'instrument pour attirer les investissements directs étrangers (IDE) en RDC.

Cet ambitieux programme requiert, bien évidemment, un approvisionnement adéquat en énergie, puisque l'activité industrielle est, par essence même, énergivore. L'absence de politique énergétique et l'obsolescence du système d'alimentation électrique occasionnent de graves problèmes d'approvisionnement en électricité, ce qui constitue une hypothèque sur la transformation économique de la RDC. Dans son deuxième article intitulé *Le rôle stratégique du secteur énergétique dans la transformation économique de la RDC*, Jean-Marc Kilolo Malambwe démontre le lien existant entre la consommation d'électricité et la croissance économique, d'une part, et celui entre la consommation d'électricité et l'IDE, d'autre part. On est dès lors plus conscient de la nécessité pour les décideurs congolais de relever le défi énergétique avant de prétendre à quelque forme d'ambition d'émergence.

Partant du postulat selon lequel les institutions internationales sont les arènes d'expression de la puissance des Etats et que ceux-ci n'agissent qu'en fonction de leurs seuls intérêts, Bertrand Ateba considère qu'il y a lieu d'être peu optimiste par rapport à une émergence économique des pays pauvres par la vertu de la gouvernance mondiale. Dans son article, *Gouvernance mondiale et émergence*, M. Ateba défend l'idée que les pays candidats à l'émergence devraient mobiliser les moyens au plan national pour que l'émergence vienne affranchir l'humain de l'emprise de la misère et du mal être qui le caractérise dans les pays non industrialisés. À ce qu'il qualifie de « mauvaise gouvernance mondiale », il faudrait, dit-il, opposer la bonne gouvernance nationale et locale, c'est à ce prix que les pays pauvres atteindront cette émergence à laquelle tous les espoirs sont suspendus.

Références bibliographiques

Cavusgil et al. (2012), Doing Business in Emerging Markets, Second Edition, SAGE Publications Ltd.

Nicet-Chenaf, D. (2014), « Les pays émergents : performance ou développement ? », accessble sur http://www.laviedesidees.fr/Les-pays-emergents-performance-ou.html, le 4 mars 2014.

Sgard J., (2008), « Qu'est-ce qu'un pays émergent ? », in Jaffrelot C. (éd.), L'enjeu mondial, les pays émergents, Paris, Presses de Sciences Po-L'Express, p. 41-54.

Van Agtmael, A. (2007), « The emerging market century: how a new breed of world class companies is overtaking the world » (N.Y.: Free Press).

Determinants of Structural Transformation of the Congolese Economy

Thaddee Badibanga and John M. Ulimwengu*

Abstract

A healthy economic transformation process requires both diversification and sophistication (specialization) of the country's production or exports basket. History shows that countries that manage to achieve only one of these without the other fail to achieve a strong and development-enhancing transformation process. This is probably the case for the Democratic Republic of Congo whose structural transformation has been at best insignificant over 1962-2008. Indeed, the country's transformation process was characterized by a reverse-diversification and temporary specialization which may explain its limited economic performance despite its abundant natural resources. The high proportion of bad products as share of total number of products exported with comparative advantage (58.3% in 1962 and 78.0% in 2008) and the lack of transition from bad products to good products in the country's export basket explain why the DRC has been unable to reach the core of the product space through structural transformation of its economy.

Keywords: structural transformation, discovery, technological change, product space, production, export.

JEL Codes: F19, O14, O33, O40.

* Researchers at the International Food Policy Research Institute

1. Introduction

There is a theoretical as well as an empirical basis for the claim that structural transformation is a key to economic development. Defined as a gradual change in the output composition and value, successful structural transformation allows countries to increase their incomes and ultimately improve their overall wellbeing. By the same token, failed structural transformation may explain why countries that lag behind have been unable to catch up with developed countries.

The nature of structural transformation observed in the Democratic Republic of Congo is the result of weak or lack of diversification and specialization which are keys for insulating the economy against shocks and their devastating effects. The challenge for the DRC[1] is how to capitalize on its abundant natural resources in order to hasten the transformation of its economy so as to reduce poverty. Obviously, its endowment of mineral resources is not enough to trigger successful structural transformation, since this change also requires intangible resources, such as entrepreneurial spirit, R&D, information coordination, quality of governance, and a conducive economic environment. These resources are in rather short supply in the DRC.

In this paper, we use the product space approach (Hausmann *et. al.*, 2006; Hausmann and Klinger, 2006; Hidalgo et al, 2007) to analyze the key features of the DRC's sluggish economic transformation in the light of structural transformation occurring in economies such as Indonesia, Malaysia, and Thailand. More specifically, we construct an index of structural transformation *(IST)* and apply it to the United Nations Commodity Trade Statistics Database (UN-COMTRADE) in order to gauge the quality of the DRC's transformation process and compare it with those of the three successful countries mentioned above. Next, we investigate the determinants of structural transformation (the trends in the *IST*) of the DRC and the three successful countries to answer the following question:

Why have the countries included in the analysis (i.e., Indonesia, Malaysia, and Thailand) been successful than DRC in fostering growth and structural change and what can DRC learn from their structural transformation processes?

The choice of the three countries for comparison with the DRC is motivated by three criteria. First, each of the three countries was at the same level of development as the DRC's at the beginning of the process (i.e., in 1962) as it can be seen through their per capita GDP presented in Table 1. Next, the industry whose GDP share is used to gauge whether a country has structurally transformed or not was the smallest sector in Indonesia, Malaysia, and Thailand; but the second largest sector after services in DRC in 1962. Forty-seven years later (i.e., in 2008), per capita GDP was 30 percent of its 1962 levels in DRC, while it was 5 times higher in Indonesia, 17 times higher in Malaysia, and 8 times higher in Thailand. Finally, the economic structure in 2008 was totally

1. The DRC harbors abundant mineral resources such as copper, cobalt, zinc, tin, diamonds, gold, silver, coal, petroleum, Colombo tantalum, uranium, and many others. The country has also 6 percent of the world's forestry reserves, not to mention a very rich ecology and abundant hydrology, which can support various farming activities.

different from the 1962's for each of the four countries. For Indonesia, Malaysia, and Thailand, the industry has become the leading sector in terms of its contribution to the GDP whereas in DRC, not only it has shrunk but also it has become the lagging sector after agriculture and services. Thus, the process of each of the three countries can provide DRC with new insights into structural transformation.

Overall, the results confirm the dynamics reflected in the evolution of sectoral contribution to GDP (see Table 1), that is, Indonesia, Malaysia, and Thailand have achieved structural transformation while DRC has not. The *IST* of the DRC increased between 1962 and 1988 at an annual average rate of 6 percent, and then experienced stagnation (i.e., an average annual rate of growth of 0 percent) between 1988 and 2008. However, average annual rates of growth of the *IST* for the period 1962-2008 were 13.1 percent, 10.0 percent, and 18.0 percent for Indonesia, Malaysia, and Thailand, respectively.

The DRC structural transformation's counter performance has been determined by a diversification into less connected and low value products, and by armed conflicts and political instability that have prevented a sustain investment in product discovery. However, the results demonstrate that Indonesia, Malaysia, and Thailand experienced each a strong transformation process explained by a diversification into products across all types of products and by specialization through gradual upgrading of products.

The present study is similar to the analysis of structural transformation that Hausmann and Klinger (2007b) conducted for Chile, Hausmann and Klinger (2008) for Pakistan, Wagstaff and Maennling (2009) for Mozambique, Usui and Abdon (2010) for the Kyrgyz Republic, Felipe, Kumar, Usui and Abdon (2010) for China, and Badibanga *et. al.* (2009) for China, Malaysia, and Ghana. However, unlike previous studies, ours characterizes the DRC's structural transformation by explicitly identifying the factors that limit the diversification, upgrading, and specialization of its exports.

The rest of this paper is organized as follows. Section 2 reviews the literature of structural transformation. Section 3 highlights economic and institutional characteristics of the DRC from 1960 to 2008. Section 4 describes the methodology of product space, and develops the index of structural transformation (IST). Section 5 applies the IST to data to analyze the key features of the DRC's structural transformation and compare it with the Indonesia's, Malaysia's, and Thailand's. Section 6 specifies a model of structural transformation and estimates it to identify determinants of structural transformation of the DRC and the three successful countries selected for comparison. Section 7 discusses the results and the lessons the DRC can learn from the structural transformation of the three successful countries. Section 7 presents the concluding remarks.

2. Literature review

In the growth and economic development literature there exist many stylized facts and regularities about structural transformation processes; which numerous authors have highlighted over and over again. A consistent feature is that,

TABLE 1

Level of development (per capita GDP) and economic structures of selected countries in 1962 and 2008

Country	Per capita GDP (constant 2000 US $)		Sector contribution to GDP (%) (A = agriculture, I = industry, S = services)					
	1962	2008	1962			2008		
DRC	333.0	100.0	20.1	32.3	47.7	40.2	28.0	32.0
Indonesia	206.6	1,052.8	45.8	16.3	37.2	15.0	48.1	37.5
Malaysia	293.0	5,073.1	33.8	21.3	43.1	10.2	48.0	42.0
Thailand	342.3	2,608.5	34	20.9	45.1	12.0	44.1	44.2

Source: Constructed by the authors from the WDI 2010 and 2011

as countries develop, production shifts away from primary goods into more sophisticated manufactured goods and services. For example, Kuznets (1973) characterizes economic growth as a process where productivity rises and is associated with a high rate of structural transformation, where production shifts away from agriculture into non-agricultural activities–and at higher levels of income per capita the shift goes from industry to services–and the distribution of employment between different sectors of the economy changes–usually away from agriculture and into industry and services. Similarly, Chenery (1960) also finds that with industrialization the relative importance of manufacturing increases and the composition of industrial output changes. More recent literature on structural change has supported these earlier findings. Duarte and Restuccia (2010) find that the common path in the development of countries involves a decline in the share of hours devoted to agriculture, an inverted U-shape in the share of hours devoted to manufacturing, and an increase in the share of hours in services as income per capita rises. Moreover, McMillan and Rodrik (2011) and Duarte and Restuccia (2010) find that *"there are sizeable and systematic differences in sectoral growth rates"* and levels *"of labor productivity across countries*[1]*"*, and that countries with different levels of income are at different stages in the structural transformation process, with poorer countries at earlier stages of this process.

An interesting feature of these stylized facts is that these empirical regularities seem to hold not only between countries across different income levels, but also within countries across time. Kongsamut, Rebelo and Xie (2001) look at the evolution of shares of total employment, GDP and total consumption expenditures for the U.S. from 1869 to 1970. They find that for agriculture all of these indicators decline, they remain stable for manufacturing and they increase for services as income

1. Duarte and Restuccia (2010).

rises. Similarly, McMillan and Rodrik (2011) find a common U-shaped pattern for the ratio of agricultural to non-agricultural labor productivities both among countries across income levels and within countries across time.

Despite the consistency of these stylized facts, for many years macroeconomic growth models offered little explanation as to why these patterns arise and what the role of each sector was in economic development. Traditionally, the (neoclassical) macroeconomic growth literature treats the structure of the economy as an irrelevant byproduct of economic growth. However, structural change has little to no effect on the future growth potential of an economy. Recently, however, the persistence of these differences in economic structure and the observed lack of convergence between developing and developed economies have raised questions about the assumptions of the standard growth model, and there has been more interest in accounting for these structural differences and explaining how they might affect growth. New theoretical models have tried to explain these stylized facts. One strand of the literature tends to emphasize the role of non-homothetic preferences as the main explanation behind the stylized facts. Hence, as economies grow, non-homothetic preferences dictate a shift from primary products to other products – like manufactured products and services. These shifts in the demands for goods and services are then reflected in the supply structure of the economy. For example, Echevarria (1997) presents a model where non-homothetic preferences give way to sectoral differences that are consistent with the stylized facts. Nevertheless, the assumption of a specific type of preferences and the fact that these preferences are the main driver of the results is somewhat disappointing.

Other models emphasize technology's role in driving structural change. These models tend to highlight differences in technological change between sectors, which tend to drive sectoral shifts in the economy as countries move from low- to high-income levels. Baumol (1967) is a classic example of this type of model. More recently, Ngai and Pissarides (2007), who assume different growth rates of technological change among sectors (modeled as differences in sectoral Total Factor Productivity (TFP) growth rates) and show that, even with similar production functions across sectors, these differences in technological change drive structural change. While this kind of model does not necessarily rely on a specific assumption on preferences, they are still driven by an exogenous rate of technological change. There are other hybrid models, such as Rogerson (2008), that use a combination of non-homothetic preferences and differentiated sectoral technological change that also provide predictions broadly in line with the stylized facts.

A major shortcoming of both these strands of the literature is that they have more to do with explaining or accounting for the stylized facts mentioned before than with explaining the role structural change could have on economic growth. Hence, models that simply aim to explain structural change as the result of demand reduce structural change to a mere residual, or an exogenous byproduct of economic development. The explanatory models and technology-driven assumptions simply see the economic structure as a consequence of economic growth, stripping it of any explanatory power and *ex-ante* assuming its exogeneity. While the assumption of non-homothetic preferences might seem reasonable, there is still no way of knowing which utility function is the most adequate; moreover, it is likely that preferences are not the only driver of structural change. Furthermore, as Echavarria (1997) points out, making the rate of sectoral technical change endogenous is an important extension for these models.

Duarte and Restuccia (2010) recently revised these models in a way that not only tries to explain how structural differences arise, but also what role they might play in growth and how the latter depends on the former. While their general equilibrium model is one where the drivers of sectoral shifts are also non-homothetic preferences and differentiated sectoral productivity growth, structural change is endogenous to initial levels and changes in sectoral labor productivity. As such, there is some path-dependency in aggregate productivity growth and countries that achieve relatively high levels of labor productivity growth in manufacturing tend to converge faster on the aggregate productivity levels of the U.S.

The non-balanced growth model of Acemoglu and Guerrieri (2008) produces results consistent with observed patterns of sectoral differences and produces them without relying on exogenous technological change. The main drivers of non-balanced growth in their model are differences in factor proportions – different capital shares, capital deepening, and faster growth of capital than of labor – between sectors.[1] They show that with sectoral differences in factor proportion and capital deepening, there will be non-balanced growth and this result holds with endogenous technological change.[2] As with models of structural change based on non-homothetic preferences or differentiated technological change, this model is good at generating predictions in line with the observed stylized facts but does not offer clear implications for policy.

While theoretical models of structural change have become more sophisticated, accounting for more nuances in stylized facts and relaxing many of the previous standard assumptions, they still leave a number of important questions unanswered. First, the question of whether there is any room for policy intervention is not addressed. These models tend to imply that growth-enhancing structural change will happen as long as the assumptions of the model hold. These assumptions are non-monotonic preferences or differences in technological progress between sectors, over which there is little government or any other agent can do. Second, and even if there were room for policy intervention within these frameworks, it is not clear which market imperfections are binding and should be targeted first. Moreover, these models provide no insight as to which sectors would allow a developing country to grow faster and why.

There is a growing body of literature that addresses these issues more directly and puts manufacturing – par-

1. In their model, non-balanced growth happens even if there is balanced technological progress (i.e. technological change is identical between sectors).

2. They specify a model of technological change with spillovers of innovations.

ticularly specialization in high-end manufactured products – as one of the main driving forces behind economic development. Its main argument is that structural change drives economic development and that manufacturers play a key role and driving growth-enhancing structural change.[1] Rodrik (2007) presents some stylized facts about economic development and develops a model that puts structural change as the main driving force of economic development. Rodrik's model also highlights non-traditional manufacturing's central role as a driver of economic growth and structural transformation.[2] He identifies a number of regularities in the empirical literature of growth and structural change. First and foremost, he highlights manufacturing's role in economic development by pointing out that not only do countries with a relatively large manufacturing sector grow faster than those with a relatively small one, but also that instances where the structure of the economy has moved toward manufacturing are associated with faster growth. Fagerberg (2000) shows that countries that have been able to move into production of the most technologically advanced manufactured products – electronics – ave had higher-than--average aggregate productivity growth. Similarly, Duarte and Restuccia (2010) show that, while catch-up in labor productivity in agriculture helps reduce the differential in aggregate productivity between developed[3] and developing countries, catch-up in manufacturing does so by a much higher proportion.

Another fact put forward by Rodrik (2007) is that, contrary to what many neoclassical trade models would predict, economic growth and development is achieved through diversification and not specialization. Rodrik cites work by Imbs and Wacziarg (2003), who empirically show that economic development implies first, diversification into different sectors and, only at relatively high per capita income levels, specialization. They find that this pattern holds across countries, income levels and time. It also holds within countries. Moreover, this same pattern arises within manufacturing, with less-developed economies first expanding the set of manufactured products they produce and only at a much later stage of development, specializing in certain manufactured products. Rodrik (2007) also argues that there seems to be path-dependence in industrialization patterns, and higher diversification raises the likelihood of successful transition to new economic activities or into the production of new goods. Furthermore, based on findings by Hausmann *et al.* (2007), Rodrik (2007) notes that countries that are able to produce and export more sophisticated goods grow faster. So developing countries should try to increase the number of manu-

1. We borrow this term from McMillan and Rodrik (2011). The term "structural change" is neutral; it can equally refer to the shift of resources from low-productivity activities to high-productivity activities (growth-enhancing) or the shift of resources from high-productivity to low-productivity activities (growth-reducing). We thus distinguish between growth-enhancing structural change and growth-reducing structural change.

2. Rodrik (2007) refers to non-traditional manufactures as those manufactures typically produced by developed ("rich") countries and not by developing ("poor") countries. While this definition is somewhat vague, "rich country" manufactures tend to be more sophisticated (e.g. electronics) and "poor country" manufactures tend to be less so (e.g. cotton fabric).

3. In their paper Duarte and Restuccia (2010) use the U.S. as the benchmark.

factured goods they produce and such diversification will raise the chances for a successful structural transformation.

Two additional observations by Rodrik (2007) also have implications for policy. First, factor endowments do not necessarily determine the type of products a country can produce. Second, convergence in productivity levels in individual manufactured products does not depend on country-specific characteristics and, the convergence speed is fast. So, there is room for policy to help shape growth-enhancing structural transformation.

Recent works by Hausmann and Klinger (2006, 2007a) and Hidalgo *et al.* (2007) draw from Rodrik's (2007) observations about economic development and diversification, and further expand the idea that the manufacturing sector – particularly the sophisticated manufacturing subsector – is key in determining economic development and structural change. To analyze structural change, Hausmann and Klinger (2006, 2007a) and Hidalgo *et al.* (2007) use the *product space* concept. In essence the product space can be thought of as a network, or "space," of products, where each product is a node in the network and the connection between the different nodes is determined by how likely it is to see that any given country exports a specific good given that it exports another specific good and vice versa. One of the main insights in Hausmann and Klinger (2006, 2007) is that it is more likely that countries diversify into new products in the product space that are "near" the set of products which they already produce. Moreover, Hausmann and Klinger (2006, 2007) show that structural change or productive transformation is more difficult for countries producing goods situated in parts of the product space that are less dense and that these countries tend to grow slower on average.

Felipe *et al.* (2010) build on the work by Hausmann and Klinger (2006, 2007a) and Hidalgo *et al.* (2007) to offer a taxonomy of commodities based on two criteria: their levels of sophistication and their connectivity to other products within the product space.

The work of Hausmann and Klinger (2006, 2007a), Hidalgo *et al.* (2007), Rodrik (2007), and Felipe *et al.* (2010), are complementary in important ways. Rodrik's (2007) observations highlight the importance of product diversification and the role that manufacturing plays in fostering structural transformation. On the other hand, the findings by Hausmann and Klinger (2006, 2007a) and Hidalgo *et al.* (2007) underscore the importance of analyzing the evolution and current state of the products exported by a country to understand its potential for future growth, as well as the available paths for faster structural transformation. Felipe *et al.* (2010) identify which products are "better" in their levels of sophistication and connectivity in the product space and, thus, can help pinpoint the most promising path toward faster structural change given a country's current position in the product space.

3. Economic and institutional characteristics of DRC (1960-2003)

Five decades after becoming an independent country,[1] the DRC is experiencing an aftermath of mismanagement

1. The Democratic Republic of the Congo accessed to the international sovereignty in 1960.

of its natural resources, corruption, bad governance, and political instability and armed conflicts. The country has been exposed to a severe socioeconomic crisis observable through its alarming economic and social indicators. Its per capita GDP dropped substantially from US$ 323 in 1960 to only US$ 100 in 2008 (World Bank, 2011). The UNDP's *Human Development Indicator* ranked in 2011 the DRC the 187th country out of the 187 countries assessed (UNDP, 2011). Nearly 71% of the Congolese population lives below the poverty line of US$ 1 per day (World Bank, 2011).

This poor socioeconomic performance of the country is in contrast with the country's potential for achieving sustained growth and development. In 1960, the DRC had the second strongest economy in Sub-Saharan Africa after that of South Africa, and its two leading economic sectors (mining and agriculture) were relatively productive. Thus, the country had the opportunity to choose among several alternative paths for its development, given the abundance of its natural/mineral resources, the large size of its territory (second largest country in Africa), and the dynamism of its population (the DRC population is dominated by a large proportion of young people who can be used in productive activities). Its natural resources include copper, cobalt, diamonds, gold, zinc, uranium, tin, silver, coal, manganese, tungsten, cadmium, Colombo tantalum, uranium, crude oil, and many others. The country also has other natural resources such as huge forest reserves (6 percent of the world endowment), extensive network of navigable waterways in Africa, vast hydroelectric potential and good ecology.

Despite all these resources and the high potential for development, several constraints seem to have prevented the DRC from following any development path to improve the living conditions of its population. Of these constraints, the political instability and the armed conflicts are the most recurrent and the most binding ones. Days only after its political independence, the country found itself caught into political chaos that disrupted its economy. From 1960 to 1965, mutinies and secession in different parts of the country disrupted the transportation networks, poisoned the business environment, and creates disincentives for investment. As a result, the GDP fell by 4 percent between 1960 and 1965.

Following this period of political turmoil, the country achieved political stability which lasted from 1966 to 1990, the year it opened up again to democracy. This period can be broken into three sub-periods that marked differently the country's economic environment. Those sub-periods are 1966-1974, 1975-1982, and 1983-1990.

The 1966-1974's sub-period was characterized by relative economic prosperity and growth due mostly to sustained investment in agriculture, manufacturing, and mining; and to the implementation of the first economic policy named "*Decennial Plan 1971-1980*." As a result, the aggregate real GDP grew on average and per annum during this sub-period by 5 percent. Also, the *Decennial Plan* was associated with huge government intervention in the economy. However, this huge intervention of government went later on beyond government actions to improve the business environment and public investment to embrace control of economic activities.

It is in this context that government implemented few key but ill-advised policies from 1973 to 1975, namely, the nationalization of private ownership (1973), the radicalization (1974), and the retrocession (1975).[1] Those policies together with adverse shocks to terms of trade[2] rushed the economy into a severe and long lasting recession starting in 1974.

Although these policies lasted only two years, they had long lasting negative effects on the economy. Those effects were observed between 1975 and 1982 and consisted mostly in a negative growth rate of aggregate GDP of -1.9% on average and per annum or its shrinking by 15% in 7 years. During this subperiod, the ambitious public investment program initiated in the context of the "*Decennial Plan*" was interrupted. Fiscal revenue dropped making thus government unable not only to maintain infrastructures and productive capital but also to service its debt used to fund its investment plan.

It is in this context of the economic and debt crises that the country solicited for the first time the assistance of the International Monetary Fund (IMF) in 1983 to help eliminate several observed distortions and stabilize its economy. The IMF assistance helped the country to return back to weak growth recovery from 1984 to 1986 with an average annual growth of the real GDP of 2.5 percent. It also helped the country to engage with the World Bank into a structural adjustment program starting 1987 for long term growth recovery. However, favorable shocks to the terms of trade of copper starting 1987 incited government to discontinue its structural adjustment program in order to take control over those unexpected additional export revenue. The discontinuity of the stabilization effort rushed again the economy into recession by the end of 1980s.

The sub-period 1990-2000 was the worst one in the country history. In fact, the rate of growth of the real GDP per capita which was -6.6% in 1990 reached its lower level in 1999, that is, -14%. This new drop in the GDP (which contracted by 43 during this decade) was associated with the disappearance of many economic activities, unprecedented circle of hyperinflation, currency depreciation, increasing dollarization and financial disintermediation, declining savings, deteriorating economic infrastructure, massive lay-offs, and the incapacity (financial and organizational) of government to insure provision of basic services such as education, health, and infrastructures. These events contributed, in turn, to the political instability, which was marked by massive looting in Kinshasa and other major cities (1991 and 1993), inter-ethnic conflicts in Katanga (1992 and 1993), and armed conflicts (1996 to 2003) that destroyed almost all the remaining country's productive capacities and social infrastructures and left at least 5 million people dead.

4. Methodology

To analyze DRC structural transformation over time, we use the product space methodology developed by

1. Radicalization consisted of government taking over mismanaged businesses granted to nationals through the nationalization policy while retrocession consisted of government turning the nationalized businesses to the owners.

2. Such conjuncture was caused by the 1973 petroleum crisis and the drop in prices of exports of minerals (i.e., copper) and some agricultural products.

Hausmann and Klinger (2006). Hausmann and Klinger (2006) characterize the world product space– the degree of relatedness among all goods produced in the world in a given year–to understand how its structure affects the specialization patterns of countries. The standard growth theory hypothesizes that this space is homogeneous, that is, products are located at equal distances in this space so that there always exists a new product a firm can jump to provided it incurs a fixed cost. If this were the case, Hausmann and Klinger (2006) note, then countries' observed patterns of structural transformation and growth would not be different. In fact, the product space (referred to as "a forest") is heterogeneous in that it includes areas which are either dense or sparse. Products in different areas of the product space will have different technological contents. Those in the dense part of the forest will have high technological content as well as more paths toward many other similar products than will those in the sparse part of the forest. For instance, a country producing a highly technological product like a computer can jump easily to several new products such as automobiles, aircraft, machinery, electronic devices, and so on. Similarly, a country producing a primary good like bananas can only jump to another, similar product, such as oranges rather than automobiles, since the latter has different production requirements and is in a different product space area. Thus, connectivity, or relatedness of a product to other products and technological content (technological intensity) are important characteristics of structural transformation, which is viewed as a process during which a country moves toward producing new products featuring upgraded technology and products of higher unit values. Whether a country can achieve structural transformation or not will depend on its initial location in the product space and on the distance to the product areas featuring technology-intensive and high value products. If the production basket of a country is in the sparse part of the product space, then the distance to products embodying higher technology and value will be a limiting factor in its transformation process.

Hausmann and Klinger (2006) develop three metrics to measure the degree of relatedness or connectivity of a product to others and two metrics to measure the level of sophistication of a product and of a country's production basket. Starting with the connectivity, they define first the *proximity* between two goods (i and j) as the probability to produce a good i given that a good j is being produced. Suppose that i is an apple and j is a vehicle. Then the proximity or the probability that a country will produce a vehicle given that it already produces an apple should be close to zero since the production requirements (capabilities) of the two products differ. But, the proximity is higher if i is a computer instead of an apple because the productive capabilities of a computer can be redeployed or adapted to produce a vehicle. The *proximity* between two goods (i and j) at time t is given by:

$$\varphi_{i,j,t} = \min\left[P(x_{i,t} / x_{j,t}), P(x_{j,t} / x_{i,t})\right]^{1} \quad (1)$$

1. The minimum of the conditional probabilities of i and j is used here to resolve the problem of asymmetry between the two probabilities, and to avoid a higher value of proximity due to a drop in the number of exporters

where $P(x_{i,t}/x_{j,t})$ is the conditional probability that a country will produce good i in period t given that it is already producing good j in the same period. The term $x_{i,t}=1$ if a country has a revealed comparative advantage *(RCA)*[1] in good i in period t and $x_{i,t}=0$ otherwise. The conditional probability is expressed as:

$$P(x_{it}/x_{j,t})=\frac{P(x_{it}\cap x_{jt})}{P(x_{jt})},\quad P(x_{jt}/x_{i,t})=\frac{P(x_{it}\cap x_{jt})}{P(x_{it})} \quad (2)$$

where the numerator of equation (2) is the joint probability of producing both goods i and j, and the denominator is the marginal probability of producing good i or good j. The measure of *proximity* is uniquely identified for each pair of commodities in the world.

Next, Hausmann and Klinger (2006) develop the metric of proximity at the country level and call it *density*. Density measures the proximity of a particular new product to the current country's export basket or the probability that a country with a given export basket will produce and export this new product in the near future. The *density* of the export basket for country c to good i at time t is expressed as:

$$density_{i,c,t}=\frac{\sum_k \varphi_{i,k,t}x_{c,k,t}}{\sum_k \varphi_{i,k,t}} \quad (3)$$

where $j_{i,k,t}$ and $x_{c,k,t}$ are defined as in (1). Unlike the proximity measure, which is the same across countries for any pair of goods, the *density* varies across countries.

Hausmann and Klinger (2006) use the metric of proximity to calculate another metric of connectivity called *paths*, that is, the number of other products that can be reached through a given product. The *paths* is the distance-weighted number of products around a product *i* (referred to as tree *i*) at time *t*. The *paths* is used to determine which good is in the dense part of the forest and which one is in the periphery, and is expressed as:

$$paths_{i,t}=\sum_j \varphi_{i,j,t} \quad (4)$$

Hausmann and Klinger also derive two metrics to measure the implicit value of a product *(Prody)* and the level of sophistication of the country's industrial structure as represented by the value of her export basket *(Expy)*. The *Prody* index of a product measures its value or level of sophistication. For a good i, the *Prody* is calculated as a weighted average of per capita GDP of countries producing it at time t, where the weights are the countries' *RCA* in that good. The *Expy* index of a country c at time t is calculated from the *Prodys* of products in the corresponding period. It is the weighted sum of all *Prodys*, where the weights are the country export shares of goods. The expressions of the *Prody* and *Expy* are as follows:

$$\text{Prody}_{i,t}=\sum_c \frac{(xval_{i,c,t}/X_{c,t})}{\sum_j (xval_{i,c,t}/X_{c,t})_j} y_{c,t}, \quad (5)$$

$$Expy_{c,t}=\sum_i (xval_{i,c,t}/X_{c,t})\text{Prody}_{i,t}, \quad (6)$$

of a given product rather than to the similarity of two goods exported by the same country.

1. According to Ballassa (1965), a country has a revealed comparative advantage (RCA) in a good *i* if the share of this country's exports of good *i* in its total exports is greater than the world share of this product in the world total product. The RCA is calculated by dividing the country share of good i by the world share of good *i*. A country whose value of RCA for good *i* is equal or greater than 1 will tend to specialize in the production of the good and export it to countries whose value of RCA for this good is less than 1.

where $xval_{i,c,t}$ is the exports of good i by country c in year t, $X_{c,t}$ is total exports by country c in year t, and $y_{c,t}$ is the per capita GDP of country c in year t. *Prody* is uniquely defined for each product while *Expy* is country-specific. Both *Prody* and *Expy* are also used to emphasize the value of the new goods a country produces over time. These new goods can either be upscale (high value) or downscale (low value) with respect to the value of the country's current production.

To analyze the structural transformation of the DRC, we need metrics that capture both changes in output composition as well as in output value. For the output value, the *Expy* metric described above measures the aggregate value of the country output or export basket. However, the three metrics of proximity defined previously (*proximity, density,* and *paths*) refer to the connectivity or relatedness of a single product to other products and cannot be used to measure the country's change in output composition or diversification. Thus we propose an aggregate metric to capture the aggregate proximity, that is, the proximity of a country's current export basket to all products in the product space that the country is not yet producing. Such a metric was developed in Badibanga *et al.* (2009) and called *Density Gravity Center* (*DGC*). The *DGC* is defined as a weighted sum of densities of all products for a country c, where the weights are the country's revealed comparative advantages *(RCA)* of products. This sum is further normalized by the sum of densities of all products. Using the density as defined in (3), we express the *DGC* metric as

$$DGC_{c,t} = \frac{\sum_i density_{i,c,t} x_{i,c,t}}{\sum_i density_{i,c,t}}, \qquad (7)$$

where $x_{i,c,t}$ is equal to 1 if $RCA_{i,c,t} \square 1$, and it is equal to 0 if $RCA_{i,c,t} < 1$.

The *DGC* is an aggregate metric that captures the performance of a country on the diversification of its production over time. It can be understood intuitively because it represents the proportion of the world product space that the country has already developed. The complement to the *DGC* represents the proportion of the product space that a country has not yet developed. An increase in the value of the *DGC* from period to period is an indication that a country is diversifying, that is, it is densely occupying the product space by jumping to a set of new products in which it has developed or is intending to develop comparative advantages.

Since structural transformation implies both changes in output composition and output value, we can map both *DGC* and *Expy* into a single space so that the distance between the origin and each coordinate in this space represents a particular value of the process for a country in a particular year. An alternative way to do this consists of constructing a new metric which will measure the geometric distances between consecutives coordinates of this space. A positive difference in the geometric distances between two successive years (two consecutive dots) suggests positive movement toward transformation, whereas a negative difference indicates a regression in transformation. We call this metric the *Index of Structural Change (ISC)* and express it as

$$IST_{c,t} = \sqrt{DGC_{c,t}^2 + Expy_{c,t}^2}, \qquad (8)$$

where *DGC* and *Expy* are defined as previously.

5. Overall features of structural transformation of the DRC economy

To implement the metrics described above, we use the United Nations Commodity Trade Statistics Database (UNCOMTRADE). This database includes the annual international trade statistics data available at the SITC at 4-digit levels of disaggregation. This database includes 625 commodities for 284 partner countries or regions over the period 1962-2008. We construct first the revealed comparative advantage index *(RCA)* and then all the other metrics described above.

We plot the structural transformation (*DGC-Expy* space) of the DRC and the other three selected countries (Indonesia, Malaysia, and Thailand) from 1962 to 2008 in Figure 1. Each dot in this figure represents a coordinate point in the *DGC-Expy* space, where the calculated *DGC* from 1962 to 2008 is on the x-axis while the calculated *Expy* over the same period is on the y-axis. We use different colors for the dots to distinguish the processes of the four countries. Also, we label the initial point/condition (1962), the midway point (1985), and the terminal point/condition (2008) for each country. A South or South-West to North-East movement in this space (i.e. an upward trend) indicates a strong transformation since a country is occupying proportionately more of the world product space and each of the new products in its export basket is of higher unit value compared with the overall value of its export basket.[1] Further, a South to North or a West to East movement indicates a transition biased toward increases in product sophistication (i.e. specialization without diversification) for the former and a transition biased toward product discovery (i.e. diversification without specialization) for the latter. Any other movement is an indication of either a process that is harder to identify or a country's failure to commensurate with the rest of the world.

From Figure 1, we can see that the countries started with quite comparable conditions (1962). Both countries had almost the same levels of sophistication of their production basket (*Expy*) but slightly different levels of diversification (*DGC*). Thailand had slightly better diversification level in comparison with the other three countries. It was followed by Indonesia. DRC and Malaysia came third and last, respectively.

Figure 1 also shows different patterns of structural transformation for DRC in comparison to the three countries over the period 1962-2008. For DRC, the process moves from South to North-West indicating a reverse diversification (decrease in the value of the *DGC*) associated with some specialization (increase in the value of *Expy*) from 1962 to 2008. However, the process for each of the three countries for the same period moves from South to North-East indicating both strong diversification and specialization of their production basket (increase in both *DGC* and *Expy* values).

Alternatively, we construct the Index of Structural Transformation (*IST*) to evaluate movement in the *DGC-Expy* space for each country using expres-

1. In principle, a country needs to include a new good in its production basket only if this good is upscale, that is, if its value is greater than the overall value of the country's production or export basket. However, a country can choose to include a downscale good in its production basket if this new good allows it to reach upscale goods in the future.

Figure 1. Structural Transformation of DRC, Indonesia, Malaysia, and Thailand: Expy-DGC space (1962-2008)

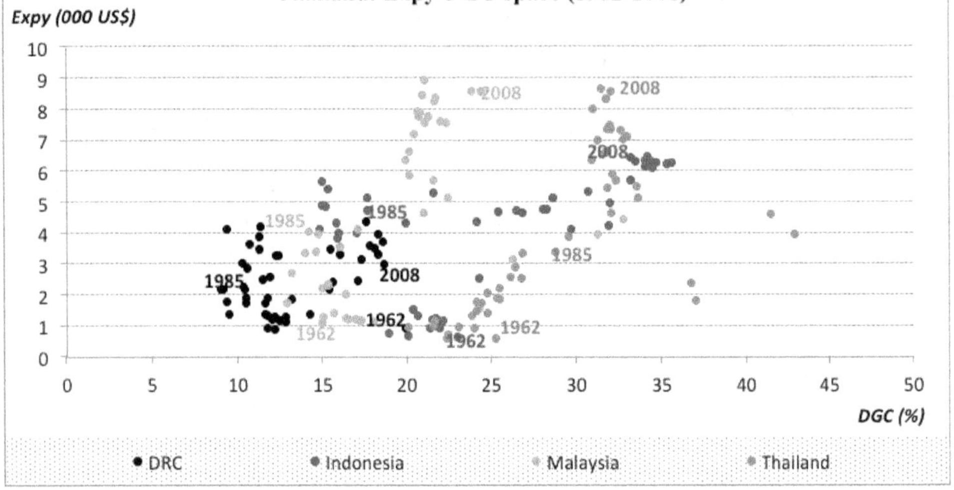

sion (8) above. We depict the results in Figure 2. As for the *DGC-Expy* space, this figure shows an impressive transformation process for Thailand and a very poor process for DRC. It also shows very good transformation processes for Indonesia and Malaysia.

From this figure, it is obvious that the transformation processes of the four countries were quite similar in 1962. However in early 1970s, Thailand started to stand out from the other countries and maintained the lead in transformation process until the end of the period under study. Its *IST* increased on average between 1962 and 2008 at an impressive growth rate of 18.0 percent per annum. As for Thailand, Indonesia started to stand out from DRC and Malaysia in early 1970s. From 1972 to 1987, it led in this process before being undertaken by Thailand starting 1987 and on. Like for Thailand, its *IST* grew on average between 1962 and 2008 at an impressive rate of 13.1 percent per year. Malaysia, on the other hand, had a very good transformation process too. Its *IST* increased on average between 1962 and 2008 at a steady rate of 10.0 percent per year.

However, the DRC process was characterized by a sub-period of good performance (1974-1982) during which its *IST* increased on average by 6.0 percent a year followed by a sub-period of stagnation (1988-2008) during which this index grew on average at a rate of 0 percent per year.

6. Determinants of structural transformation in DRC

The results of the previous section show that not only the DRC was a laggard in the transformation processes but also that the gap between its pro-

Figure 2. Index of Structural Transformation (IST) of DRC, Indonesia, Malaysia, and Thailand (1962-2008)

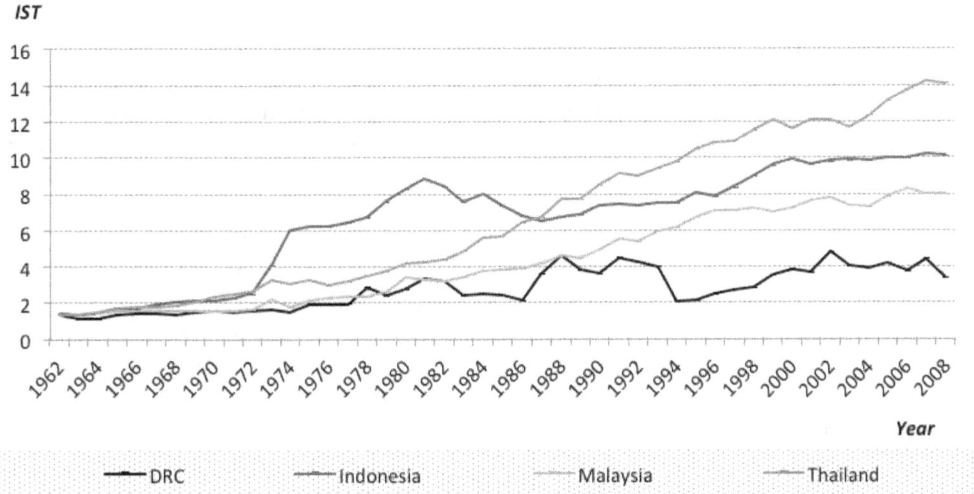

cess and those of the three successful countries widened substantially during the period under study. Thus, we need to identify the factors explaining the success of the three countries (Indonesia, Malaysia, and Thailand) as well as the counter performance of DRC. To do so, we use the model of structural transformation described in Hausmann and Klinger (2006, pp. 6-8). This model is an extension of the overlapping generations' model of firms developed by Diamond (1989) and Cabral (2000).[1] Accordingly, the process of structural transformation depends on the distance or the proximity of the country production basket to the more connected products in the product space, the cost of jumping to such products, and the degree to which the price of the new good exceeds that of the standard good that the country is already producing.

We specify this model of structural transformation as follows:

$$IST_t = \beta_0 + \beta_1 DGC_t + \beta_2 CJNP_t + \beta_3 DPE_t$$

$$+ \beta_4 GDPpc_t + \beta_5 DUMCONF + \varepsilon_t$$

where:

- *IST* is the index of structural transformation which we use as our measure of structural transformation;
- *DGC* is our measure of proximity of the country production basket to the rest of products in the product space. *DGC* is also used as an index of diversification;
- *CJNP* is the cost of jumping to the new product.
- *DPE* is the differential between the price of new product and that of the standard product;

1. Diamond (1989) and Cabral (2000) are cited in Haussman and Klinger (2006).

- *GDPpc* is the per capita GDP which is introduced in the model to control for the level of development;
- *DUMCONF* is the dummy variable introduced in the case of the DRC to take into account the impact of conflicts and political instability on structural transformation;
- ε is the disturbance term. ε follows a normal distribution with mean zero and with variance 1, that is, $\varepsilon \sim N(0,1)$, and
- β_i is a coefficient which measures the marginal impact of the associated variable on structural transformation, i =1, 2,.., 5.

The expected signs and magnitudes of the coefficients are as follows:

- β_i is unrestricted. First, a positive sign $(\beta_1 > 0)$ indicates a good diversification process consisting for a country to include into its production basket new goods or new clusters of goods which are more connected and of at least of the same value as that of its production basket. Next, a negative sign on the other hand $(\beta_1 < 0)$ reflects a diversification process characterized by a jump to products which are not only of low value with respect to the value of the country production basket. Finally, a neural sign $(\beta_1 = 0)$ indicates stagnant diversification process.
- β_3 is unrestricted. It can take on a positive sign $(\beta_3 > 0)$ when the new good is upscale (i.e., a good of higher value with respect to the value of the country production basket) or a negative sign $(\beta_3 < 0)$ when the new good is downscale (i.e., a good of lower value with respect to the value of the country production basket).
- β_4 is unrestricted. We expect an economy to structurally transform with the level of development $(\beta_4 > 0)$. However, when the increase in the GDP is the result of favorable shocks to the terms of trade of natural resources or the discovery of new mineral deposits, structural transformation may regress $(\beta_4 < 0)$ as export revenues that may result from those shocks are allocated to the capital deepening in the mining sector, creating thus a bias against product discovery and innovation.
- β_2 is expected to be negative $(\beta_2 < 0)$ to reflect the two possible scenarios in product discovery. Each new generation of product requires a firm to incur a cost. However, this cost can be less or greater than that of the previous generation of product. The first case (lower cost) correspond to the situation where the new product is close technologically to the old product so that the cost of adapting capabilities to bring it out is lower compared with that incurred for the previous generation. Another plausible explanation is that knowledge on the previous generation of product is not internalized or is public so that new product developer will pick up from where the developer of the old generation left off (i.e., the new developer will incur partial cost) without having to start over and incur the total cost. The second case, on the other hand, corresponds to the situation where the new product is technologically distant from the country's current technology and thus requires a total redeployment of production capabilities to be brought out. In this case, the cost will be

higher than that incurred for the previous generation of product. In either of the two cases, the negative coefficient reflects the inverse relationship between structural transformation and the cost of bringing out a product.

- β_5 is expected to be negative $(\beta_5 < 0)$ since conflict poisons the economic environment and reduce business confidence which in turn prevents any investment in product discovery.

To estimate our model, we need times series data on variables appearing in the model. We use the *IST* and *DGC* constructed earlier and the per capita GDP from the WDI 2012 database. We also construct the *DPE* using the *Expy* of each country and the *Prody* of each product constructed earlier. For each year, we calculate first the difference between the *Prody* of each new product included in the country basket in that year and the *Expy* of the country in that year. Next, we calculate the *DPE* by averaging the differences between *Prody* and *Expy* across all the new products included in the country production basket in that year. Next, we construct the dummy of conflict for DRC by setting *DUMCONF – 1* if there was at least an armed conflict or a political instability of major importance in a particular year and *DUMCONF* – 0 otherwise. Finally, we need data on *CJNP*. However, these data are not available for the countries included in the analysis. Instead, we use the net number of products developed in a country – *NNP* (the difference between the total number of products in which a country has developed comparative advantages in particular year and the total number of products abandoned by a country in that year) as a proxy of *CNJP*. The interpretation of the coefficient associated with *NNP* is described as follows. A positive coefficient will mean that a unit increase in the net number of new products a country jumped to improves structural transformation when the cost of jumping is low, that is, when a new product is close to the country basket so that that country has to just adapt its capabilities to produce the new product. However, a negative coefficient will mean that a unit increase in the net number of new products a country jumped to affects negatively structural transformation when the cost of jumping is high, that is, when a new product is technologically far from the country basket so that it has to abandon some old products in order to redeploy all its capabilities to produce the new product.

We estimate our model using the robust regression method and present the results in Table 2. As it is reflected in this table, the fit of the model to data is satisfactory. For each country, the adjusted R-squared is extremely high (close to 1) indicating variations in structural transformation (*IST*) are jointly determined by variations in all variables included into the model. Next, the coefficients associated with *DPE* and *GDPpc* are each statistically significant at 1 percent level for each country, while that associated with *NNP* is statistically significant at 5 percent significance level only in the case of Indonesia. Further, the coefficient associated with *DGC* is statistically significant at 1 percent significance level for all countries except for the DRC where it is not statistically significant. Finally, the coefficient associated with

TABLE 2

Results of estimation of the model of structural transformation

	Dependent variable: *IST* (1962-2008)			
	DRC	INDONESIA	MALAYSIA	THAILAND
Constant	5.481* (0.000)	-1.238* (0.013)	0.164 (0.507)	-0.468 (0.344)
DGC	-3.066 (0.438)	10.367* (0.002)	5.336* (0.000)	8.120* (0.000)
NNP	0.005 (0.764)	0.033** (0.021)	-0.010 (0.261)	0.003 (0.778)
DPE	-0.001* (0.000)	-0.002* (0.000)	-0.001* (0.001)	-0.001* (0.000)
GDPpc	-0.010* (0.000)	0.007* (0.000)	0.001* (0.000)	0.004* (0.000)
DUMCONF	-0.428** (0.031)			
Adjusted R-squared	0.81	0.98	0.99	0.99
N	46	46	44	46

Numbers in parentheses are P-values. * indicates the coefficient is statistically significant at 1 percent level of significance while ** indicates it is significant at 5 percent significance level.

DUMCONF is statistically significant at 5 percent level of significance.

The results in Table 2 call for the following observations. Except for the marginal effect of the price differential (*DPE*) on structural transformation which is similar across both countries, the other determinants of structural transformation were different for DRC in comparison to the other countries. First, increasing proximity of the country production basket to the rest of products in the product space seems to be the major determinant of the steady structural transformation of Indonesia, Malaysia, and Thailand. A marginal increase of 1 percent in the *DGC* has a huge impact on structural transformation, that is, it results in an increase in *IST* of 10 point in Indonesia, 5 point in Malaysia, and 8 point in Thailand. For DRC, however, not only the coefficient associated with *DGC* is not statistically significant but also its sign is opposite to that of the three countries. Nonetheless, its magnitude is large and suggests that a marginal increase of 1 percent in the *DGC* causes a decrease in the *IST* of 3 points. This results is an indication that the DRC diversified into products of lower value and difficult to upgrade overtime, causing thus a regression in its transformation process.

Second, the level of development has a positive effect on structural transformation in Indonesia, Malaysia, and Thailand, but a negative effect in the case of DRC. For each of successful countries, 1 dollar increase in per capita GDP has a small effect (i.e., less than 1 percent) on *IST.* In the DRC case, however, an increase (a decrease) of 1 dollar in per capita GDP results in 1 percent decrease (1 percent increase) in *IST.* Intuitively, this negative effect reflects a bias against diversification into non-mineral products during periods of favorable shocks to terms of trade of key minerals (i.e., copper and cobalt) or movement toward diversification into non-mineral products during periods of adverse shocks to terms of trade of mineral products.

Third, an increase of 1 unit in the *NNP* improves the *IST* by 3.3 percent in Indonesia. This implies the new product was close technologically to this country' capabilities so that it did not cost much to adapt those capabilities in order to bring it out. For the rest of countries, this effect is null and indicates the cost of bringing out a new product was the same as the cost of the old product.

Fourth, an increase of 1 dollar in price differential between the new and standard products results in a decrease of less than 1 percent in the *IST* for each of the 4 countries. This implies that the new good included in the country' production basket was downscale (i.e., low value with respect to the value of the country's production basket).

Fifth, conflicts seem to have impacted negatively the transformation process of DRC. A prevalence of a major conflict results in a decrease of the *IST* of 0.43 point.

7. Discussion

The results of the previous section have confirmed the claim that the types of products a country specialized into matter for structural transformation and growth (Hausmann et. al, 2007). Although the four countries included in this analysis had similar transformation processes as well as levels of development in 1962, the outcomes of their diversification processes were different by 2008. Indonesia, Malaysia, and Thailand increased in 47 years their indices of structural transformation (*IST*) by 7 folds, 6 folds, and 9 folds, respectively. At the same time, their per capita GDP in 2008 was in comparison to the 1962's 5 times higher in Indonesia, 17 times higher in Malaysia, and 8 times higher in Thailand. However, the corresponding figures for DRC confirm its downhill fate. Its per capita GDP in 2008 was a third of its 1962 levels and its *IST* was stagnant from the mid-1980s to 2008.

The results of estimation show also that diversification has a positive effect in the three successful countries but a negative effect in the DRC case. To get a sense of why diversification has an opposite effect in DRC compared with the three successful countries, we construct a product distribution for each country using the connectivity (diversification) and sophistication (specialization) criteria. We define four types of products. The "best product" is a good in the dense part of the product space (more connected) that is also upscale (sophisticated or advanced technologically or of higher value with respect to the value of e country production basket). A good is qualified as a "bad product" if it is in the sparse part of the forest (less connected) and is downscale (less sophisticated). Between the two groups, there exist goods that are either more connected but downscale ("transition good products") or less connected but upscale ("biased good products"). Unlike transition good products which can help to sustain the transformation process in the long run by shortening the distance to the best products, biased good products can limit transformation process since they can lock the country into the sparse areas of the product space.

We construct the distributions of goods for each country in 1962 and in 2008 using the connectivity and sophistication criteria and we present the results in Table 2. Overall, the results confirm the counter performance of DRC. Although the number of products exported with comparative advantage increased slightly (from 36 in 1962 to 47 in 2008), the DRC product discovery seems sluggish. In 47 years, the country's number of the best products exported with comparative advantage increased by only three products. Furthermore, bad products dominated the country's basket in 1962 as well as in 2008. These products represented 58.0 percent and 76.0 percent of the total number of products exported with comparative advantages in 1962 and 2008, respectively. Also, the cell of transition good products shows no product in 1962 but a single product in 2008. This implies that the country did not have any opportunity to escape the bad product trap. The products it produced/exported were not only in the sparse part of the forest but also transition good products through which the country could transition to reach the denser part of the forest (i.e. the core of the product space) were technologically distant from its basket.

The good performance observed for each of the three successful countries is reflected in Table 3 as well. Starting with the number of products each country exported with comparative advantage, Indonesia shows the lead with an impressive cumulative growth rate of 366.0 percent (from 38 products to 177 products) between 1962 and 2008. It is followed by Thailand with a cumulative growth rate of 206.0 percent (from 54 products to 165 products), and then by Malaysia with a cumulative growth rate of 166.0 percent (from 44 products to 116 products). Meanwhile, each of the three countries reduced the proportion of bad products in the total of products exported with comparative advantages between 1962 and 2008. The proportion of bad products in that total fell from 61.0 percent in 1962 to 32.2 percent in 2008 in Indonesia, from 55.0 percent in 1962 to 28.0 percent in 2008 in Malaysia, and from 41 percent in 1962 to 26.1 percent 2008 in Thailand.

The most interesting results in this table relate to the increase in exports of the best products and the transition good products between 1962 and 2008, with Thailand leading the way for both. In Thailand, the number of best products exported with comparative advantage increased from 5 in 1962 to 32

Table 3: Distributions of Products for the DRC, Indonesia, Malaysia, and Thailand in 1962 and 2008						
DR Congo						
	1962			**2008**		
	Upscale	Downscale	**Total**	Upscale	Downscale	**Total**
High Paths	2	0	2	5	1	6
Low Paths	13	21	34	3	31	34
Total	15	21	36	8	32	40
Indonesia						
	1962			**2008**		
	Upscale	Downscale	**Total**	Upscale	Downscale	**Total**
High Paths	2	0	2	31	46	77
Low Paths	13	23	36	43	57	100
Total	15	23	38	74	103	177
Malaysia						
	1962			**2008**		
	Upscale	Downscale	**Total**	Upscale	Downscale	**Total**
High Paths	9	0	9	22	28	50
Low Paths	11	24	35	34	32	66
Total	20	24	44	56	60	116
Thailand						
	1962			**2008**		
	Upscale	Downscale	**Total**	Upscale	Downscale	**Total**
High Paths	5	0	5	32	55	87
Low Paths	27	22	49	35	43	78
Total	32	22	54	67	98	165

in 2008. The best products represented 9.3 percent and 19.4 percent of the total of products exported with comparative advantages in 1962 and 2008, respectively. Also, exports of transition good products increased from 0 in 1962 to 55 products in 2008.

Indonesia and Malaysia on the other hand show each significant performance but of less magnitude than Thailand. The number of the best products exported increased from 2 products in 1962 to 31 in 2008 in Indonesia and from 9 products in 1962 to 22 products in 2008 in Malaysia. The proportion of the *best products* in the total number of exported products increased in Indonesia (i.e., from 5.3 percent in 1962 to 18.0 percent in 2008) but decreased in Malaysia (i.e. from 20.4 percent in 1962 to 19.0 percent in 2008). Still, the number of transition good products between the two periods increased from 0 in 1962 in each of the two countries to 46 in Indonesia and 28 in Malaysia in 2008.

The transformation processes of Indonesia, Malaysia, and Thailand provides several insights from which DRC can learn from. First, diversification into best products (i.e., more connected and upscale products) is the first best for achieving a steady structural transformation. However, this type of products may not be easily reachable as countries in their early stage of transformation may not have the required capabilities to jump to such products. This is the reason why country can opt for the second best, that is, the country can transition through the transition good products (more connected but downscale products) provided these products are upgraded over time or they allow a country to cut the distance to the best products. The three successful countries seem to have followed these patterns too. Indeed, the results of regression indicate new product included in each of the four countries' production basket was on average downscale in the year of its inclusion (i.e. the estimated coefficient associated with the price differential *DPE* is negative for each country). However, the patterns of sophistication or specialization of the production basket (i.e., *Expy*) of each of the three successful countries indicate each upgraded products previously included since this index increased steadily for each of them (see Figure 3).

Finally, political stability is an important determinant of structural transformation. Firms invest in product discovery or in R&D because of profit motives or incentives. Any political instability creates uncertainty which in turn creates disincentives for investing in product discovery. Indonesia, Malaysia, and Thailand have experienced political stability that may have helped their transformation while the DRC has not.

8. Conclusion and policy implications

In this paper, we have extended the product space methodology (Hausmann and Klinger, 2006) to empirically analyze the transformation process of the DRC from 1962 to 2008 and compare it with those of Indonesia, Malaysia, and Thailand. Both DRC and the three countries included in the analysis were at the same levels of development in 1962 and their transformation processes in that year were comparable. This study has also identified determinants of

Figure 3: Expy of DRC, Indonesia, Malaysia, and Thailand (1962-2008)

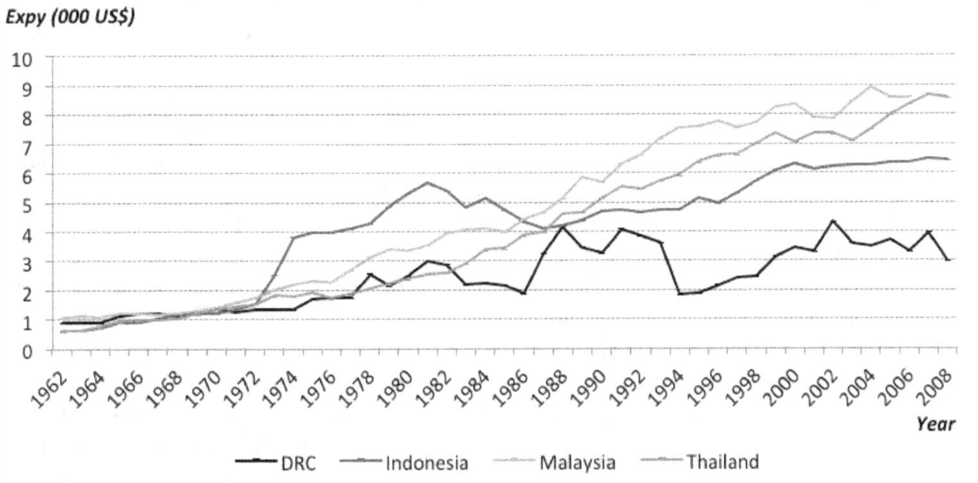

structural transformation in DRC and in each of the other three countries.

The results show a very slow or even stagnant transformation process for DRC but very impressive ones for the other three countries. Indeed, the DRC's *IST* indicates that the country not only lagged but also that the gap widened between its process and those of the three successful countries. Its *IST* grew annually at an average rate of 6 percent only between 1974 and 1982 and then stagnated between 1988 and 2008, while those of Thailand, Indonesia, and Malaysia grew over 1962-2008 at average annual rates of 18.0 percent, 13.0 percent, and 10.0 percent, respectively.

Further, the estimation of the model of structural transformation has helped to get insights into constraints to the DRC's structural transformation. The types of products a country specializes into, the cost of bringing out a new product, the price differential between new and standard goods, and conflicts are determinants of structural transformation.

Diversification advanced structural transformation in Indonesia, Malaysia, and Thailand; but caused it regression in DRC. In DRC case in particular, the country diversified into bad products, that is, products that were not only poorly connected to others but also downscale (low-value products). The proportion of these products in total products exported with comparative advantage increased from 58 percent in 1962 to 76 percent in 2008. Such products do not provide any opportunity for sustainable structural transformation. The only way to escape the "bad product trap" consists of jumping to the transition good products (more-connected but downscale products) so as to cut the distance to the best products (more connected and upscale products). By essence, the latter help to accelerate transformation since they allow a country to diversify its basket while increasing the basket's value. Our results show that the DRC export basket was not surrounded by transition good products. The number of transition good products increased from 0 products in 1962 to only 1 product in 2008. Further, the number of best products increased only by 3 units in 47 years (i.e., from 2 to 5 products). In this context, achieving diversification and thus transformation of the economic structure was left to chance.

Furthermore, conflicts seem to have limited the DRC's opportunities for structural transformation.

What can DRC do to transform its economic structure? There is no one-size-fits-all prescription to move a country with constraints like the DRC's back to a sustainable growth-enhancing transformation. The DRC needs to learn from the experiences of countries that have achieved a successful transformation such Indonesia, Malaysia, and Thailand. Indeed, these countries followed more realistic strategies. Neither of them started off with the sort of advanced productive capabilities that enable a country to jump to the best products with comparative advantage. So they opted to jump to the nearby products, whether these products were upscale or not. In particular, both countries jumped to more connected, but downscale, products. They then invested in product development and R&D to develop comparative advantage in these products over time. In this way, they ended up upgrading their products. Also, jumping to such products gave them the opportunity to cut the distance to the best products, which they ended up developing years later. To achieve their spectacular performance, Indonesia, Malaysia, and Thailand implemented policies that the DRC can try to customize. First, the strategy consisted of attracting foreign firms with advanced capabilities to develop transition good products. This strategy was combined with the creation of special zones with special fiscal regimes. These countries also implemented local content requirements' policies that encourage foreign firms to develop local markets of inputs in a reasonable time period. Technology development strategies that promoted the sharing of information and technology between foreign firms and local research centers were also crucial.

All these strategies may not seem a novelty for DRC which seems to have tried some in the past. For instance, DRC had auto assembly factories in late 1960s until the mid-1980s. Also, the country had an impressing fiscal incentives' regime for those firms intending to invest in product discovery and/or use local inputs. However, the country failed to organize the provision of complementary inputs such as basic infrastructures, market institutions of necessary inputs, market information system, and others. The lack or short supply of these complementary inputs made it harder for these foreign firms to use efficiently their capabilities to develop more connected products. Further, fiscal incentives granted in what has been called "Zone Franche" were used by the Administration for rent seeking reasons so that product developers ended up with higher cost of bringing out new product. Finally, all these policies were contradicted by the Zaireanisation policies in 1974 which consisted of transferring private foreign ownership either to the citizens or to the state.

Further, government should also implement policies that create incentives for local firms to invest in product discovery. Such policies should include for instance the creation of an enabling business environment, the implementation of government based insurance against risks associated with investment in high tech product discovery, the set-up of information system on products newly developed, the government support to new product developers (fiscal incentives, information, and marketing) to increase their competitiveness in the local and international markets.

Finally, any of the proposed policies will not work unless political instability the country has been facing is ended. The country has implemented since 2003 several peace consolidation programs to end the war and armed conflicts. To date, political instability is still prevailing in the Eastern part of the country. These programs need to be complemented with strategies that address the triggers of conflicts including poverty, unemployment, and so on.

One of the weaknesses of the product space approach is the lack of mechanisms that explain how well-identified policies impact structural transformation. It is unclear how specific policies might have affected the structural transformation metrics. For future research, not to mention policy guidance, the product space approach can also be extended by developing a transition matrix. This matrix will describe an optimal path for a given country producing a particular good in a given time. Thus, a monitoring and evaluation system can be developed to track progress over time against the optimal path.

References

Acemoglu, D., & Guerrieri, V. (2008). Capital Deepening and Nonbalanced Economic Growth. *Journal of Political Economy*, 116(3), 467-498.

Badibanga, T., Diao, X., Roe, T., & Somwaru, A. (2009). Dynamics of Structural Transformation: An Empirical Characterization in the Case of China, Malaysia, and Ghana. IFPRI Discussion Papers, 00856. Washington (DC): International Food Policy Research Institute.

Baumol, W.J. (1967). Macroeconomics of Unbalanced Growth: The Anatomy of Urban Crisis. *The American Economic Review*, 57(3), 415-426.

Chenery, H.B. (1960). Patterns of Industrial Growth. *The American Economic Review*, 50(4), 624-654.

Duarte, M., & Restuccia, D. (2010). The Role of the Structural Transformation in Aggregate Productivity. *Quarterly Journal of Economics*, 125(1), 129-173.

Echevarria, C. (1997). Changes in Sectoral Composition Associated with Economic Growth. *International Economic Review*, 38(2), 431-452.

Fagerberg, J. (2000). Technological Progress, Structural Change and Productivity Growth: A Comparative Study. *Structural Change and Economic Dynamics*, 11, 393-411.

Felipe, J., Kumar, U., & Abdon, A.M. (2010). How Rich Countries Became Rich and Why Poor Countries Remain Poor: It's the Economic Structure. The Levy Economics Institute Working Paper Collection, 644. Annandale-on-Hudson (NY): Bard College.

Felipe, J., Kumar, U., & Abdon, A.M. (2010). Why Has China Succeeded – And Why it Will Continue to do so. The Levy Economics Institute Working Paper Collection, 611. Annandale-on-Hudson (NY): Bard College.

Hausmann, R., Hwang, J., & Rodrik, D. (2007). What You Export Matters. *Journal of Economic Growth*, 12(1), 1-25.

Hausmann, R., & Klinger, B. (2006). Structural Transformation and Patterns of Comparative Advantage in the Product Space. Center for International Development Working Paper Series, 128. Cambridge (MA): Harvard University.

Hausmann, R., & Klinger, B. (2007a). The Structure of the Product Space and the Evolution of Comparative Advantage. Center for International Development Working Paper Series, 146. Cambridge (MA): Harvard University.

Hausmann, R., & Klinger, B. (2007b). Structural Transformation in Chile. Quantum Advisory Group. <http://www.bligoo.com/media/users/0/32886/files/Hausman%20et%20al%20Structural%20Transformation%20in%20Chile.pdf> (cited 16 April 2011).

Hausmann, R., & Klinger, B. (2008). Pakistan: Competitiveness and Structural Transformation in Pakistan. Technical Assistance Consultant's Report. Asian Development Bank. <http://www.adb.org/Documents/Reports/Consultant/PAK/41661/41661-01-pak-tacr.pdf> (cited 16 April 2011).

Hidalgo, C.A., Klinger, B., Barabási, A.L., & Hausmann, R. (2007). The Product Space Conditions the Development of Nations. *Science*, 317(5837), 482-487.

Imbs, J., & Wacziarg, R. (2003). Stages of Diversification. *The American Economic Review*, 93(1), 63-86.

Kuznets, S. (1973). Modern Economic Growth: Findings and Reflections. The American Economic Review, 63(3), 247-258.

Kongsamut, P., Rebelo, S., & Xie, D. (2001). Beyond Balanced Growth. Review of Economic Studies, 68, 869-882.

McMillan, M., & Rodrik, D. (2011). Globalization, Structural Change, and Productivity Growth. <http://www.hks.harvard.edu/fs/drodrik/Research%20papers/Globalization,%20Structural%20Change,%20and%20Productivity%20Growth.pdf> (16 April 2011).

Ngai, L.R., & Pissarides, C.A. (2007). Structural Change in a Multisector Model of Growth. American Economic Review 97(1), 429-443.

Rogerson, R. (2008). Structural Transformation and the Deterioration of European Labor Market Outcomes. Journal of Political Economy, 116, 235-259.

Rodrik, D. (2007). Industrial Development: Stylized Facts and Policies. Industrial Development for the 21st Century: Sustainable Development Perspectives, 7-28. New York: United Nations.

United Nations Comtrade database. Available at http://Comtrade.un.org/db/default.aspx.

UNDP (2011), Human Development Report 2011. New York: UNDP.

Usui, N., & Abdon, A.M. (2010). Structural Transformation in the Kyrgyz Republic: Engineering Future Paths to Capability Accumulation. ADB Economic Working Paper Series, 200.

Wagstaff, T., & Maennling, N. (2009). Spatial Awareness: What can Mozambique Learn from the Product Space?

Paper presented at the II IESE Conference on Dynamics of Poverty and Patterns of Economic Accumulation in Mozambique. IESE Conference Papers, 48. <http://www.iese.ac.mz/lib/publication/II_conf/CP48_2009_Wagstaff.pdf> (cited 16 April 2011).

World Bank (2011), République Démocratique du Congo: Accélérer la croissance et l'emploi. Rapport de Synthèse, Mai 2011. Rapport No. 59631-ZR.

World Bank (2012), World Development Indicators, 2012. Washington, D.C.: World Bank.

Le capital humain et la trajectoire économique de la République démocratique du Congo

Andrianasy Angelo Djistera*

Résumé

L'augmentation de la qualification de la main-d'œuvre grâce à des investissements dans le secteur éducatif a contribué au décollage économique de certains pays, notamment en Asie. Le capital humain apparaît bien comme un facteur majeur dans le processus de production d'une économie. L'objet de cette étude est d'examiner les implications de ce facteur dans l'évolution de l'économie congolaise. La population active dispose en moyenne d'un faible niveau d'instruction en RDC. Cette situation s'explique par plusieurs facteurs parmi lesquels le manque de financement des investissements éducatifs et l'instabilité macroéconomique liée à la guerre. L'insuffisance de l'accumulation et la faiblesse de l'efficacité dans l'utilisation du capital humain limitent ainsi le potentiel de croissance et de développement du pays.

Mots clés : Capital humain, développement, éducation, République démocratique du Congo

* Maître de conférences en sciences économiques Université de Toamasina, Madagascar

Introduction

La République Démocratique du Congo (RDC) fait partie des pays les plus pauvres du monde, malgré l'importance de sa dotation en ressources naturelles. Contrairement à certains pays d'Asie, elle n'a pas réussi à décoller. Les économistes ont depuis longtemps étudié les problèmes du développement. Ils participent ainsi progressivement à la compréhension et à la résolution de ces problèmes. Selon Bresser-Pereira (2009) : « Il est possible de concevoir l'évolution tant des théories que des politiques économiques comme l'expression d'un lent processus d'apprentissage en réaction aux crises économiques et financières majeures. » Il serait ainsi intéressant d'examiner les conditions favorables à l'émergence et au développement de la RDC en s'appuyant sur les connaissances des pays émergents d'Asie (PEA).

La croissance et le développement économique résultent de la combinaison de plusieurs facteurs. La Banque mondiale (1993, 1999) met en lumière l'importance de l'investissement en capital physique, de la stabilité macro-économique, de l'effort éducatif et de l'absorption des technologies provenant des pays plus avancés dans les performances économiques des pays émergents. Le capital humain est particulièrement important dans la mesure où il agit sur les autres facteurs du développement. Il affecte par exemple l'efficacité des investissements en capital physique et constitue un des facteurs de stabilité. Par ailleurs, les nouvelles théories de la croissance économique démontrent qu'il constitue un déterminant majeur du développement (Boccanfuso et *al.*, 2009 ; Seka, 2013). Il agit sur le processus de croissance par l'intermédiaire de la productivité de la main-d'œuvre (Lucas, 1988), d'une part et de l'innovation (Romer, 1990), d'autre part. Pour Hussain et *al.* (2000), le capital humain est d'autant plus important que l'amélioration de la productivité grâce à l'investissement dans l'éducation, la santé et la nutrition constitue un volet essentiel des politiques d'élimination de la pauvreté. Le savoir est devenu un déterminant majeur de la productivité des individus et des nations.

Cet article a pour objet d'analyser les implications de la qualité de la main-d'œuvre dans la trajectoire de la RDC. Au lieu de se limiter aux spécificités des économies africaines, il propose un cadre général d'analyse à partir des comparaisons avec les évolutions des PEA. La recherche sur le rôle du capital humain dans le décollage de l'économie congolaise est effectuée ici en s'inspirant des expériences des pays dynamiques d'Asie.

La première section présente un état des lieux de l'alphabétisation des adultes en RDC. La deuxième section analyse le niveau d'instruction de la population en âge de travailler. La troisième section est consacrée à la recherche des explications de la situation du niveau de scolarisation du pays. La dernière section aborde la question des incidences du capital humain sur la trajectoire de l'économie congolaise.

1. L'alphabétisation des adultes

La revue de la littérature économique révèle que les indicateurs liés à l'éducation formelle sont généralement utilisés pour approximer le capital humain. Les économistes s'accordent à utiliser les statistiques en matière d'éducation afin de mesurer le capital humain. Les données relatives à l'éducation formelle offrent ainsi une vue d'ensemble de l'évolution de ce facteur. L'objet de la présente section est d'examiner l'état de l'alphabétisation des adultes en République Démocratique du Congo.

L'alphabétisation des adultes permet d'avoir une première idée sur la situation du capital humain en RDC. Le taux d'alphabétisation de la population active ou en âge de travailler peut être défini comme la proportion de la population âgée de 15 ans et plus qui est capable de lire et écrire. Il s'agit d'un indicateur relatif à l'état du stock de capital humain dans une économie. En effet, en admettant que la lecture et l'écriture sont des facteurs explicatifs importants de la productivité dans les différents secteurs d'activité d'une économie, l'utilisation de cet indicateur est justifiée. Plusieurs auteurs considèrent cet indicateur comme une mesure du capital humain (Romer, 1989 ; Middendorf, 2005). L'alphabétisation est en particulier liée à l'éducation de base et plus généralement à la formation professionnelle. L'intérêt de cet indicateur est sa disponibilité pour un grand nombre de pays et pour une période relativement longue.

Selon Lututala Mumpasi et Ngondo a Pitshandenge (2003), 32% de la population congolaise âgée de 15 ans et plus ne sait ni lire ni écrire ni sans doute calculer. De plus, l'analphabétisme en RDC est beaucoup plus prononcé chez les femmes (44%) que chez les hommes (19%). Et quel que soit le sexe, il touche davantage les milieux ruraux (55% de femmes, 21% d'hommes) que les milieux urbains (20,6% de femmes contre seulement 7,3% d'hommes). L'auteur a également mis en évidence une progression de l'analphabétisme dans le pays : il connaît une légère augmentation en 2001 par rapport à 1995 tant chez les hommes que chez les femmes. L'augmentation de l'analphabétisme est plus visible en milieu urbain qu'en milieu rural. Par ailleurs, le pourcentage d'analphabètes varie d'une province à l'autre.

Durant le Colloque sur la Société Civile de la Reconstruction au mois d'août 2003, Mulyumba wa Mamba a également souligné que le taux d'analphabétisme est très élevé en RDC. D'après les données de l'Institut de statistique de l'UNESCO (ISU), le taux d'alphabétisme des adultes (population âgée de 15 ans et plus) augmente légèrement, mais il reste faible en 2001 (67,2%). Par ailleurs, l'indicateur se dégrade en 2007 en passant à 61,2%.

Cependant, l'alphabétisation ne constitue qu'une composante du stock courant de capital humain, et ne reflète pas les aptitudes ou les compétences des individus qui vont au-delà des niveaux de scolarisation élémentaires. Pour Van Leeuwen (2006), elle ne permet pas de rendre compte de l'effet du capital humain, notamment lorsque le processus de développement de l'éducation de masse est achevé et remplacé par l'accroissement des niveaux d'éducation secondaire et tertiaire. Le *et al.* (2005) ont également noté que l'utilisation d'un indicateur relatif à l'alphabétisation conduit à ignorer la contribution des compétences et connaissances plus avancées à la productivité. Selon ces auteurs, même si l'alphabétisation constitue un élément fondamental du capital humain, elle ne prend pas en compte d'autres composantes essentielles du capital humain parmi lesquelles le raisonnement logique, analytique et la connaissance technologique. Il semble ainsi opportun d'examiner des indicateurs plus pertinents tels que le nombre moyen d'années de scolarisation et la répartition de la population active par niveau d'éducation.

2. Le niveau d'éducation de la main-d'œuvre

La distribution de la population active selon le niveau atteint d'éducation donne une vision générale du niveau moyen de capital humain d'un pays. Barro et Lee (2013) fournissent cette distribution pour un grand nombre de pays et pour plusieurs années.

L'observation des évolutions dans le tableau ci-dessous montre qu'il y a une amélioration globale du niveau d'instruction de la population active en RDC. La fraction de la population âgée de 25 ans et plus n'ayant reçu aucune éducation est notamment passée de 91,94% en 1950 à 48,14% en 2010. Toutefois, des efforts restent à réaliser dans la mesure où un grand nombre d'individus ne sont pas instruits : 48,14% de la population âgée de 25 ans et plus seulement ont atteint le niveau primaire, 14,83% le niveau secondaire et 1,71% le niveau supérieur en 2010.

Tableau 1
Répartition de la population selon le niveau d'éducation

Année	Aucune	Niveau le plus élevé atteint					
		Primaire		Secondaire		Tertiaire	
		Total	Complet	Total	Complet	Total	Complet
		(% de population âgée de 25 et plus)					
1950	91,94	7,57	0,60	0,51	0,20	0,02	0,01
1960	86,62	12,36	1,20	1,00	0,41	0,05	0,03
1970	80,17	18,10	2,14	1,65	0,67	0,06	0,04
1980	72,71	23,89	3,38	3,02	1,35	0,32	0,20
1990	61,49	29,20	4,92	8,54	4,12	0,70	0,45
2000	51,58	30,87	6,18	16,20	8,17	1,26	0,81
2010	48,14	35,23	8,41	14,83	7,89	1,71	1,08

Source : Barro et Lee (2013)

La faiblesse du niveau de scolarisation de la population congolaise est d'autant plus marquante lorsqu'on compare sa situation par rapport aux PEA. Le tableau 2 met en évidence un retard conséquent de la RDC par rapport à ces pays. En effet, presque la moitié de la population congolaise âgée de plus de 25 ans ne fréquente pas l'école en 2010 selon les données de Barro et Lee (2010). 35,23% de la population ont atteint le niveau primaire ; 14,83% le secondaire et seulement 1,71% le supérieur. Ces statistiques mettent en évidence d'importantes déficiences en matière de niveau d'instruction de la population.

Est-ce que le nombre moyen d'années de scolarisation, qui est l'indicateur généralement utilisé pour approximer le stock de capital humain de la population active dans un pays, confirme cette constatation ? Le tableau 3 présente l'évolution de cette variable en RDC et dans les pays émergents d'Asie (à titre de comparaison). Les données de Barro et Lee (2013) mettent en lumière un accroissement du niveau de capital humain de la RDC, mais il reste faible. La comparaison avec les économies dynamiques asiatiques révèle en particulier un retard important du pays en la matière. Malgré des efforts notables dans le domaine de l'éducation, le pays reste défavorisé en matière de capital humain comme la plupart des pays africains. Par ailleurs, l'écart entre le nombre moyen d'années de scolarisation de la population active en RDC et celui que l'on peut trouver dans les pays émergents d'Asie augmente. Les statistiques montrent qu'il passe de moins de 2 années en 1950 à 4 années et plus en 2010.

Tableau 2
Répartition de la population selon le niveau d'éducation en 2010

Pays	Aucune	Niveau le plus élevé atteint					
		Primaire		Secondaire		Tertiaire	
		Total	Complet	Total	Complet	Total	Complet
		(% de population âgée de 25 et plus)					
RDC	48,14	35,23	8,41	14,83	7,89	1,71	1,08
Chine	8,16	29,20	17,65	56,59	40,32	6,05	3,91
Corée du Sud	4,11	10,48	10,18	46,95	36,78	38,45	17,92
Inde	42,22	19,14	16,60	32,28	0,84	6,37	4,07
Indonésie	20,64	51,70	32,04	24,94	11,05	2,71	1,73
Malaisie	10,30	20,30	12,90	55,47	33,84	13,93	5,03
Philippines	4,82	30,40	18,00	35,28	19,86	29,50	22,37
Singapour	8,39	30,67	16,56	42,19	15,82	18,76	12,19
Thaïlande	12,60	57,90	27,35	20,54	10,07	8,92	8,77

Source : Barro et Lee (2013)

Tableau 3
Nombre moyen d'années de scolarisation de la population âgée de 25 ans et plus

	1950	1960	1970	1980	1990	2000	2010
RDC	**0,30**	**0,51**	**0,78**	**1,16**	**1,98**	**2,93**	**3,07**
Chine	0,74	1,47	2,48	3,75	4,85	6,60	7,54
Corée du Sud	4,01	3,23	5,38	7,29	8,95	10,58	11,69
Inde	0,92	0,94	1,23	1,87	2,96	3,58	4,43
Indonésie	0,75	1,11	2,26	3,09	3,21	4,59	5,50
Malaisie	1,81	2,27	2,99	4,43	6,53	8,16	9,53
Philippines	2,33	3,68	4,83	6,05	7,07	7,97	8,66
Singapour	2,14	2,80	3,74	3,72	5,76	7,59	8,82
Thaïlande	2,19	3,42	3,04	3,71	4,57	5,37	6,55
Moyenne des PEA	**1,86**	**2,37**	**3,24**	**4,24**	**5,49**	**6,81**	**7,84**

Source : Barro et Lee (2013)

Toutefois, il convient de noter que le nombre moyen d'années de scolarisation ne permet pas de mesurer la qualité de l'éducation. Pourtant, comme le PNUD (2013, p. 35) a souligné dans le Rapport sur le développement humain, « la qualité de l'éducation est encore plus importante que la durée de scolarisation. Il s'agit d'un facteur clé pour le développement des capacités de l'être humain. »

En résumé, le niveau d'éducation de la population active est faible en RDC. Cette constatation est confirmée par d'autres travaux. Lututala Mumpasi et Ngondo a Pitshandenge (2003) ont, par exemple, apporté des statistiques démontrant la faiblesse du niveau et des déficiences importantes en matière d'instruction de la population congolaise. Par ailleurs, compte tenu de la situation actuelle de la RDC, notamment concernant sa jeunesse, le risque de voir la qualification de la population active du pays atteindre un niveau élevé à court terme et moyen terme est faible. L'analyse de la situation des enfants et des adolescents congolais effectuée par Bashir (2009) a présenté un bilan très négatif :

- le nombre de jeunes déscolarisés qui ne feront pas davantage d'investissement en matière d'éducation si la situation actuelle continue est importante, soit environ 69% des jeunes de 12 à 14 ans et près de 80% des jeunes de 15 à 19 ans ;
- le niveau d'instruction le plus élevé atteint par la majorité de ces jeunes n'atteint pas le cycle primaire ;
- parmi ceux qui sont actuellement scolarisés, la moitié au moins est inscrite aux niveaux d'enseignement situés en dessous des niveaux théoriques correspondant à leur groupe d'âge. Dans un tel contexte, le niveau d'instruction le plus élevé dans le futur de ces jeunes sera ainsi inférieur à ce qu'il devrait être.

Tableau 4
Taux bruts de scolarisation par niveau en RDC (en %)

	1999	2009	2010	2011	2012
Primaire	52,5	102,1	102,7	105,2	110,9
Secondaire	...	41,1	40,9	43,1	43,3
Supérieur	...	6,0	...	...	...

Source : ISU

La faiblesse extrême du niveau d'instruction de la jeunesse congolaise ne permet pas d'espérer un accroissement rapide du capital humain au sein de la population active dans les années à venir, si les tendances actuelles se maintiennent. Selon Bashir (2009) : « le stock de capital humain parmi les futurs nouveaux arrivants sur le marché du travail au cours des dix prochaines années sera très bas. »

3. Explications de la situation du capital humain

Pour commencer, l'état global du capital humain de la RDC est en grande partie lié aux efforts effectués en matière d'éducation dans le passé. Le niveau de la scolarisation des jeunes détermine le niveau d'éducation de la population active dans le futur. En matière de scolarisation, la RDC n'est pas un très bon élève. Le tableau ci-dessous présente le niveau les taux bruts de scolarisation récents par niveau. Les statistiques de l'ISU révèlent que le taux brut de scolarisation est élevé au niveau primaire, 102,1% en 2009. Pourtant, les taux bruts de scolarisation sont faibles dans les niveaux supérieurs : 41,1% au secondaire et 6,0% au supérieur pour la même année.

Malgré les efforts en matière de scolarisation dans le primaire, la faiblesse de la scolarisation dans les deux autres niveaux limite la progression du niveau de capital humain de la population active en RDC.[1]

Pour expliquer l'état de l'éducation, et donc du capital humain, de la population congolaise, Lututala Mumpasi et Ngondo a Pitshandenge (2003) mettent l'accent sur « l'insuffisance persistante de l'offre par rapport à la demande ou aux contraintes liées à la demande de la part des parents ». Ils soulignent en particulier l'incapacité de l'offre à faire face à la demande, la faiblesse de la demande scolaire à cause de la pauvreté des parents et la faiblesse de la demande scolaire dans certaines provinces en raison de l'implantation scolaire.

Ces explications continuent à agir négativement sur l'accumulation de capital humain en RDC. La disponibilité en main-d'œuvre qualifiée est limitée à cause de l'inefficience du système éducatif. L'offre scolaire en RDC est caractérisée par l'insuffisance des res-

1. Par ailleurs, le taux net de scolarisation en primaire n'est pas excessivement élevé. Il est par exemple égal à 74,8% en 2010 d'après le Document UNESCO de programmation pays : République Démocratique du Congo 2011-2013.

sources humaines sur le plan surtout qualitatif, d'une part et les problèmes d'infrastructures, d'autre part. En RDC, l'UNESCO (2014) a noté : « le personnel enseignant souffre d'une formation initiale jugée peu professionnalisante et de l'absence quasi-totale de système national fonctionnel de formation continue. Selon les données statistiques 2008/2009, un tiers des enseignants du primaire et 64% des enseignants du secondaire n'ont pas la qualification requise pour enseigner. » La faiblesse de la qualification académique des enseignants du secondaire est également mis en évidence par Bashir (2009). Concrètement, un grand nombre d'enseignants dans ce niveau d'instruction n'ont qu'un diplôme de deuxième cycle du secondaire (51% des enseignants de mathématiques et 38% des enseignants de science dans les écoles publiques)[1].

Le pays est également confronté à d'importants problèmes en matière d'infrastructures. Comme dans la plupart des pays africains, il y a un manque d'infrastructures en RDC. Elles sont également vétustes et très inégalement réparties sur le plan géographique.

Dans un tel contexte, un grand nombre d'enfants, notamment dans les milieux défavorisés, sont exclus de l'école en RDC. Le Rapport de l'enquête nationale sur les enfants et adolescents en dehors de l'école (EADE) dans le pays en 2012 met en évidence l'importance du phénomène de déscolarisation : 71,1% des enfants de 5 à 17 ans fréquentent l'école en 2011-2012. Il y a ainsi une grande proportion d'enfants et d'adolescents qui sont en dehors de l'école[2]. L'ampleur du phénomène des enfants et adolescents en dehors de l'école est plus significative chez les filles.

La pauvreté des parents influe négativement sur la scolarisation en RDC. Il est évident que la situation en matière d'éducation est mauvaise dans un pays où il y a une pauvreté extrême.[3] Le taux net de scolarisation augmente avec le niveau de revenu d'après l'UNESCO (2014) : 65,1% pour le plus pauvre contre 91,6% pour le plus riche en 2010.[4]

L'accumulation du capital humain, via l'éducation, nécessite enfin un contexte favorable, notamment un environnement macroéconomique stable. Cette accumulation est fortement affectée par les années de crises. Selon la Fiche pays Education Pour Tous de la RDC en 2012 : « Plus de trois décennies de déclin économique, de chaos politique et de guerre ont malheureusement valu à la RDC le dernier rang sur l'indice de développement humain du PNUD, et créé des conditions extrêmement difficiles pour l'éducation. »

D'autres facteurs, tels que le phénomène migratoire et les guerres, aggravent le déficit en matière de capital humain en République Démocratique du Congo.

L'accumulation du capital humain paraît difficile dans le contexte congolais. En effet, le pays est confronté à des

1. La situation est moins mauvaise dans les écoles privées. En effet, selon Bashir (2009), 88% des enseignants de mathématiques et de science dans ces écoles ont un niveau universitaire.

2. Parmi les enfants et adolescents en dehors de l'école (28,9%), 6,8% sont déscolarisés et 22,1% n'ont jamais fréquentés l'école.

3. Plus de 70% des congolais vivent en dessous du seuil de pauvreté selon l'UNESCO (2014).

4. Bashir (2009) met en lumière des statistiques démontrant les effets du revenu, mais aussi du niveau d'instruction, des parents sur l'éducation des parents.

guerres qui empêchent toute perspective de développement depuis son indépendance (Mulyumba wa Mamba, 2003). Dans une étude sur la relation entre le capital humain et la lutte contre la pauvreté en Afrique, Hussain et *al.* (2000) ont fait remarquer que le développement du capital humain dans de nombreuses régions du continent africain a été freiné par les conflits sociaux. L'instabilité dans l'Est la RDC est en particulier peu favorable à l'accroissement du niveau de capital humain de la population congolaise. Jacquemot (2010) a ainsi mis l'accent sur les conséquences désastreuses sur l'éducation de l'insécurité qui règne dans le Kivu à cause des conflits armés: les taux de scolarisation sont très faibles dans le niveau de scolarisation primaire (environ 53%).[1]

4. Les implications économiques de l'insuffisance du capital humain

Dans une étude sur la situation de la jeunesse en RDC, Bashir (2009) note que le capital humain peut améliorer la croissance économique du pays. Les ressources humaines jouent un rôle essentiel dans le processus de développement socio-économique. L'accumulation et l'exploitation du capital humain devraient avoir des impacts majeurs sur l'évolution d'une économie. L'expérience des PEA peut donner des enseignements intéressants sur l'importance de la valorisation du capital humain dans le décollage économique. En effet, les performances de ces pays fascinent : ils ont un excédent commercial et maîtrisent leur croissance économique. Cette situation a permis à ces pays d'acquérir le statut de « modèle ». En effet, l'Asie de l'Est et du Sud-Est constitue un cadre particulièrement intéressant pour examiner le processus de croissance économique. Après la Deuxième Guerre mondiale, cette région connaît une forte croissance qui est comparable à aucune autre, ni dans l'espace ni dans le temps. D'ailleurs, pour décrire le développement rapide des économies de la région, la Banque mondiale (1993) utilise la notion de « miracle asiatique ». Toutefois, ces pays subissent bien sûr parfois des crises. Nous allons nous intéresser particulièrement aux implications du capital humain dans cet essor et d'en tirer des enseignements pour la RDC.

Le capital humain a joué un rôle crucial dans le décollage des pays émergents d'Asie. Il s'agit d'un facteur particulier dans le sens où il agit sur les autres variables déterminantes dans le processus de croissance. Les théories de la croissance examinent les mécanismes par lesquels ce facteur affecte l'augmentation de la production, mais l'analyse des évolutions historiques devrait fournir des éclaircissements supplémentaires. Boccanfuso et *al.* (2009) rappellent en particulier que, dans la théorie économique, les modèles de croissance néoclassiques et les modèles de croissance endogène, soulignent l'importance du capital humain pour le développement d'une économie[2].

Les nouvelles théories de la croissance mettent en évidence deux approches pour lesquelles le capital humain agit

1. Par ailleurs, les taux de mortalité maternelle et infantile y sont également très élevés selon Jacquemot (2010).

2. Plusieurs études mettent en évidence l'existence des deux approches quant à l'impact du capital humain sur la croissance (Aghion et Howitt (1998), Gurgand (2000), Altinok (2006), etc.).

sur la croissance économique : l'effet accumulation, d'une part et l'effet niveau, d'autre part. Selon Boccanfuso et *al.* (2009), « Ces différents modèles peuvent être regroupés suivant deux catégories selon leur approche de la relation liant le capital humain à la croissance. La première catégorie concerne les modèles qui considèrent le capital humain comme un facteur d'accumulation au même titre que le capital physique dans la fonction de production et dont l'accumulation favoriserait la croissance, de sorte que les différences dans les niveaux de capital humain sont liées aux différences dans les niveaux de production entre les pays. La deuxième catégorie de modèles considère qu'un plus grand stock de capital humain affecte principalement la croissance économique en facilitant l'innovation et l'adoption de nouvelles technologies, de sorte que les différences dans les niveaux de capital humain causent des différences dans la croissance de la production dans les différents pays. »

L'évolution historique des expériences des économies dynamiques d'Asie démontre non seulement l'existence des effets des investissements éducatifs sur l'accroissement de la productivité, mais aussi le fait que la dotation en matière de main-d'œuvre qualifiée facilite l'adaptation de nouvelles technologies issues des économies plus avancées. En se penchant sur le cas de la RDC, Masoka Wamtu (2007) a également formulé la même conclusion, suite à une revue de la littérature théorique sur le capital humain et la croissance économique. Selon l'auteur, le capital humain influence positivement la croissance économique d'un pays. En effet, les dépenses publiques allouées à l'éducation agissent favorablement sur cette croissance. Après avoir revue la littérature (théorique et empirique), il est parvenu aux conclusions suivantes : l'investissement dans le capital humain contribue de façon significative à la croissance économique ; le capital humain joue un rôle essentiel en faveur de l'évolution et la diffusion technologique ; l'investissement dans le capital humain apparaît comme attractif par rapport à d'autres avoirs, tant au niveau individuel qu'agrégé ; les politiques qui augmentent la quantité et la qualité du stock du capital humain sont compatibles avec l'amélioration de la cohésion sociale.

Masoka Wamtu (2007) a enfin estimé un modèle de croissance économique prenant en compte le taux de scolarisation secondaire. Les tests économétriques ont permis de vérifier les hypothèses de base : compte tenu de l'effet que le capital humain a sur la croissance, l'investissement dans le secteur éducatif ne fera qu'augmenter la croissance économique et la maintenir durant une longue période. Hussain et *al.* (2000) rappellent également que les études macroéconomiques démontrent que les périodes de croissance économique soutenue vont de pair avec des améliorations en matière d'instruction, de nutrition, de santé et de mobilité : il existe une corrélation positive entre l'investissement qu'un pays effectue dans l'éducation et sa croissance économique. Comme le savoir est devenu un facteur primordial de la productivité des individus et des nations, le développement du capital humain constitue un outil essentiel afin d'assurer une croissance économique soutenue et lutter contre la pauvreté. Selon une étude de la Banque mondiale de 1993 portant sur 113 pays, l'éducation primaire est le facteur qui contribue le plus à la croissance des pays d'Asie de l'Est. La situation actuelle de l'éducation en Afrique se caractérise par le fait qu'un pourcentage non négligeable de la main-d'œuvre n'est pas bien préparé à contribuer au développement. La contribution de l'éducation au développement économique est souvent évaluée en fonction des avantages privés et sociaux de l'investissement dans l'éducation. L'observation des faits montrent que les investissements publics et privés dans l'éducation primaire de base et l'éducation secondaire comportent des avantages relativement élevés dans plusieurs pays africains.

Un regard sur le processus de développement des pays en développement suffit à comprendre que l'accumulation du capital humain n'aboutit pas systématiquement à l'émergence économique. L'amélioration du niveau d'instruction de la population active a contribué au décollage des pays émergents d'Asie alors que la plupart des pays africains stagnent. Pour Hussain et *al.* (2000), « l'investissement dans les ressources humaines sera voué à l'échec si très peu d'opportunités d'emploi sont créées pour utiliser pleinement le capital humain. » Au-delà des impacts de la qualification de la main-d'œuvre sur le processus productif, l'engagement ou l'implication de ce facteur joue également un rôle déterminant dans le développement d'une économie. L'importance de l'intérêt accordé par les congolais aux évolutions de la situation de leur pays pourrait également avoir une influence sur la trajectoire économique de ce dernier.

Selon Mulyumba wa Mamba (2003), le manque de personnes formées, capables et engagées dans la construction du pays constitue le problème de le RDC depuis son indépendance. En effet, le pays est en difficulté pour l'auteur car la « déviation est totale dans la mobilisation du capital humain. » L'individualisme a pris la place du souci du travail collectif et de la production communautaire que les Belges avaient si bien exploité ; l'amour de l'argent facile et mal acquis a remplacé la solidarité légendaire des Africains ; le tribalisme exclusif a substitué la cohésion communautaire qui devrait conduire au sentiment de patriotisme à l'échelle nationale. Pourtant, pour Mulyumba wa Mamba (2003) : « Le capital humain est la base de tout développement, de tout progrès social que vise le projet de reconstruction. » Les différents problèmes de la République Démocratique du Congo sont liés au niveau de mobilisation de son capital humain (le patriotisme, l'unité ou l'inspiration à l'intégration culturelle, l'intégration socio-politique, la culture politique). L'auteur a enfin noté que les congolais ont agit défavorablement au développement de leur pays dans la mesure où ils ont des responsabilités dans les crises qui ont frappé le pays.

Conclusion

L'analyse de l'alphabétisation des adultes et du niveau d'instruction de la population âgée de 25 ans et plus permet de démontrer que le niveau moyen de capital humain de la population active congolaise est faible. Pourtant, il s'agit d'un facteur nécessaire à l'amélioration du système productif et au développement du pays. L'éducation pourrait participer à une modification profonde des mentalités ou des comportements et apporter de la stabilité en République Démocratique du Congo. La situation du capital humain du pays limite ainsi son potentiel de croissance et développement. Il convient de noter que des efforts ont été effectués depuis l'indépendance en matière d'éducation, même si ils sont très modérés, mais les impacts sont limités à cause de l'environnement macroéconomique et des contextes social et de gouvernance. Masoka Wamtu (2007) souligne également que l'assainissement de l'environnement politico-économique devrait concourir à l'augmentation et au maintien de la croissance économique de la RDC.

Cette étude montre que le capital humain constitue un des facteurs de blocage de l'émergence économique. Pourtant, il devrait être un des facteurs majeurs de l'essor économique du pays. Plusieurs conditions nécessaires méritent ainsi d'être mises en place pour que l'éducation favorise enfin l'émergence et le développement de la RDC. Elle devrait transmettre un certain nombre de connaissances et de valeurs utiles au développement national. Le système éducatif devrait inciter les congolais à s'intéresser et à contribuer à l'amélioration de la situation de leur pays. Une personne éduquée suit davantage les règles générales de la société (constitution) et les règles au sein de l'entreprise où elle travaille. Par ailleurs, l'éducation devrait être liée au système productif, et donc satisfaire aux besoins de celui-ci. Mulyumba wa Mamba (2003) a également noté que l'éducation est un investissement rentable car la personne instruite et formée constitue un atout pour son pays, mais il faut déterminer un certain nombre de choses avant d'investir en éducation (le nombre de personnes à instruire, la répartition des personnes formées entre les différentes disciplines menant aux professions variées indispensables au développement, la répartition au sein de chaque discipline entre les divers niveaux d'instruction, la qualité de l'instruction à donner, les attitudes à développer dans les personnes à former).

Références

Altinok, Nadir (2006), "Capital humain et croissance : l'apport des enquêtes internationales sur les acquis des élèves", *Revue économie publique*, No. 18-19 – 2006/1-2.

Banque mondiale (1993), *The East Asian Miracle : Economic Growth and Public Sector Policy*, Oxford University Press, New York.

Banque mondiale (1999), *Rapport sur le développement dans le monde 1999 : Le savoir au service du développement*, Banque mondiale et Éditions ESKA, Washington et Paris.

Barro, Robert, Lee, Jong-Wha (2013), "A New Data Set of Educational Attainment in the World, 1950-2010", *Journal of Development Economics*.

Bashir, Sajitha (2009), "Changer de trajectoire : Education et formation de la jeunesse en la république démocratique du Congo", *Document de travail de la Banque mondiale No. 169*, Série : Le développement humain en Afrique.

Boccanfuso, Dorothée, Savard, Luc et Savy, Bernice, "Capital humain et croissance : Evidences sur données de pays africains", Université de Sherbrooke.

Gurgand, M. 2000. "Capital humain et croissance : la littérature empirique à un tournant ?", *Économie Publique*, 6, 71-93.

Hussain, M. N., Moyo, S. S., Oshikoya, T. W. (2000), "Capital humain et lutte contre la pauvreté", Premier Forum International sur les Perspectives Africaines, L'Afrique émergente : 3-4 Février 2000, Banque Africaine de Développement et Centre de Développement de l'OCDE, Paris.

Jacquemot, Pierre (2010), "Les dynamiques de l'instabilité dans l'Est de la RDC", *Revue des Migrations Forcées No. 36*, p. 6-7, Décembre.

Lucas, Robert E., 1988, "On the Mechanics of Economic Development", *Journal of Monetary Economics*, Vol. 22(1), p. 3-42.

Masoka Wamtu, Bibish (2007), "L'impact du capital humain sur la croissance économique en République Démocratique du Congo", Institut Africain du Développement Economique (IDEP).

Middendorf, Torge (2005), "Human Capital and Economic Growth in OECD Countries", *Rhine-Westphalia Institute for Economic Research Discussion Papers No. 30*, Allemagne.

Mulyumba wa Mamba, Barnabé (2003), "Le capital humain : Gage ou entrave pour la reconstruction du Congo après la guerre", Colloque sur la Société Civile et la Reconstruction de la R.D.C. après la guerre, Bukavu, 21-24 août.

Pereira, Luiz C. (2009), *Mondialisation et compétition. Pourquoi certains pays réussissent et d'autres non ?*, Editions La Découverte.

Romer, Paul M. (1989), "What Determines the Rate of Growth and Technological Change?", *Policy Research Working Paper Series No. 279*, Banque mondiale, Washington.

Romer, Paul M. (1990), "Endogenous Technological Change", *Journal of Political Economy*, 98, p. 71-102.

Seka, Pierre R., 2013, "Corruption, croissance et capital humain : quels rapports ?", *Afrique et développement*, Vol. XXXVIII, No. 1&2, 2013, p. 133-150.

UNESCO (2012), "Fiche Education Pour Tous : République démocratique du Congo", *Bureau à Dakar - Bureau régional pour l'éducation en Afrique*.

UNESCO (2014), "Document UNESCO de Programmation Pays : République Démocratique du Congo 2011-2013", *BSP/UCPD/3 REV*, Kinshasa - République Démocratique du Congo.

La contribution de la diaspora à l'émergence de la RD Congo : la promotion de l'investissement dans le secteur privé

Claude Sumata*

Résumé

Cette étude procède à une évaluation de la contribution des investissements de la diaspora congolaise au profit de leur pays d'origine, lesquels pourraient servir de canaux de transmission de la croissance et du développement économique. Les retombées bénéfiques de ces investissements peuvent être cernées en termes d'entrepreneuriat et de création d'emploi. Les entrepreneurs potentiels et les hommes d'affaires de la diaspora constituent des valeurs sûres sur lesquelles les autorités gouvernementales congolaises doivent compter pour assurer la promotion du secteur privé. L'expertise et les ressources financières emmagasinées dans les pays d'accueil constituent des atouts majeurs face au tarissement de fonds et aux conditionnalités des programmes d'aide imposées par les instances financières internationales. Leur rôle peut être crucial dans l'essor des PME/PMI si des mesures appropriées sont adoptées pour attirer leurs ressources vers des secteurs porteurs de l'économie. Des mesures incitatives doivent être prises en leur faveur pour mieux canaliser leurs ressources dans l'optique de la création d'une classe moyenne d'entrepreneurs. Dans ce contexte, les incubateurs d'entreprises transnationales demeurent dès lors des catalyseurs majeurs.

Mots-clés : entrepreneuriat, investissements directs étrangers, diaspora, incubateurs, émergence.

* Professeur à l'Université Catholique du Congo Facultés d'Économie et Développement Kinshasa/RD Congo.

1. Introduction

Les problèmes relatifs à la diaspora et à sa contribution au commerce international demeurent des sujets de prédilection de nombreuses études (Doen et al., 1998 ; Zhou, 2004 ; Shifft, 2007 ; Mundra, 2005 ; Sumata, 2014b). La diaspora se trouve dès lors au centre du processus de promotion des relations commerciales entre les pays d'origine et d'accueil des migrants. Les migrants favorisent dans ce cadre la réduction des coûts de transaction, et par conséquent, accroissent la confiance avec les natifs du pays hôte. Dans ce contexte, ils peuvent constituer des vecteurs majeurs de l'émergence de leurs pays d'origine du fait de leurs implications personnelles dans les transferts de fonds et dans la promotion de l'entrepreneuriat (Diop, 2003 ; Meyer, 2004 ; Sumata, 2004 et 2008 ; Nielsen et Riddle, 2009).

Le recours aux investissements de la diaspora se justifie à plusieurs titres : d'abord, il convient de mentionner leur prépondérance comme vecteur majeur de développement économique du fait des potentialités à mobiliser dans ce contexte ; ensuite, il faut considérer le manque de conditionnalité lié à leur dynamique propre ; enfin, il apparait judicieux d'amplifier une tendance existante dont les retombées restent perceptibles au niveau des secteurs prioritaires de l'économie de la RD. Congo.

Cette étude porte essentiellement sur l'évaluation des opportunités réelles que les entrepreneurs congolais de la diaspora peuvent saisir en RD Congo pour stimuler la promotion des investissements dans le secteur privé. En effet, de nombreux immigrés congolais se sont établis en Occident en créant des entreprises dans les domaines de la production et/ou de la commercialisation des denrées. D'autres se sont spécialisés dans les secteurs de l'exportation et de l'importation entre le pays d'accueil et le pays d'origine. Ils peuvent assurer la promotion de l'entrepreneuriat dans le cadre de l'implantation des PME/PMI en RDC.

Signalons qu'un nombre croissant d'entre eux ont franchi le pas en procédant à la promotion des activités entrepreneuriales au niveau de leurs pays d'origine. Il convient donc d'encourager cette initiative dont l'impact sur la croissance et le développement économique peut être substantiel. Notre démarche vise à suivre la trajectoire des entrepreneurs congolais de la diaspora au niveau de la République Démocratique du Congo afin de stimuler l'impact de leur contribution à l'essor économique de ce pays dans le cadre d'un processus de « Brain gain ».

L'ambition majeure de cette analyse est de procéder à une évaluation judicieuse de la contribution économique des investissements réalisés par la diaspora congolaise au profit de leur pays d'origine, lesquels pourraient servir de canaux de transmission de la croissance et du développement économique.

Cette étude est articulée autour de cinq étapes essentielles. Dans un premier temps, nous essayerons de dresser le profil de la diaspora congolaise. Cette démarche nous permettra d'évaluer par la suite les potentialités de la diaspora en termes d'investissements. Dans le troisième volet de notre travail, il sera question d'aborder les créneaux des investissements de la diaspora en RD Congo. Nous allons nous attarder par la suite sur les mécanismes visant à assurer la promotion de ces investissements dans leur pays d'origine. Finalement, nous conclurons cette étude en dégageant quelques perspectives d'avenir pour l'émergence économique de la RD Congo.

2. Profil de la diaspora congolaise

L'émigration congolaise constitue un phénomène récent qui remonte à la fin des années 70 et au début de la décennie 80. Cette réalité sociale résulte de plusieurs faits majeurs dont la persistance du marasme économique et la dégradation drastique des conditions matérielles des populations restent des facteurs primordiaux. L'émigration s'est amplifiée à partir des années 90 marquées par le processus de démocratisation tumultueux, lequel a entrainé des instabilités sociopolitiques et, notamment, le maintien par la suite des conflits armés sur une portion importante du territoire congolais.

Par conséquent, le profil du migrant congolais couvre toutes les strates de la société congolaise. De ce point de vue, les individus sans qualifications précises (étudiants, chômeurs....) côtoient les cadres bardés de diplômes (professeurs d'universités, médecins, infirmiers, ingénieurs....) à la quête d'un avenir radieux alors que les entrepreneurs plus ou moins aguerris essayent également de saisir des opportunités d'affaires dans les pays d'accueil. Les pays qui exercent dans ce contexte une force d'attraction particulière demeurent la Belgique, l'ancienne puissance coloniale, la France, du fait des liens linguistiques, l'Angleterre, compte tenu de sa politique sociale généreuse et l'Afrique du Sud. Ce dernier va servir dans la plupart des cas de zone tampon ou de tremplin pour le processus d'émigration vers les pays occidentaux.

Il est difficile de se prononcer sur le nombre exact de migrants congolais vivant dans les pays occidentaux compte tenu de la faiblesse des statistiques en RD. Congo. Selon le Gouvernement congolais, le nombre de congolais vivant à l'étranger peut atteindre en moyenne 7 millions de personnes.

Les migrants congolais représentent dès lors des atouts majeurs dans la reconstruction du pays en situation de post-conflit du fait de leurs compétences dans divers domaines notamment dans les technologies de pointe comme les Nouvelles technologies de l'information et de Communication (NTIC), l'ingénierie médicale et dans les techniques de création et de gestion des entreprises. Il convient de remarquer que la RD. Congo a organisé dans ce contexte les premières assises des congolais de l'étranger et le forum de la diaspora de la santé en 2008 ainsi que le forum économique de la diaspora congolaise en 2009. Cette démarche vise à encourager leurs initiatives en faisant prévaloir l'importance de leurs actions dans le développement du pays d'origine.

Il est judicieux de mentionner que la création de la Maison des Congolais de l'Etranger et des Migrants (MCDEM) relève de la volonté de mieux gérer et rentabiliser les flux des ressources et les initiatives de la diaspora congolaise de manière à les intégrer dans les stratégies de développement de la RD Congo.

3. Les potentialites de la diaspora en termes d'investissements

3.1 Migration[1] et développement

Les disparités de niveaux de développement entre les Etats constituent des vecteurs majeurs à la base des trajectoires migratoires des agents économiques. Elles déterminent dès lors les tendances de la migration internationale et les ressources transitant par ces canaux. Par conséquent, la libéralisation des échanges commerciaux constitue une avancée significative dans le sens de la réduction de la mobilité des individus. Le commerce peut être considéré dans ce cadre comme une alternative face à la mobilité des agents économiques dans un horizon plus ou moins lointain.

Selon une étude de l'OCDE parue en 1994, le développement consécutif à l'ouverture favorise dans un premier temps la propension à émigrer. Cependant, la dynamique de développement économique observée par la suite tend à améliorer les conditions de vie de la population et constitue par conséquent un frein majeur au processus d'émigration La contribution de la diaspora à la promotion du commerce international a été mise en exergue dans de nombreuses études (Doen et al., 1998 ; Zhou, 2004 ; Shifft, 2007).

La diaspora constitue une courroie de transmission majeure des relations commerciales entre les pays d'origine et d'accueil des migrants. En effet, ils favorisent dans ce cadre la réduction des coûts de transaction, et par conséquent, accroissent la confiance avec les natifs du pays hôte. Ils peuvent donc être des vecteurs prépondérants de l'essor de la dynamique de développement dans leurs pays d'origine du fait de leurs implications personnelles dans les transferts de fonds et dans la promotion de l'entrepreneuriat (Diop, 2003 ; Meyer, 2004 ; Sumata, 2014b).

Les migrants influent également de manière positive sur les flux des Investissements Directs Etrangers (IDE) au profit de leurs pays d'origine dans la mesure où ils peuvent fournir, en temps réel, des informations appropriées aux natifs du pays d'accueil sur les opportunités d'investissements. En effet, ils facilitent, dans ce contexte, la maîtrise des lois et du système de réglementation, ainsi que la connaissance de la culture et des pratiques commerciales en vigueur dans leurs pays d'origine (Shifft, 2007).

La migration internationale constitue dès lors un rempart pour de nombreux ménages en Afrique dans la mesure où son impact sur l'allégement de la pauvreté demeure globalement positif. L'allocation des transferts aux secteurs économiques prioritaires a permis dans certains cas de stimuler les motivations entrepreneuriales des agents au niveau local. Les immigrés vivant en Occident agissent dans une certaine mesure comme des pourvoyeurs des ressources en dernier ressort du fait de la quasi-inexistence des marchés financiers formels. Par ailleurs, leurs transferts inondent parfois les circuits parallèles des changes en ayant une incidence majeure sur l'évolution de marchés financiers.

1. Il convient de préciser que notre étude concerne essentiellement la migration internationale en dehors de toute considération relative aux phénomènes de déplacements des populations à l'échelle nationale. De ce point de vue, les problèmes récurrents d'exode rural ne sont pas pris en compte.

Les migrants demeurent des acteurs de Co-développement compte tenu de l'importance de leurs transferts financiers et de leur expertise. Cette réalité est désormais prise en compte par divers gouvernements à travers le monde au niveau à la fois des pays occidentaux et moins développés ainsi que des agences multilatérales de développement. Il convient donc de considérer les potentialités réelles des migrants à juste titre pour les canaliser de manière efficiente vers la redynamisation du secteur privé dans leurs pays d'origine.

Selon une étude récente conjointe de la Banque Mondiale (BM) et de la BAD, les transferts de fonds des africains résidant à l'étranger ont représenté 40 milliards de dollars en 2010. Les bénéficiaires au niveau des pays d'origine les ont utilisés essentiellement dans l'achat des terres, l'amélioration des conditions d'habitation et le démarrage des affaires à petite échelle. De même, l'utilisation de ces ressources pour le financement de l'éducation constitue une priorité majeure dans des nombreux pays (Nigeria, Uganda, Burkina-Faso et Kenya). En règle générale, les flux de ces fonds au profit de l'Afrique continuent de croitre malgré le maintien des coûts exorbitants dans les opérations de transferts (Migrant Remittances, 2011).

3.2 Le processus d'immigration internationale et la création d'entreprises

La création d'entreprises est un moyen permettant de combattre l'exclusion sociale en améliorant les conditions de vie des immigrés. Les activités commerciales et de production leur permettent d'avoir des revenus plus ou moins décents et de procéder à la création d'emplois en brisant le cercle vicieux de la pauvreté. Cependant, cette dynamique demeure aléatoire car les entrepreneurs immigrés rencontrent souvent des barrières insurmontables qu'il faut mentionner.

En effet, le financement des activités demeure hasardeux dans un environnement où la discrimination constitue la règle. Certains analystes affirment que les problèmes des entreprises d'immigrés ne sont pas différents de ceux des autres gestionnaires des petites et moyennes entreprises (PME). Cependant, leurs problèmes demeurent tangibles à toutes les phases de leurs activités, compte tenu des difficultés substantielles rencontrées au niveau du démarrage de leurs entreprises et des étapes successives de croissance.

Les entreprises des migrants font face à d'autres barrières qui affectent leur dynamisme, y compris des difficultés linguistiques, les problèmes d'immigration et de xénophobie, la concentration sectorielle des entreprises et le manque de vision sur l'avenir des affaires. Les entrepreneurs immigrés d'Afrique en Occident sont pénalisés par rapport à l'accès au crédit. De même, les problèmes liés à la fidélisation de la clientèle en l'occurrence l'étroitesse du marché les confine dans la plupart des cas dans des enclaves ethniques (Borjas, 1999&2000).

3.3 La mise en place des incubateurs d'entreprises transnationales

Pour assurer l'essor des innovations au sein des PME/PMI et l'émergence d'entreprises sur des créneaux porteurs, les autorités gouvernementales doivent mettre à la disposition des entrepreneurs potentiels notamment les jeunes entrepreneurs, un réseau de compétences et d'expertises. Il existe différents programmes à mettre en place pour accompagner les entreprises dans la construction et le renforcement de partenariats ou de coopérations, pour encourager les processus interactifs favorables au développement d'innovations.

Les incubateurs d'entreprises mis en exergue notamment par Hackett et Dilts (2004) et Aerts et al. (2007) demeurent des recours considérables dans l'expansion et la prolifération des PME/MPI. Ces mécanismes de partenariat ou de coopérations peuvent s'établir à l'échelle nationale, ou internationale par le biais d'incubateurs, de pépinières ou de technopoles, en tant que structures d'hébergement et/ou d'accompagnement des créateurs d'entreprises innovantes. Cette démarche est censée leur permettre de se familiariser avec les processus d'innovation et établir les partenariats nécessaires avec les centres de compétences et accéder à l'annuaire de compétences technologiques et scientifiques.

De nombreuses études ont mis en évidence l'importance des incubateurs d'entreprises dans la promotion des entreprises à l'échelle domestique dans certaines nations (Bergek and Norrman, 2008 ; Aernoudt, 2004; Allen and McCluskey, 1990).

Il est opportun de signaler, par exemple, les diasporas chinoises et indiennes ont joué un rôle prépondérant dans le processus d'émergence de leurs pays respectifs, en maitrisant notamment les technologies importées et en les intégrant, par la suite, dans des programmes de développement de leurs pays d'origine. Dans ces conditions, les indiens ayant évolué à la Silicon Valley (Etats-Unis), ont procédé, ensuite, à l'implantation d'unités de production et commerciales dans le domaine des Nouvelles Technologies d'Information et de Communication (NTIC) en Inde.

Les ressources de la diaspora peuvent être utilisées pour servir de catalyseurs majeurs dans le cadre de la relance des investissements. Dans ce contexte, une nouvelle dynamique s'est créée autour des incubateurs d'entrepreneurs transnationaux (Sumata, 2014 ; L. Riddle et al., 2010 ; Molenaar and Joosten, 2006).

La matérialisation des projets d'investissement de la diaspora peut se faire sous l'égide des programmes d'incubation d'entreprises transnationales au niveau des pays hôtes des migrants en vue d'encourager leurs initiatives entrepreneuriales dans leurs pays d'origine. De même, certains Etats facilitent également l'implantation des incubateurs et des pépinières d'entreprises pour attirer les potentialités de leurs ressortissants vivant à l'étranger.

La mise en place des incubateurs d'entreprises entraine généralement l'essor des échanges et le maintien d'un système de partage d'informations du fait de la mise en réseau des créateurs d'entreprises. Cette dynamique peut favoriser le développement des synergies favorables car des contacts peuvent se nouer entre les porteurs de projet, les entrepreneurs expérimentés, les organismes financiers et les centres de recherche.

Les centres d'incubation constituent des lieux par excellence facilitant la collaboration au niveau international notamment avec les technopoles des pays européens ou émergents afin de bénéficier de leur expertise. On peut envisager des programmes d'échange Sud-Sud en partenariat avec les entreprises ou les incubateurs des autres pays en développement.

4. Les créneaux des investissements de la diaspora en RDC

4.1 L'impact des investissements des immigrés sur l'entrepreneuriat

Les transferts des fonds des immigrés allègent la souffrance des individus face à la pérennisation de la crise socio-économique caractérisée par une pénurie persistante de ressources financières. En RD. Congo, ces ressources ont représenté environ 135 millions de dollars américains en 2009. Ce montant constitue une régression par rapport à l'année précédente car ces transferts avaient atteint 212 millions USD. L'utilisation des ces transferts des fonds dépend des priorités immédiates des familles dans la mesure où ils sont utilisés pour des motifs divers allant de la consommation à l'investissement. En ce qui concerne les projets d'investissement, ils concernent pour l'essentiel l'implantation des activités commerciales à faibles coûts.

Le secteur du transport de la capitale congolaise, Kinshasa, a toujours bénéficié des transferts des immigrés vivant en Occident dont l'investissement a permis de maintenir un système privé en dépit de l'inexistence du transport public officiel durant plusieurs années. En effet, l'acquisition des minibus, des camions ou des taxis dans le cadre de ces transferts semble être le point saillant de ce processus en facilitant la promotion des entreprises familiales. Par conséquent, les transferts demeurent des sources de financement de l'entrepreneuriat au démarrage des activités comme au renforcement du cash-flow lors du processus de consolidation des affaires. En situation de pénurie croissante de ressources, les transferts des immigrés peuvent représenter le seul apport en capital pour des microentreprises.

4.2 Les secteurs porteurs des investissements de la diaspora congolaise

Il est difficile de séparer les transferts des immigrés alloués à la consommation et ceux investis directement dans les activités commerciales et de production. Certaines activités destinées a priori à la consommation comme le paiement des frais scolaires, la prise en charge des soins médicaux ou la construction d'une maison peuvent avoir des effets d'entraînement considérables à terme sur les activités économiques aux niveaux local et national. La prise en charge des soins médicaux et des frais de scolarité par la diaspora, par exemple, demeure une réponse urgente face aux besoins immédiats des membres de leurs familles. Néanmoins, les dépenses opérées dans ce cadre peuvent avoir un impact considérable à terme du fait du capital humain.

La coexistence de deux types de financement liés aux investissements à petite échelle et ceux de gabarit supérieur. La part des transferts des migrants congolais allouée au financement des microcommerces relève de la sphère domestique, dans la mesure où ces activités procurent une soupape de sécurité pour les familles bénéficiaires dans le cadre de leur survie. Par contre, les ressources plus importantes sont canalisées vers des projets plus perceptibles (magasins d'habillement ou d'alimentation, chambres froides) ou vers des vecteurs plus porteurs (hôtellerie, télécommunications, bureautique).

De même, les investissements de la diaspora couvrent des champs majeurs des services publics à l'instar des domaines de la santé, de l'agriculture et du transport où les défaillances de l'Etat demeurent flagrantes. De ce point de vue, la promotion des Partenariats Public-Privé (PPP) serait salutaire pour améliorer l'offre disponible sur le marché des biens et services et satisfaire dans une certaine mesure la demande pléthorique.

Il convient d'évaluer les retombées positives de la contribution des investissements de la diaspora congolaise en RD. Congo. Un inventaire non-exhaustif semble indiquer que la majorité des projets réalisés relèvent essentiellement du secteur des services de base alors que les secteurs de l'agriculture et de l'industrie occupent la part congrue.

Le secteur des services

Le secteur de transport demeure à l'aune des réalisations entreprises par les immigrés au sein de l'économie congolaise. Ce secteur survit grâce au dynamisme de la diaspora du fait de la prolifération des moyens de communication non conventionnels alors qu'on assiste à la dégradation des services étatiques et à l'essoufflement du parc d'automobiles « formel ». À Kinshasa, comme on l'a évoqué plus haut, le transport urbain bénéficie des transferts réalisés par les immigrés qui acheminent des « kombis » (minibus) assurant l'essentiel des déplacements des citoyens face à la faillite du système de transport public.

Le nombre de véhicules à Kinshasa tend à augmenter grâce au dynamisme du secteur non structuré et du transfert des marchandises en provenance de la Diaspora. La vitalité des minibus dépend des transferts de fonds et d'équipements des immigrés congolais vivant en Europe et en Amérique du Nord. Parmi les biens transférés par ces derniers, on compte également les moulins à manioc, les matériels informatiques (ordinateurs et imprimantes), les appareils téléphoniques et les moteurs des chambres froides.

L'appui inconditionnel des fonds et des équipements en provenance de la diaspora demeure primordial et le recours aux opérateurs qualifiés issus du système scolaire officiel constitue une donnée incontournable. Le problème récurrent du chômage des personnes qualifiées trouve une réponse partielle même si les offres d'emploi ne correspondent pas toujours à la formation initiale. Au cours de l'année 2000, par exemple, une agence située dans la région parisienne a expédié plus de 300 véhicules d'occasion en RD. Congo (Musila, 2003).

En dehors du domaine de transport, la majeure partie des investissements réalisés par la diaspora se concentre sur des activités commerciales et des services regroupant pour l'essentiel des boutiques des vêtements, des services informatiques (cafés Internet) et le secteur alimentaire (Chambres froides). De même, l'acheminement des médicaments et des équipements médicaux demeure à la base de la création de certaines cliniques privées et les soins prodigués aux membres de leurs familles constituent une des facettes de leur contribution à leur survie.

Le secteur de l'immobilier est aussi un domaine de prédilection dans lequel les ressources financières de la diaspora sont canalisées. L'achat des maisons et/ou la construction des villas pour les membres des familles et pour les immigrés eux-mêmes constituent un autre volet primordial de leur contribution au développement économique de la RD. Congo. La construction des villas peut prendre plusieurs années et la prolifération des nouveaux logements dans les quartiers périphériques de Kinshasa par exemple constitue une réalité flagrante. Cependant, de nombreux immigrés ont été victimes des supercheries de la part des membres de leurs familles dans la mesure où les transferts peuvent être détournés de leur trajectoire initiale en retardant du même coup les travaux de construction en cours.

Plus récemment, l'expansion des Flats à louer et des Hôtels reste perceptible face à une demande en pleine progression notamment celle émanant de la diaspora elle-même. En effet, les migrants congolais en vacances constituent une clientèle sûre pour ce parc immobilier. Le boom immobilier observé en RD. Congo à partir de l'année 2001 est un indicateur de la rentabilité du secteur immobilier. Plusieurs membres de la diaspora y ont trouvé un créneau porteur. Il convient de se référer à cette agence de transfert établie en Suisse dont la succursale à Kinshasa spécialisée dans le domaine du bâtiment a pu construire 77 maisons dans les quartiers huppés de Binza et Limete (Bagalwa et Monnier, 2002).

Le secteur de l'agriculture

Le financement des activités agricoles (agriculture de base, élevage domestique et pisciculture) constitue également un autre volet de l'intervention des migrants compte tenu de la forte demande de produits alimentaires. Les congolais résidant au pays ont la possibilité de bénéficier dans ce cadre des apports financiers et des transferts d'équipements agricoles ainsi que des intrants et des produits pharmaceutiques à usage vétérinaire de la part des migrants. L'acheminement du capital financier sert aussi à maintenir le développement des petites activités commerciales informelles notamment dans les secteurs alimentaires et de l'artisanat. Le démarrage de ces activités ne nécessite pas la mobilisation de ressources financières substantielles.

Le secteur de l'industrie

Il convient de remarquer la modicité ou l'inexistence des investissements de la diaspora congolaise dans le secteur de l'industrie alors que les besoins y demeurent pharamineux du fait de la déliquescence des unités de production. En effet, les migrants congolais peuvent jouer un rôle majeur dans ce cadre en mettant en valeur leurs compétences et leur maitrise des technologies ainsi que leurs capacités managériales. Cependant, leur participation dans ce domaine reste dérisoire.

4.3 L'étroitesse du marché de l'emploi : Encourager la Diaspora à investir dans le secteur privé

La mise en place d'une stratégie de croissance et d'emploi est de nature à assurer le maintien des revenus stables à la population. Elle constitue par conséquent une garantie stable dans l'optique des stratégies de réduction de la pauvreté. En effet, la lutte contre le chômage endémique est de nature à favoriser la redistribution des ressources et à diminuer la bipolarisation sociale. L'offre d'emploi au niveau du secteur formel nous permet d'avoir une indication sur l'ampleur du phénomène. En effet, le taux de chômage a atteint plus de 50 % de la population active en moyenne annuelle sur la période allant de 2000 à 2009, selon la Banque Centrale du Congo[1].

Parmi les pesanteurs majeures qui empêchent le maintien d'une politique efficace en termes de création d'emploi et de réduction de pauvreté en R.D.Congo, il convient de mentionner la faiblesse du taux d'investissement. Cette réalité demeure une barrière considérable au maintien de la croissance économique à un niveau élevé sur une période longue. Par conséquent, la promotion de l'investissement privé constitue un vecteur majeur du renversement de tendance espéré. La mise en œuvre de cette politique se heurte à l'étroitesse du mode de financement des entrepreneurs privés. En effet, la modicité de l'épargne intérieure empêche le maintien d'une stratégie d'allocation optimale des fonds. Par ailleurs, l'existence des taux d'intérêt faibles ou négatifs constitue également une barrière dans le processus d'attraction des fonds vers les instances financières formelles.

À la lumière de ce qui précède, force est de reconnaitre que la mise en place des politiques volontaristes de promotion de l'entrepreneuriat s'impose pour résorber le chômage en R.D.Congo. La réussite de cette stratégie est conditionnée par le maintien d'une fiscalité favorable au profit du secteur privé en général et de la diaspora en particulier. De même, la construction des infrastructures au niveau du territoire national s'impose ainsi que l'accès aux innovations techniques pour les opérateurs privés.

1. Voir Condensé d'informations statistiques n° 52/2009.

La promotion de l'emploi passe par le maintien d'un cadre légal et institutionnel favorisant l'essor de l'investissement privé. La revitalisation de l'emploi au niveau du secteur public ne doit pas être négligée même si la réputation de l'Etat-providence reste compromise. La réforme des entreprises publiques est de nature à préserver des entités viables notamment dans le cadre des Partenariats Public Privé (PPP). La contribution de la diaspora peut être décisive compte tenu de ses capacités financières et de ses compétences techniques.

Par ailleurs, le gouvernement congolais devra s'engager davantage dans la mise en œuvre d'une politique efficace visant à attirer les Investissements Directs Etrangers. De même, l'usage des mesures fiscales et incitatives ciblées au profit du secteur privé et de la diaspora peut constituer une alternative dans le cadre de la politique de création d'emplois. Cette dynamique est de tendance à créer des synergies favorables pour canaliser les ressources des migrants congolais vers les secteurs porteurs de l'économie.

Selon notre enquête réalisée en Juillet 2011, la majorité des entrepreneurs de la diaspora congolaise proviennent essentiellement des pays suivants : France, Belgique et Grande-Bretagne, et dans une moindre mesure des Etats-Unis (Graphique 1).

Il convient d'analyser les domaines dans lesquels les investissements de la diaspora sont orientés afin de mettre en place une politique économique appropriée. En effet, cette stratégie est de nature à mobiliser davantage leurs ressources vers les secteurs porteurs par le biais d'une politique volontariste.

Les dispositifs d'appui aux entrepreneurs de la diaspora ne sont pas

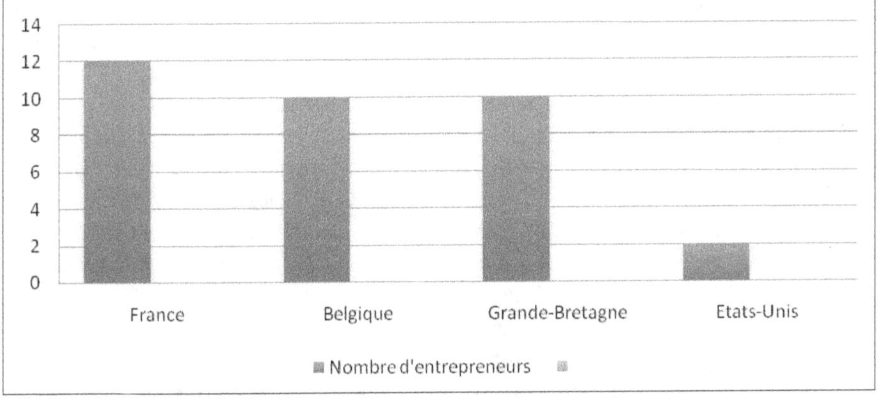

Graphique 1 : Répartition des entrepreneurs de la diaspora selon leurs pays de résidence

uniformes à l'échelle nationale. Cette dynamique demeure la conséquence de l'absence d'une politique d'envergure au niveau national. Certaines provinces comme le Bas-Congo dispose d'un cadre cohérent de promotion des investissements alors que d'autres comme l'Equateur et le Bandundu en sont dépourvues.

Selon notre enquete de Juillet 2011, le secteur de l'immobilier constitue le domaine de prédilection des investissements de la diaspora alors que la presse semble attirer également un nombre considérable d'entrepreneurs. En règle générale, on observe la prédominance des activités du secteur des services (Transport, Presse, Frêt.). Par contre, le secteur secondaire semble inexistant dans le tableau des investissements de la diaspora congolaise. En effet, cette dynamique traduit la faiblesse de l'implication des entrepreneurs immigrés dans le processus d'industrialisation de leur pays d'origine (Figure 2).

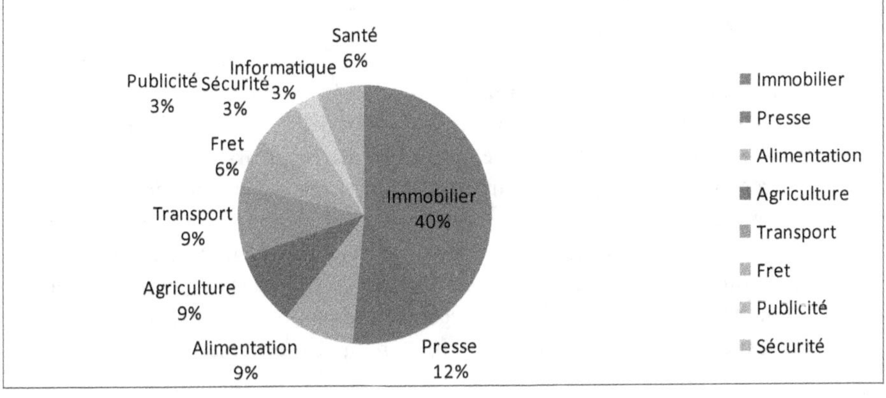

Graphique 2 : Répartition des entrepreneurs de la diaspora selon les domaines d'activités

5. Quelques perspectives d'avenir dans le cadre de l'émergence de la RDC

La RD Congo dispose de potentialités énormes pour hisser son économie vers l'émergence à l'horizon 2030. Elle dispose de ressources naturelles importantes (mines, hydrocarbures, faune, flore) et d'une population jeune. Elle a connu une croissance régulière au cours de la dernière décennie. Cependant, cette dynamique positive ne s'est pas accompagnée d'avancées sociales. Il faut inverser la tendance en dotant le pays d'infrastructures de base et en procédant à l'industrialisation de l'économie. La relance de l'agriculture et la promotion de l'entrepreneuriat (PME/PMI) doivent jouer un rôle majeur dans la recherche d'une croissance soutenue pro-pauvre. Cette dynamique suppose également le respect de la bonne gouvernance et le maintien de la paix. La vision de la RD Congo à l'horizon 2030 est censée concevoir et disposer d'un référentiel stratégique à long terme, à partir d'un consensus national sur une vision future, et promouvoir un mode de gouvernance rénovée dans la gestion du développement du pays.

L'expérience récente des BRICS démontre que le leadership et la planification restent des vecteurs essentiels de l'émergence économique. La relance des activités et la croissance économique dépendent de quatre facteurs primordiaux :

- La promotion des activités tournées vers l'exportation et l'accroissement des réserves de change pour financer les importations ;
- La redynamisation du secteur agricole pour assurer l'autosuffisance alimentaire et favoriser dans une certaine mesure les exportations ;
- Le rôle déterminant de l'éducation pour maintenir un système de formation orienté vers l'acquisition des connaissances techniques et scientifiques ;
- Le recours à la technologie en provenance de l'extérieur par l'acquisition des licences de fabrication et l'appel aux services du personnel qualifié étranger et/ou à la diaspora.

L'émergence de la RD Congo suppose également l'essor d'une classe d'entrepreneurs transnationaux capables de saisir des opportunités d'affaires. Il s'agit de créer un environnement propice à l'entrepreneuriat en investissant dans les équipements et dans la formation pour augmenter la productivité de la main-d'œuvre. De même, il convient de garantir la propriété privée et le maintien d'un environnement propice à l'expansion des affaires. La politique de promotion du secteur privé doit intégrer la dynamique des Investissements Directs Etrangers dont le rôle semble déterminant dans la relance des activités économiques.

5.1 La mise en œuvre des actions stratégiques

Il convient de mentionner quelques suggestions pour assurer la promotion des initiatives de la diaspora au profit de la RD. Congo notamment en faveur de l'investissement privé. Il s'agit dans ce contexte d'utiliser leurs ressources financières, leurs réseaux d'affaires et leur expertise pour faciliter des synergies favorables permettant de stimuler l'entrepreneuriat. Leur rôle dans la dynamique de la croissance et, par conséquent, de la réduction de la pauvreté sera déterminant. En effet, leur contribution pourra être jugée à l'aune des emplois générés dans ce contexte.

Il est judicieux de mettre en œuvre des actions stratégiques pour appuyer les axes prioritaires définies précédemment. Cette démarche peut se traduire dans les éléments énoncés dans le tableau suivant :

Tableau 1 **Mesures pour favoriser l'essor des investissements privés de la diaspora congolaise**
Objectif global
Assurer la promotion des investissements privés de la diaspora en RD. Congo
Objectifs spécifiques
Augmenter le flux des investissements directs de la diaspora
Favoriser la création des PME/PMI de la diaspora
Accroitre le nombre d'emplois et réduire le chômage urbain et rural
Maintenir une croissance économique pro-pauvre Valoriser les innovations technologiques
Mesures à adopter dans ce cadre
Eliminer les goulets d'étranglement et accroître le nombre des entreprises de la diaspora (court terme)
La réforme du cadre réglementaire (loi foncière et réforme agraire) Le maintien d'un système d'information fiable au profit de la diaspora L'organisation des forums économiques dans les grands foyers de résidence de la diaspora congolaise pour attirer les investissements directs de la diaspora La mise en service d'un site internet recensant les opportunités d'affaires à saisir par la diaspora
La réforme du secteur financier en favorisant l'octroi du crédit et des facilités aux entrepreneurs de la diaspora
La levée des options stratégiques pour la réhabilitation et la construction des infrastructures
Le renforcement des capacités du Ministère des Affaires Etrangères à travers la MCEM
L'accroissement de la coopération entre l'ANAPI, la COPEMECO et la MCEM
La création d'un cadre légal et institutionnel viable pour la promotion des investissements de la diaspora
Diversifier les domaines d'intervention des entreprises de la diaspora pour élargir leur base productive. Elargir leurs débouchés et renforcer le Partenariat Public Privé (PPP) (moyen terme)
Le soutien aux initiatives privées en matière d'encadrement, d'approvisionnement et de commercialisation
La professionnalisation des interventions de la diaspora (changer progressivement les systèmes traditionnels d'exploitation)
La mise en place d'un programme de production et distribution de nouvelles technologies
La diversification des secteurs d'intervention de la diaspora
L'organisation et à l'encadrement des entrepreneurs immigrés en associations
Assurer la pérennisation des entreprises de la diaspora et consolider leur contribution à la croissance économique. Accentuer leur rôle dans la création d'emplois et la réduction de la pauvreté
Insérer des clauses spécifiques dans le Code des Investissements favorisant les investissements de la diaspora
Renforcer le rôle du Ministère des PME/PMI en créant un cadre propice à la promotion des investissements de la diaspora

5.2 L'adoption des mesures incitatives en faveur de la diaspora congolaise

Restaurer le statut de la diaspora congolaise

Le rétablissement de la confiance entre les autorités congolaises et leur diaspora constitue un préalable à la mise en place des mesures économiques concrètes visant à promouvoir les investissements des congolais de l'étarnger. Il s'agit de redorer le blason des relations tumultueuses existant entre les deux partis en instaurant la confiance réciproque et en insistant sur les intérêts mutuels. La construction sociale de la confiance passe également par l'organisation systématique des campagnes d'information et de sensibilisation au profit de la diaspora.

De ce point de vue, la création ou la valorisation des services économiques au sein des ambassades ou des missions diplomatiques (Consulats) de la RD. Congo constitue une priorité majeure. Dans ce contexte, la création ou la maintenance des sites web pourra garantir le maintien de ce lien en permettant un dialogue régulier. Les missions diplomatiques sont censées établir le contact avec les enterpreneurs congolais de la diaspora en leur proposant des plans d'actions précis pour les inciter à investir dans leur pays d'origine dans les secteurs porteurs en fonction de leurs compétences et de leurs activités dans le pays hôte.

Mettre en place des mesures douanières favorables à la diaspora congolaise

Il convient de procéder dans un premier temps à la mise en place d'un dispositif d'information permettant à la diaspora congolaise de s'enquérir facilement des mesures existant dans le cadre de la législation douanière. Il s'agit de leur faire bénéficier d'exonérations éventuelles dans le processus de dédouanement des marchandises. Ensuite, il est judicieux de s'attaquer à bras le corps aux pesanteurs majeures liées aux procédures douanières afin d'assurer la fluidité des échanges et de faciliter l'entrée des biens en RD. Congo. Enfin, les redevances perçues en termes de droits de douanes demeurent exorbitants pour certains types de denrées ; il convient dès lors de revoir à la baisse des prix afin d'accroitre le volume des échanges et ce faisant, maximiser le flux des ressources financières au profit de l'Etat congolais.

Adopter des mesures fiscales ou parafiscales favorables à la diaspora congolaise

La mise en œuvre d'un plan national de valorisation des investissements de la diaspora s'impose. Il s'agit d'éliminer progressivement toutes les pesanteurs liées à la persistance des barrières administratives et de faciliter les procédures de création des PME/PMI. De même, l'octroi des avantages fiscaux aux membres de la diaspora congolaise constitue une mesure salutaire dans ce sens.

Le maintien d'un système fiscal déclaratif demeure une pesanteur majeure à l'expansion du secteur privé dans la mesure où les processus de contrôle deviennent hasardeux compte tenu des limites des procédures de redressement. Par conséquent, il est souhaitable de procéder aux amendements et aux ajustements du Code d'investissements afin d'attirer les entrepreneurs immigrés. En effet, on pourra y insérer par exemple des clauses spécifiques en leur faveur notamment dans le processus de création d'entreprises au pays.

Le respect des textes juridiques en vigueur demeure un passage obligé pour stimuler l'entrepreneuriat national en considérant par exemple la discrimination positive exercée dans le cadre du commerce de détail. Les avantages dont bénéficient les congolais résidant au pays doivent être élargis à ceux de l'étranger même lorsqu'ils jouissent d'une autre nationalité.

La réussite de cette démarche positive dépend également de la reconnaissance explicite de leur rôle d'agents de Co-développement, ce qui les inciterait à s'engager davantage dans le processus de reconstruction de la RD. Congo en situation de post-conflit. Par conséquent, le gouvernement congolais devrait être proactif et mettre en place des programmes d'insertion des migrants congolais avec le concours de ses partenaires bilatéraux et multilatéraux.

L'embellie observée récemment sur le plan macroéconomique en RD. Congo ne s'est pas accompagnée des avancées significatives au niveau du climat des affaires et surtout de la promotion du secteur privé. Par conséquent, il est opportun de cibler les opérateurs économiques censés jouer un rôle majeur dans ce contexte. Il s'agit de développer des synergies favorables en adoptant des mesures incitatives afin de les attirer davantage vers les secteurs porteurs de l'économie. La mise en œuvre d'une politique proactive en direction des Congolais de l'Etranger s'impose pour cibler les entrepreneurs viables et leur proposer des créneaux dans lesquels ils pourront investir en tenant compte de leurs avantages concurrentiels et compétitifs.

L'élaboration d'un plan de promotion des investissements de la diaspora en RD. Congo demeure une priorité majeure pour valoriser les potentialités énormes dont regorge le pays et résoudre par conséquent les problèmes récurrents de chômage. En effet, la valorisation des ressources naturelles à entreprendre dans ce contexte est de nature à inverser dans une certaine mesure la tendance catastrophique qui y prévaut. Il s'agit d'orienter, par exemple, les ressources de la diaspora vers l'exploitation des plantations abandonnées dans les provinces agricoles de l'Equateur et du Bandundu qui subissent un appauvrissement croissant.

On pourra initier des programmes ambitieux d'industrialisation du pays en impliquant le secteur privé dans le processus de transformation des produits de base au niveau du territoire national afin de créer davantage de plus-values. Cette dynamique suppose également le maintien d'une classe moyenne efficace capable de saisir les opportunités afin de stimuler le secteur privé. De ce point de vue, son absence constitue un frein majeur à la prolifération de l'entrepreneuriat.

5.3 Les canaux de transmission des investissements de la diaspora

L'acheminement des ressources de la diaspora vers les investissements au niveau du secteur privé constitue une ambition légitime en RD. Congo dans la mesure où les PME représentent 80% de ses potentialités réelles. Il convient de déplorer l'inexistence des clauses spécifiques favorisant les investissements de la diaspora dans le nouveau code des investissements promulgué en 2002. En effet, les efforts ont été entrepris pour éliminer dans une certaine mesure les faiblesses du code d'investissement de 1986 en mettant en exergue le role fondamental du secteur privé dans le nouveau code de 2002.

Au niveau national, des efforts supplémentaires doivent être déployés pour prendre en compte l'importance de la diaspora congolaise dans le processus de reconstruction nationale en canalisant leurs ressources vers les secteurs porteurs. Dans ces conditions, l'ANAPI devrait adopter des mesures adéquates en faveur de la diaspora congolaise afin de stimuler la créativité et les innovations nécessaires à l'essor d'une classe d'entrepreneurs performants. En effet, l'élaboration d'une politique de discrimination positive s'impose dans ce contexte afin d'impulser une dynamique nouvelle dans le cadre de la promotion du secteur privé. Il s'agit de faciliter par exemple les conditions de création d'entreprises par la diaspora congolaise en allégeant les procédures administratives et en raccourcissant les délais nécessaires à l'obtention des autorisations requises.

A l'échelle internationale, il convient de mobiliser les partenaires bilatéraux et multilatéraux à s'impliquer davantage dans le processus de financement des entrepreneurs potentiels issus de la diaspora. Le maintien des projets spécifiques dans le pays d'origine des migrants constitue dès lors une contribution majeure au processus de développement et par conséquent un frein tangible à la migration internationale. En effet, la promotion du secteur privé et la création d'emplois consécutifs constituent des éléments majeurs d'une stratégie visant à fournir aux individus des revenus décents et à réduire les flux migratoires.

Par ailleurs, le recours aux sociétés multinationales s'impose également afin de canaliser leurs ressources financières vers les investissements de la diaspora congolaise dans leur pays d'origine. Il s'agit de mettre en place des systèmes de sélection des candidats potentiels appropriés de façon à leur accorder des dons ou des bourses pour créer des entreprises en RD. Congo. De même, l'amélioration des circuits bancaires et financiers formels peut constituer un moyen efficace de drainer davantage les flux des transferts des fonds. On pourra mettre en place par la suite des titres rémunérateurs pour renforcer les capacités de captation de ces institutions financières et allouer ces ressources vers des prêts à l'investissement pour favoriser l'entrepreneuriat.

L'octroi de microcrédit peut constituer une voie salutaire dans le cadre de la politique de financement des unités de production ou commerciales. Par ailleurs, les ressources financières de la diaspora peuvent être recyclées de manière efficiente dans le cadre des marchés financiers par l'acquisition des actions et des obligations en supposant que des bourses de valeurs mobilières existent et fonctionnent dans de bonnes conditions.

6. Conclusion

L'investissement joue un rôle majeur dans la croissance économique et le développement des nations, comme on peut s'en rendre compte, en analysant l'expérience récente des pays émergents à l'instar des BRICS (Brésil, Russie, Inde, Chine et Afrique du Sud). Le recours aux IDE constitue le socle d'une stratégie visant à favoriser le maintien de la compétitivité des économies. La faiblesse des investissements constitue une faiblesse majeure pour la plupart des pays africains dont l'enracinement dans

Encadré 1
Les programmes de promotion des entrepreneurs immigrés à l'échelle internationale

1) Le partenariat USAID et WESTERN UNION pour la promotion des investissements privés de la diaspora africaine dans leurs pays d'origine

Dans le cadre du programme d'aide à la création d'entreprises par la diaspora africaine dans leurs pays d'origine mis en place par le gouvernement américain (USAID° et la compagnie Western Union, 14 bourses dont la valeur se situe entre 50 000 et 100 000 dollars ont été accordées aux candidats sélectionnés dans le cadre de cette compétition au cours d'une cérémonie qui a eu lieu à Washington, du 12 au 13 janvier 2010. Il s'agit d'un programme visant à assurer l'épanouissement des initiatives privées au sein de la communauté africaine aux Etats-Unis en leur offrant les capitaux nécessaires au démarrage des investissements en Afrique subsaharienne. Cette dynamique se situe dans le cadre de la stratégie du gouvernement américain de favoriser la croissance économique dans ce continent par la création des PME/PMI dont les capacités de création d'emplois sont importantes. De ce point de vue, cette démarche constitue une avancée significative dans le processus de réduction de pauvreté dans la mesure où elle permet aux agents économiques d'accroitre leurs revenus. Dans ce contexte, les entrepreneurs issus de la diaspora saisissent des opportunités dans leurs pays d'origine pour mettre en pratique des idées novatrices par le biais des investissements dans le secteur privé.

2) Le Programme Migrations et Initiatives Economiques Nord/Sud en France

L'objectif majeur du Programme Migrations et Initiatives Economiques (PMIE) est de faciliter la mise en place des projets économiques des migrants dans leurs pays d'origine et en France. Il a commencé en 2001 sous l'égide de l'association pS-Eau (Programme Solidarité Eau). Il bénéficie des financements du gouvernement français par le biais du Ministère des Affaires Etrangères et de celui du Travail, de l'Emploi et de la Cohésion Sociale ainsi que d'autres institutions comme la Commission européenne et le Comité Catholique contre la Faim et pour le Développement (CCFD). Depuis 1996, le Ps-Eau anime un réseau d'opérateurs d'appui : Le GAME (Groupe d'Appui à la Micro Entreprise). Deux actions d'envergure ont été mises en place dans ce contexte :

Les bourses d'étude de faisabilité : Elles facilitent la réalisation d'étude dans les pays d'origine pour la collecte des informations indispensables au projet. Elles offrent aux migrants la possibilité d'en vérifier la pertinence et la viabilité. L'étude en question est effectuée par un opérateur local spécialisé dans le domaine de la création d'entreprises. Les montants de l'ordre de 1300 euros sont alloués en dehors de la prise en charge des frais de voyage, d'hébergement dans le pays et de prestation à verser à l'organisme d'appui.

L'action « Investissement à distance » : Elle est opérationnelle au Sénégal et au Mali en partenariat avec les banques locales. Elle permet aux migrants travaillant en France et disposant d'une épargne de cautionner le crédit accordé par une banque locale à un membre de famille ou à un partenaire pour créer une entreprise. Le montant de la caution représente la moitié de la valeur totale du prêt.

3) Le soutien des initiatives de développement des migrants dans leurs pays d'origine d'OCIV en Belgique

Il s'agit d'un programme mis en place par « OCIV-Migration et Développement », un des départements d'OCIV (Overlegcentrum Integratie Vluchtelingen), la plate-forme de concertation des associations d'aide aux réfugiés et aux demandeurs d'asile basées en Flandre. Ce programme a été créé en 2000 pour accompagner les migrants dans le processus de création d'entreprises et d'élaboration de projets au profit des populations locales de leurs pays d'origine.

le cercle vicieux de la pauvreté reste dans ce cadre une réalité flagrante.

Par conséquent, les entrepreneurs issus de la diaspora peuvent constituer des acteurs majeurs de la stratégie de création d'emplois et de stimulation des investissements dans leur pays d'origine, car ils peuvent prendre des risques considérables en saisissant des opportunités dans ce contexte. En effet, leur maitrise des techniques de gestion et des innovations technologiques sont des facteurs déterminants dans l'élaboration d'une classe de promoteurs des PME/PMI. Il convient donc de les encourager et de leur offrir un cadre légal et institutionnel favorable à leur épanouissement.

Il revient donc aux autorités gouvernementales congolaises de mettre en place des politiques économiques ambitieuses à la hauteur des défis majeurs qui soustendent les flux des investissements de la diaspora congolaise afin d'accroitre leurs effets positifs sur l'entrepreneuriat. Il s'agit d'adopter une stratégie proactive visant à faciliter les mécanismes de création d'entreprises par les migrants congolais. Ces derniers peuvent ainsi être des partenaires viables dont l'attitude peut être décisive dans le processus de création d'unités de production et commerciales. De même, leur engagement demeure souhaitable dans les stratégies à mettre en place pour persuader les investisseurs potentiels à saisir les opportunités d'affaires en RD. Congo. Il s'agit de stimuler leur rôle en tant qu'« ambassadeurs » de ce pays censés encourager les opérateurs privés étrangers à saisir des opportunités d'affaires dans ce contexte et assurer la promotion des IDE.

Préalablement, les autorités gouvernementales puissent user de leur pouvoir de séduction afin d'impliquer ces migrants dans des programmes adéquats de partenariat en leur faisant jouer le rôle crucial d'agents de Co-développement. Il s'agit à la fois de restaurer la confiance et d'assurer la visibilité de ces programmes à mettre en place sous l'égide des autorités gouvernementales et des acteurs de la diaspora.

Les entrepreneurs potentiels et les hommes d'affaires de la diaspora constituent dans ce contexte des valeurs sûres sur lesquelles les autorités gouvernementales congolaises devraient compter pour assurer la promotion de l'investissement privé. Il convient de remarquer que l'expertise et les ressources financières emmagasinées dans les pays d'accueil constituent des actifs surs face au tarissement de fonds et aux conditionnalités des programmes d'aide des instances financières internationales. En effet, les entrepreneurs congolais de la diaspora demeurent dès lors des catalyseurs majeurs dans la stratégie de revitalisation de l'entrepreneuriat en RD. Congo. En effet, leur rôle peut être crucial dans la promotion du secteur privé si des mesures appropriées sont adoptées pour attirer leurs ressources vers des secteurs porteurs de l'économie en vue de stimuler la croissance et créer des emplois. De ce point de vue, ils occupent donc une place prépondérante dans les programmes de lutte contre le chômage et de réduction de pauvreté.

7. Bibliographie

AERNOUDT, R. (2004), "Incubators: Tool for entrepreneurship?", *Small Business Economics*, 23 (2), 127–135.

AERTS, K., MATTHYSSENS, P., VANDENBEMPT, K., (2007), "Critical role and screening practices of European business incubators", *Technovation*, 27 (5), 254–267.

ALLEN, D. N., McCLUSKEY, R. (1990), "Structure, policy, services, and performance in the business incubator industry", *Entrepreneurship: Theory and Practice*, 15 (2), 61–77.

ALLEN, D. N., RAHMAN, S. (1985), "Small business incubators: A positive environment for entrepreneurship", *Journal of Small Business Management*, 23 (3), 12–22.

BAGALWA MAPATANO, J. (2007), *Crise de l'Etat et migration. La diaspora congolaise-zaïroise en Suisse 1980-2005*, Genève, Institut Universitaire d'Etudes du Développement (IUED): 366.

BERGEK, A., NORRMAN, C. (2008), "Incubator best practice: A framework", *Technovation*, 28 (1–2), 20–28.

BORJAS, G. J. (2000), "Ethnic enclaves and assimilation". *Swedish Economic Policy Review*, 7:89-122.

BORJAS, G. J. (1999), *Heaven's Door: Immigration Policy and the American Economy*. Princeton University Press, Princeton.

DIOP C. (2003), « Rôle du secteur informel et des sénégalais de l'extérieur : stratégie de mobilisation de l'épargne et sécurisation des investissements », Forum sur l'investissement et l'emploi, CPDS-GES ? Dakar, Mai.

DOEN M., GORTER C., NIJKAMP P. et RIETVELD P. (1998), "Ethnic Entrepreneurship and Migration: A Survey from Developing Countries", *Tinbergen Institute Amsterdam Discussion Paper*, No 98081, 14 p.

DOING BUSINESS 2011(2010), Congo *Dem. Rep. Making a difference for entrepreneurs*, Banque Internationale pour la Reconstruction et le Développement/Banque mondiale.

HACKETT, S. M., DILTS, D. M. (2004), "A systematic review of business incubation research", *Journal of Technology Transfer*, 29 (1), 55–82.

MAISON DES CONGOLAIS DE L'ETRANGERS/MCDEM (2009), Résultats du Forum Economique de la Diaspora Congolaise, Kinshasa, 8 p.

MEYER J. B. (2004), « Le rôle des migrants hautement qualifiés dans le développement de leur pays d'origine », Journées scientifiques de Dialogue 'Afrique et Mondialisation', le rôle des diasporas dans le développement de l'Afrique subsaharienne, Tervuren, Belgique, 9 mai, pp. 14-14.

MIGRANT REMITTANCES (2011), Vol. 8, No 1, Mai.

MOLENAAR, K., JOOSTEN, M. (2006) *A Challenging Future for Enterprising Migrants*, IntEnt, The Hague.

MUNDRA, K.. (2005), "Immigration and international trade: A semi parametric empirical investigation", *Journal of International Trade and Economic Development*, 14 (1), 65–91.

NIELSEN, T.M., RIDDLE, L. (2009), "Investing in peace: The motivational dynamics of diaspora investment in post-confict economies", *Journal of Business Ethics*.

CADICEC (2000), « Micro-entreprise, stratégie de lut33te contre la pauvreté », *bulletin nr. 979/80*.

De BRUYN, T. et WETS J. (2006), *Remittances in the Great Lakes Region. Migration Research Serie,*. Geneva, International Organisation for Migration.

ELLIS S., Y.-A. FAURE (Ed.) (1995), *Entreprises et Entrepreneurs Africains,* KARTHALA/ORSTOM, Paris, 1995.

FAURE Y.-A. (1991), « Entrepreneurs d'Afrique Subsaharienne : Communautés entrepreneuriales dans les travaux anglophones (Ghana, Nigéria, Kenya, Zaïre, etc...) et comparaisons avec la Côte-d'Ivoire », *Notes de Recherche de l'UREF/AUPELF*, n° 91 - 19.

HERNANDEZ M. (2011), "Can Public-Private Partnership Work? Western Union's View", *Migrant Remittances*, Vol. 8, No 1, Mai.

LUTUTALA, B. (2006). « L'ubiquité résidentielle des migrants congolais. Une enquête auprès des migrants à Paris », *Civilisations*. LIV: 117-124, No 9-10, Juillet-Décembre.

OCDE (1994), *Migration et développement. Un nouveau partenariat pour la coopération,* Paris, OCDE.

PECOUD A. (2012), « Immigration, entreprenariat et ethnicité », *Métropoles* [En ligne], 11 | 2012, mis en ligne le 12 décembre 2012, consulté le 21 octobre 2014. URL : http://metropoles.revues.org/4560

RIDDLE L., HRIVNAK G. A., NIELSEN T. M. (2010), "Transnational diaspora entrepreneurship in emerging markets: Bridging institutional divides", *Journal of International Management 16 (2010) 398–411*

SANTOS N. (2003), « Financing Small, Medium, and Micro-enterprises in a Post-conflict Situation: Microfinance opportunities in the DRC », papier présenté à la conférence «Partenariat Public-Privé pour le Développement de la République Démocratique du Congo».

SHIFFT M. (2007), « Migration, investissement et commerce : substituts ou compléments ? », *Revue d'Economie du Développement*, 2 Vol. 21, p. 7-34.

SOENEN, H. (2006). "How to Make Ice-Cream? An Anthropological Economic Study of Remittance Practices among Congolese and Ecuadorian Migrants." Kolor 6(1): 41-57.

SUMATA C. (2014a), *La gestion macroéconomique de la République Démocratique du Congo durant et après la transition démocratique*, Cahiers africains no 85, L'Harmattan-MRAC, Paris-Tervuren.

SUMATA C. (2014b) (Ed.), *Les migrants et l'investissement en Afrique*, L'Harmattan, Paris.

SUMATA C. et DZAKA-KIKOUTA T. (2013), « The determinants of China's foreign direct investment in Central Africa: evidence from the Republic of Congo and DRC?», *African East-Asian Affairs* 2 : 15-38.

SUMATA C. (2012), « La dynamique économique de la guerre et de la paix dans la région des Grands Lacs : Le processus de reconstruction post-conflit en RD. Congo », *Congo-Afrique*, No 469, Octobre, pp. 664-680.

SUMATA C. (2010), "Parallel Market for Foreign Currency and Hyperinflation: The case of Congo-Kinshasa", *International J. of Trade and Global Markets*, Vol. 3, No. 1, pp. 115-131.

SUMATA C. (2008), "Migrant remittances as a new source for development finance: The case of sub-Saharan Africa", *OSSREA Bulletin*, Volume V, No 1, Février.

SUMATA C. (2004-2005), « Les enjeux de la migration et de l'entrepreneuriat : Les transferts des migrants peuvent-ils financer l'entrepreneuriat au Congo-RDC ? », *Revue Congolaise de Gestion.*

SUMATA C. (2004), « Images et Usages de l'argent de la diaspora congolaise : Les transferts comme vecteur d'entretien du quotidien à Kinshasa » (avec Théodore Trefon et Serge Cogels) dans T. Trefon (Ed.), *Ordre et Désordre à Kinshasa : Réponses populaires à la faillite de l'Etat*, L'Hamattan-Paris, Cahiers Africains, Numéro 61-62.

SUMATA (2002), «Migradollars and poverty alleviation strategy issues in Congo-DRC», *Review of African Political Economy* (ROAPE), 93, Novembre-Décembre.

SUMATA C. (2001), *L'Economie Parallèle de la RDC : Taux de Change et Dynamique de l'Hyperinflation au Congo*, L'Harmattan, Paris.

SUMATA C. (1993a), «Les effets pervers de l'hyperinflation sur la performance de l'entrepreneuriat au Zaïre», *Notes de Recherche de l'UREF/AUPELF*, n° 93 - 36, 22 p.

SUMATA C. (1993b), «Les circuits financiers extra-bancaires et l'entrepreneuriat au Zaïre», dans PONSON B., SCHAAN J. L.: *L'esprit d'Entreprise, Aspects Managériaux dans le Monde Francophone*, AUPELF/UREF et JOHN LIBBEY EUROTEXT, p. 447-459.

ZHOU M. (2004). "Revisiting Ethnic Entrepreneurhip: Convergencies, Controversies, and Conceptual Advancements", *International Migration Review*, Numéro de l'automne, 30 p.

Les défis de la transformation économique de la RD Congo

Jean-Marc Kilolo Malambwe

1. Introduction

Le gouvernement congolais a pour ambition de faire de son pays en une économie émergente à l'horizon 2030. Cet objectif suppose une réelle transformation économique, soutenue par des politiques industrielles et de main-d'œuvre. En effet, le terme « pays émergents » ou « nouveaux pays industrialisés » (NPI) a été employé pour la première fois pour qualifier les pays d'Asie de l'Est qui ont connu une croissance économique soutenue et qui ont réussi à s'insérer dans le commerce mondial, en saisissant les opportunités qu'offrent les chaînes de valeur mondiale et en diversifiant leur économie. Trois éléments majeurs semblent être à l'origine du développement économique des tigres est-asiatiques, à savoir : un taux d'épargne élevé, l'accumulation du capital physique, ainsi que l'investissement dans le capital humain à travers leurs systèmes publics d'éducation (Sarel, 1997). Pourtant, ces trois facteurs font cruellement défaut à la RDC[1]. D'où l'intérêt de cet article qui vise à répondre à la question suivante : quelles orientations générales le gouvernement de la RDC a déjà prises ou devrait-il prendre pour faire de ce pays une économie émergente ? Mais avant d'y répondre, il convient de dresser un portrait de l'économie congolaise. Ainsi, la première section de cette étude présente un bilan économique sommaire de la RDC, mettant en lumière les limites d'un système économique basé sur l'extraction des matières premières pour ré-

1. L'article d'Angelo DJISTERA publié dans ce volume dresse un portrait exhaustif du capital humain en RDC.

pondre à des besoins extérieurs, suivant le vieux modèle des échanges basés sur les avantages comparatifs. Les sections suivantes examinent successivement trois facteurs de succès d'une politique industrielle, à savoir le positionnement dans la chaîne des valeurs, la localisation des activités économiques ainsi que la qualification de la main-d'œuvre. Concernant le premier facteur, cet article met l'emphase sur l'agriculture et le secteur des mines qui constituent le fer de lance de la politique industrielle du gouvernement.

2. L'ÉCONOMIE CONGOLAISE : UN BREF DIAGNOSTIC

En dépit de son énorme potentiel en ressources naturelles, la RDC est un pays pauvre; le niveau de vie moyen de sa population est en deçà de la moyenne de l'Afrique subsaharienne. Au cours des trente dernières années, le niveau de vie des Congolais s'est continuellement dégradé : en 2010, le PIB par tête de la RDC (148 $) représente à peine le tiers de ce qu'il était en en 1970 (459 $) ! Comme on peut le voir sur le graphique 1, la chute du PIB par tête a été continue sur la période 1970-2002, contrairement à la moyenne subsaharienne et à ses voisins zambien et rwandais. En particulier, on peut voir que les deux pays suivent la tendance africaine, où une reprise s'amorce dès la moitié des années 1990, contrairement à la RDC. Selon le Oxford Poverty & Human Development Initiative (OPHI, 2010), le revenu journalier par habitant en RDC est le plus faible de l'Afrique subsaharienne : le citoyen congolais vit avec moins de 2 $ par jour.

Depuis 1970, l'économie congolaise s'est montrée très vulnérable face à différents « chocs économiques » (évènements) : le graphique 1 montre comment la zaïrianisation a été néfaste. Il s'agit de l'expropriation des biens appartenant aux expatriés au profit des proches du régime; cette mesure qui a suivi la nationalisation des industries minières du Kasaï et du Katanga en 1966, et le recours à l'authenticité amorcé en 1971, a accéléré la chute du niveau de vie des Congolais. En effet, le graphique 1 montre une forte baisse du PIB par tête à partir de 1974, année de la zaïrianisation; cette chute se poursuit jusqu'au début des années 1980, étant donné le fait que les nouveaux propriétaires n'avaient aucune connaissance du monde des affaires. Le PIB par tête s'est maintenu à peu près à un niveau moyen de 350 $, jusqu'au début des années 1990, marquées par la transition politique et par les pillages de 1991 et 1992 qui ont détruit l'appareil de production. Ces deux épisodes de l'histoire économique ont longtemps entaché l'image du Congo auprès des milieux d'affaires. Jusqu'à ce jour, la RDC est considérée par les milieux financiers comme une destination risquée, en raison de la faible protection juridique des investissements étrangers. En fait, les pillages et les conflits armés ont exacerbé la désindustrialisation.

À la lumière de ces observations, une question vient à l'esprit : qu'est-ce qui explique la contreperformance économique de l'Afrique et de la RDC en particulier ? Michel Norro (1998) constate que « le secteur moderne de l'économie ne s y'est pas constitué à partir d'une transformation progressive de l'économie locale, mais s'y est implanté à l'initiative de l'étranger, pour

Figure 1: Évolution du PIB per capita de la RDC de 1970 à 2010

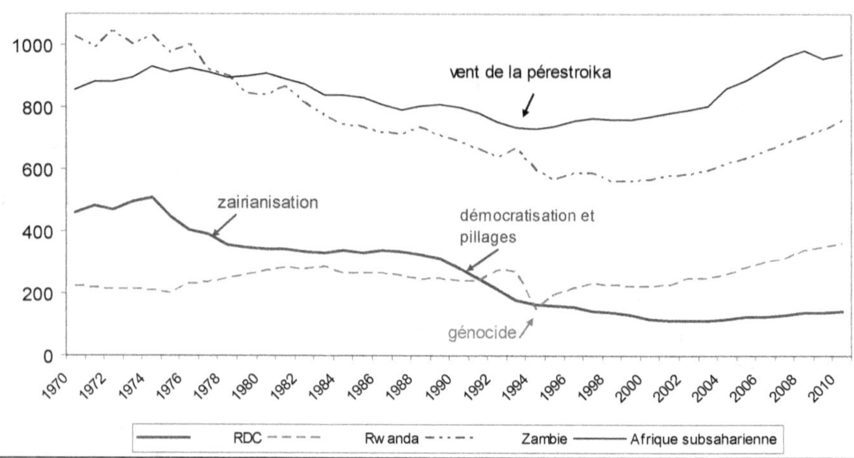

Source de données : UNCTADstat, données exprimées Dollars des États-Unis aux prix constants (2005) et taux de change constant (2005) par habitant

répondre à une demande et donc à des besoins extérieurs. De plus, pour ce faire, ce secteur a généralement recouru de façon intensive à des facteurs étrangers de production, principalement des cadres gestionnaires et des capitaux. Ce qui explique à la fois son dynamisme et sa vulnérabilité[1].» Paraphrasant les propos de Norro, on s'aperçoit que la chute quasi continue du PIB par tête débute après l'effondrement des prix internationaux des matières premières (notamment le cours du cuivre) dans les 1970. Ce qui atteste de la vulnérabilité des pays exportateurs de ces produits. Rappelons que la structure de l'économie congolaise est héritée de la colonisation : elle est dominée par le secteur primaire, en particulier l'industrie extractive (cobalt, le cuivre, le diamant et le pétrole) qui représente 78 % de la valeur des exportations du pays en 2008 et contribue à concurrence de 20 % à 40 % des recettes fiscales. Ainsi, les matières premières à faible valeur ajoutée constituent l'essentiel des exportations congolaises depuis les années 1960. Par ailleurs, l'industrie extractive a un rendement limité, compte tenu de l'équipement qui est désuet et de la faible diversification de la production.

Il est bien connu que le secteur primaire est à forte intensité capitalistique, c.-à-d. qu'il requiert des investissements majeurs en capital physique et génère peu d'emplois; par ailleurs, il est souvent mal relié au reste de l'économie, comme le laisse entendre Norro (1998). L'industrie primaire accapare l'essentiel des

1. Michel Norro (1998), « Économies africaines: analyse économique de l'Afrique subsaharienne », De Boeck Université, 307 pages.

investissements directs étrangers (IDE) avec le secteur des banques et celui des télécommunications. Par ailleurs, le secteur manufacturier, qui est rudimentaire, dessert presque exclusivement le marché local; il représente à peine 5 % du PIB et couvre l'agroalimentaire, la chimie, le textile et les biens d'équipement (Organisation mondiale du commerce, OMC, 2011). Comme dans la plupart des pays africains, le secteur manufacturier congolais fabrique des produits simples non élaborés, qui ne nécessitent pas d'investissements importants ni des compétences élevées.

La faible contribution du secteur manufacturier congolais au PIB s'explique par la vétusté de l'outil de production, le faible recours aux nouvelles technologies, sa faiblesse face à la concurrence étrangère ainsi que des coûts engendrés par le double déficit d'infrastructures et d'accès à l'énergie, en l'occurrence des coupures intempestives de courant (Banque africaine de développement (BAfD) et al., 2014). Dans ce contexte, il n'est pas surprenant que le secteur privé congolais occupe une place très marginale dans les réseaux internationaux de production et intervient essentiellement au bas de la chaîne de valeur.

S'il est vrai que depuis peu (2003), la RDC a renoué avec la croissance économique, cette dernière est non inclusive, puisqu'elle contribue très peu à la création d'emplois et à l'amélioration des conditions de vie des populations congolaises. Par ailleurs, un récent rapport de la BAfD (2014) qualifie la croissance en RDC de volatile à court et à moyen terme compte tenu de la faible diversification des activités de production, d'une forte dépendance vis-à-vis des marchés internationaux et d'une faible capacité de réaction face aux chocs externes. Dans ce contexte, il n'est dès lors pas surprenant que le taux de chômage moyen du Congo soit estimé à plus de 50 % (BCDC, 2013)[1].

Selon un rapport la Commission économique pour l'Afrique (ECA, 2011), au moins quatre facteurs peuvent être invoqués pour expliquer la faiblesse du secteur manufacturier en Afrique, à savoir : le manque de capacités technologiques, des ressources financières limitées, un avantage comparatif dans la production et l'exportation de produits de base (compte tenu de l'abondance des ressources naturelles) ainsi que la faiblesse du capital humain du continent. Dans ce cas, la transformation de la structure économique de la RDC est-elle possible ? Par où commencer et quels exemples suivre ?

3. Progresser dans la chaîne des valeurs dans le secteur des mines et dans l'agriculture

Comme le note la Commission économique pour l'Afrique (CEA, 2013), la forte demande internationale pour les produits de base donne aux états une marge budgétaire à consacrer aux programmes de transformation économique. Conscient des limites d'un modèle de développement axé sur l'exportation de matières premières[2], le gou-

1. Le taux de chômage s'explique aussi par la structure de l'économie congolaise dominée par l'agriculture non mécanisée et par le secteur primaire à forte intensité de capital, deux industries qui ne nécessitent pas des travailleurs très scolarisés (problème de capacité d'absorption des travailleurs diplômés).

2. Plusieurs travaux de recherche montrent que la croissance économique à long terme d'un pays dépend du type de produit qu'il exporte (Hausmann, Hwang et Rodrik, 2007).

Figure 2 : La transformation industrielle de la RDC requiert une montée dans la chaîne de valeur

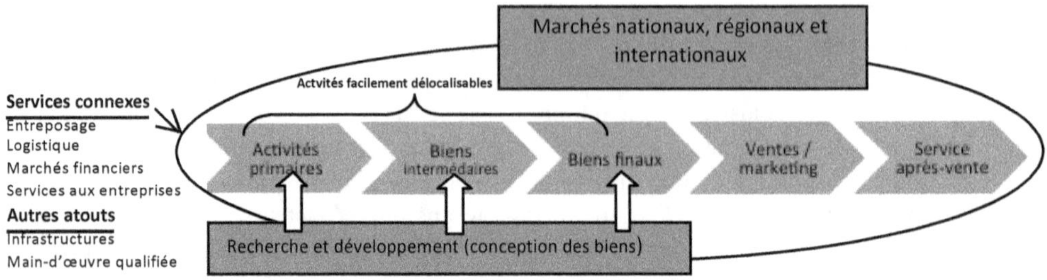

Source : l'auteur.

vernement congolais a entamé l'élaboration de la nouvelle politique industrielle de la RDC en 2012, axée notamment sur l'agroalimentaire, les textiles et la transformation des métaux. Compte tenu du potentiel de création d'emplois et des liens avec d'autres secteurs d'activité, le développement de ces industries peut générer des externalités positives pour l'ensemble de l'économie.

En vue de promouvoir le traitement et le raffinement des minerais à l'intérieur du pays, le gouvernement a interdit l'exportation des concentrés de cuivre et cobalt (BAfD et al., 2014). Ce type de mesure permettrait de monter dans les chaînes de valeurs mondiales (CVM), en passant de la simple extraction des minerais du sous-sol à la transformation de ces derniers en produits intermédiaires et finaux.

La figure 2 présente un schéma de la chaine de valeur. Celle-ci fait référence aux différentes étapes menant de la conception d'un produit ou service à sa vente au consommateur final. Les activités primaires, qui forment le socle de l'industrie congolaise, se trouvent au début de la chaîne de valeur. Grâce à la fragmentation géographique du processus de production, les entreprises peuvent délocaliser une partie des activités dans différents pays, en fonction de leurs avantages comparatifs respectifs (main-d'œuvre bon marché, présence d'infrastructures et services connexes). D'où l'expression « chaîne de valeur mondiale ». Les activités au début de la chaine sont les plus facilement délocalisables. Un exemple ci-dessous permet de mieux comprendre le concept. Compte tenu de la richesse du sous-sol congolais, le Congo exporte des minerais dont le coltan (activité primaire); ce dernier sert notamment à la fabrication de condensateurs de tantale (bien intermédiaire) qu'on retrouve dans les ordinateurs, les jeux vidéo, dans les avions, les véhicules ainsi que dans des équipements militaires (biens finaux).[1] Une fois que le produit est fabriqué, il faut le promouvoir sur le marché (ventes / marketing) et s'assurer de la satisfaction des clients (service après vente). Tout ceci est bien évidemment supporté par la recherche et développement, qui

1. Voir Martineau (2003).

permet de concevoir le projet et d'identifier les composants nécessaires à la fabrication d'un produit.

La transformation industrielle initiée par l'état congolais, qui suppose une meilleure intégration dans les chaines de valeur mondiales, s'accompagne d'une création d'emplois et d'une amélioration des conditions plus ou moins qualifiés, d'un transfert de technologie, mais aussi une amélioration de la valeur des exportations. Toutefois, le succès de cette politique industrielle dépend fortement des services qui permettent un fonctionnement effectif des CVM, en l'occurrence la logistique, les services financiers, les services aux entreprises (SAE) ainsi que les services de communication. Or le mauvais état des infrastructures (routières, portuaires et aéroportuaires, etc.) et la mauvaise fourniture d'électricité constituent de sérieuses entraves à l'efficience et la flexibilité que recherchent les firmes multinationales à travers la fragmentation de la chaîne de production à l'échelle internationale. Pour se faire une idée de l'efficience des infrastructures de transport et de la logistique, on peut comparer le coût d'exporter un conteneur de 20 pieds. En consultant la base de données World Development Indicators (2013), on constate que ce coût s'élève à 3 155 $ US en RDC, ce qui est largement supérieur à la moyenne subsaharienne (2 108 $ US). Ce coût est environ le triple de la Tanzanie (1 090 $ US), un pays ayant un bon accès à la mer, mais un peu moins du double de celui du Swaziland (1 880 $ US) qui est enclavé comme la RDC. Signalons que ce coût ne s'élève qu'à 620 $ pour la Chine. Cet exemple montre en fait que cet indicateur reflète des aspects géographiques (accès à la mer ou non), mais aussi d'autres dimensions telles que les procédures douanières et la logistique.

Dans sa stratégie industrielle, le gouvernement de la RDC devrait penser à créer toutes les capacités nécessaires visant à rencontrer les normes de qualité et les spécifications des entreprises multinationales (EMN) afin de faire face à la concurrence d'autres pays émergents ou en voie de le devenir. En effet, dans la gestion de leur chaîne de valeur, ces entreprises cherchent à optimiser le processus d'affaires, en réduisant les coûts à travers la CVM. Ainsi, il importe pour la RDC de démontrer clairement ces avantages comparatifs, en développant, par exemple, des produits qui se démarquent de ceux de la concurrence (différenciation de produits).

Le choix de transformer localement les minerais s'avère judicieux et très réaliste, puisqu'il se fonde sur le potentiel de la RDC (ses ressources naturelles), tout en tenant compte des contraintes de capacités de production et d'innovation qui pèsent sur le pays. Par ailleurs, les entreprises de droit congolais n'ont pas encore été suffisamment connectées aux marchés mondiaux afin de s'imposer comme plateforme pour la fabrication de composants de haute technologie ou comme distributeur mondial de biens. Le parcours de l'économie chinoise est très inspirant à ce propos : la Chine, qui est parfois qualifiée d' « usine du monde », est progressivement passée de la production de produits à faible valeur ajoutée aux activités d'assemblage de biens finaux de haute technologie – l'ipad étant un bel exemple. Cette transition a été réalisée, grâce notamment à politique de formation de la main-d'œuvre. Aujourd'hui, il existe des multinationales chinoises qui opèrent dans des secteurs à forte valeur ajoutée. Progressivement, ce pays a amélioré la qualité de ses produits d'exportations. En plus, la Chine, tout comme l'Inde, tente de percer des secteurs à forte concurrence monopolistique tels que le domaine pharmaceutique ou l'avionique, après avoir assez bien réussi dans l'automobile.

L'évolution récente du commerce international offre de bonnes opportunités à qui sait les saisir : en effet, la hausse de la rémunération de la main-d'œuvre en Asie, en particulier en Chine et en Inde, réduit leur avantage coût, ainsi que leur attrait comme plateforme de la production manufacturière à forte intensité de main-d'œuvre. La RDC est donc en compétition avec d'autres pays africains et d'ailleurs, qui visent aussi à capter plus de valeur dans les CVM. La réflexion stratégique à faire, c'est de savoir que la RDC a à offrir de plus que ses concurrents.

La nouvelle politique industrielle du gouvernement de la RDC accorde une place de premier choix à l'agriculture. Bien que 70 % de la population vit de celle-ci, l'agriculture congolaise demeure une agriculture de subsistance avec des niveaux de production faibles; de ce fait, la malnutrition et l'insécurité alimentaire sont des réalités bien présentes. Malgré son un immense potentiel agricole, la RDC importe aujourd'hui la plupart ses produits alimentaires qui se vendent sur le marché local.

Dans son rapport sur la politique commerciale de la RDC paru en 2011 (TPR, No WT/TPR/S/240/Rev.1), l'OMC indique que l'agriculture, qui représente environ 50 % du PIB congolais, regorge d'un potentiel immense. Les espaces disponibles pour le pâturage permettraient d'élever plus 40 millions de têtes de bétail; actuellement, la RDC n'en comptait que 700 000 en 2008, c.-à-d. près de la moitié du cheptel de 1990. Par ailleurs, le réseau hydrographique des eaux intérieures (lacs, fleuves et rivières) permettrait de produire annuellement plus de 1 million de tonnes de poissons, soit 5 fois plus que la production actuelle. Ceci témoigne du potentiel agricole du Congo pour, premièrement, garantir l'autosuffisance alimentaire et ensuite, pour l'exportation vers les marchés régionaux et émergents, qui imposent des normes sanitaires, de qualité ou de sécurité moins contraignantes que celles en vigueur dans les économies industrialisées.

Le gouvernement a lancé l'initiative des parcs agro-industriels (PAI), en vue de transformer le secteur agricole congolais de l'agriculture de subsistance en de pôles stratégiques agricoles pour une croissance économique durable ; à terme, cette stratégie permettrait de réduire la vulnérabilité de l'économie face à la volatilité des prix internationaux de matières premières, dont elle est fortement dépendante. Par ailleurs, la politique des PAI, qui fait partie du Plan national d'investissement agricole (PNIA 2013-2020) doté d'un budget de plus de 5,73 milliards de dollars US, vise la création de 20 millions d'emplois ainsi que la réduction de plus de 20% des Congolais souffrant de la famine[1].

Les PAI sont en fait des zones économiques spéciales (ZES) à vocation agro-industrielle. Pour attirer les investisseurs dans les ZES, les gouvernements offrent généralement une batterie de mesures incitatives au secteur privé, il s'agit de

1. Les informations sur l'initiative de PAI sont tirées du site Internet de la Primature www.primature.cd (voir bibliographie).

la prise de participation dans le capital, de subventions à l'exportation, de prêts à faible taux d'intérêt et de mesures protectionnistes ciblées. Ils offrent aussi des incitations fiscales (exonérations d'impôts, allégements fiscaux et crédits d'impôts) qui ont pour revers la réduction des recettes fiscales disponibles pour investir dans les infrastructures et la formation de la main-d'œuvre. En l'absence d'avantages comparatifs basés sur le coût et la qualité de la main-d'œuvre et/ou les coûts indirects (électricité, transport, SAE, etc.), les investisseurs peuvent délocaliser leurs activités, une fois que l'état décide de mettre fin aux subventions.[1] Dans ce cas, le manque à gagner en termes de recettes fiscales et les fonds publics investis dans le projet constitueraient une perte sèche.

Le renforcement du secteur agricole congolais pourrait stimuler l'expansion des supermarchés en RDC et ce faisant, la desserte en aliments à la population congolaise à des prix abordables. À l'heure actuelle, plusieurs supermarchés de Kinshasa, la capitale, s'approvisionnent auprès des chaînes étrangères (européennes ou sud-africaines, notamment). En vue de favoriser l'essor de l'agriculture congolaise, le gouvernement congolais peut imposer des exigences de contenu local ; cette exigence peut mener à des interactions entre les firmes nationales et les firmes étrangères, ce qui constitue un moyen d'apprentissage et de gain d'expertise. S'il est vrai que l'OMC milite en faveur du libre-échange et donc, de la levée des entraves au commerce, les accords commerciaux comportent généralement des clauses permettant aux signataires de déroger à leurs engagements pour protéger une industrie naissante, par exemple (en anglais, « escape clause »). Dans le cas de la RDC, il ne s'agirait pas de fermer l'accès au marché congolais aux entreprises étrangères, mais plutôt de favoriser l'investissement étranger pour créer des emplois.[2,3]

Le gouvernement a ainsi lancé un projet pilote pour la construction du premier PAI à Bukanga Lonzo, dans la province du Bandundu en 2014. Dans ce projet, l'État contribue à l'aménagement des infrastructures publiques (ex. : routes, système d'irrigation, électricité, de l'eau, etc.) et invite les investisseurs privés, tant nationaux qu'étrangers à s'implanter dans cet espace (Lukambil, 2014). Le défi, c'est d'attirer des entrepreneurs locaux compétents en grand nombre.

4. Choisir judicieusement la « localisation industrielle »

Le succès d'un parc industriel dépend de la présence d'infrastructures qui permet aux locataires du PAI de réaliser des économies d'échelle, grâce au partage des équipements industriels

1. Basu et Srinivasan (2002) constatent d'ailleurs que la décision d'investissement des firmes dépend davantage des facteurs tels que la taille du marché, l'accès aux matières premières et la disponibilité d'une main-d'œuvre qualifiée que des incitations qui sont offertes.

2. Il est bien connu en économie internationale que les entreprises multinationales ont au moins deux façons de desservir un marché étranger : elles peuvent soit exporter, soit y établir des filiales. L'option choisie parmi les deux est généralement la moins onéreuse.

3. Dans la même veine, l'état congolais peut imposer un pourcentage de travailleurs congolais aux EMN. Cette pratique est assez courante ailleurs. Au Canada, par exemple, une entreprise doit faire la démonstration qu'elle n'a pas été en mesure d'embaucher un canadien ayant les compétences nécessaires avant d'offrir un emploi à un non-résident.

de production ou de traitement des déchets. En effet, la « nouvelle économie géographique » (NEG) montre que la localisation des firmes est un choix stratégique majeur. En fait, les firmes tant nationales qu'internationales choisissent de se localiser dans des endroits spécifiques où elles bénéficient d' « économies d'échelles externes » (EEE), c.-à-d. que la concentration des firmes d'une industrie dans un district ou pôle industriel permet à chaque firme du secteur de réduire ses coûts de production.[1] Les concentrations géographiques d'entreprises et d'institutions inter-reliées dans un domaine particulier sont mieux connues sous le nom de « grappes industrielles » ou « clusters » (en anglais). Porter (1998) constate qu'au sein de celles-ci, on retrouve, par exemple, des fournisseurs de produits spécialisés tels que les composants, les machines et les services, et les fournisseurs d'infrastructures spécialisées, ainsi que leurs clients et des fabricants de produits complémentaires. C'est cette proximité géographique qui abaisse les coûts de transaction des différents participants de la grappe et promeut la compétition entre les concurrents. Par ailleurs, elle offre un meilleur accès à l'information et favorise la coopération en favorisant l'intégration verticale des firmes et la complémentarité. L'interdépendance entre les entreprises complémentaires d'un écosystème d'affaires fait en sorte que le succès des uns fasse le bonheur des autres.

Parmi les grappes industrielles les plus connues dans le monde, citons l'avionique dans la région de Toulouse et Montréal, la finance à Londres ou New York. Bien avant les tenants de la NEG (Krugman, Fujita et Thisse), Alfred Marshall relevait déjà la concentration géographique des activités économiques dans les années 1920. Il convient de signaler ici que la présence d'un bassin de main-d'œuvre qualifiée, formée et spécifique à l'industrie lui permet de réaliser des EEE. Elle permet de prévenir non seulement une pénurie de main-d'œuvre, mais aussi le chômage des travailleurs qualifiés.[2]

Toutefois, il convient d'éviter les erreurs du passé. On se souviendra que dans les années 1970, l'état congolais créait la *Société nationale de sidérurgie*, dont la mission était d'exploiter l'usine sidérurgique de Maluku, aux alentours de Kinshasa. En raison des problèmes de rentabilité, l'usine, qui ne fonctionnait qu'à 10 % de sa capacité, ferma ses portes 5 ans plus tard, parce que le Congo ne produisait pas de fer et en importait d'Italie, pays fournisseur de l'équipement (Muissa-Camus, 2005). Pourtant, l'objectif poursuivi était la création d'un pôle industriel pour le marché intérieur congolais, en traitant le minerai de fer de Banalia, en province Orientale. Cet éléphant blanc laisse penser qu'il n'y a pas eu d'études de rentabilité rigoureuses. À la lumière de l'argument théorique développé ci-dessus, on peut difficilement faire le choix de construire une usine à Maluku, alors que les intrants proviennent de la province Orientale, surtout si on tient compte du mauvais état des infrastructures routières ou

1. Le lecteur intéressé par le sujet peut consulter le chapitre 10 du manuel d'économie internationale de Krugman et Obstfeld traduit en français par Capelle-Blanchard et Crozet (2009).

2. Croyant au potentiel d'innovation des grappes industrielles, plusieurs pays africains ont adopté cette approche, notamment le Nigeria pour le secteur des composants automobiles et l'île Maurice pour le textile (voir CEA, 2011).

fluviales qui complique l'approvisionnement en intrants. Par ailleurs, cette initiative ne s'inscrivait pas dans une stratégie industrielle cohérente.

De ce qui précède, les décideurs publics devraient faire des choix éclairés dans la localisation des activités de transformation des minerais, en tenant compte à la fois de la géographie et de la nécessité de bâtir des écosystèmes d'affaires.

5. Viser également des secteurs de haute technologie

Si l'agriculture et l'industrie minière devraient servir de fer de lance à la transformation économique, cette dernière ne s'arrête pas là. La RDC doit viser également des secteurs de haute technologie, pour mettre en valeur les talents dont le pays regorge, en dépit de son système éducatif très inefficace. En 1997, le monde avait les yeux braqués sur la RDC lorsque le Dr Lurhuma expérimentait un traitement contre le virus du sida avec un collègue égyptien.[1] Malheureusement, le bilan de la recherche scientifique en général est très peu reluisant, en raison de la précarité des fonds de recherche, l'absence d'une masse critique de chercheurs compétents, de la fuite des cerveaux et de la mauvaise qualité des infrastructures et des équipements (IMF, 2013).

Plus récemment, des ingénieurs issus de l'Institut supérieur des techniques appliquées (Ista) ont mis au point un « robot roulage intelligent ». L'organisation qui les emploie, *Women technologies*, sollicite le soutien du gouvernement pour faire de cette invention un succès commercial *made in RDC*; ce qui requiert une production industrielle de cette technologie, sa commercialisation ainsi que la prospection des marchés d'exportation (Radio Okapi, en ligne). La réussite commerciale de ce projet pourrait générer des emplois de qualité, en plus de servir de précédent pour la RDC.

Ces deux exemples, quelque peu anecdotiques, témoignent du potentiel scientifique du congolais. Rappelons que tant les pays industrialisés que ceux dits émergents ne ménagent aucun effort pour consolider leur avantage concurrentiel. En effet, dans ces pays, l'état soutient la recherche et développement, grâce aux incubateurs d'entreprises notamment. Le but est de soutenir les jeunes entreprises qui ont un potentiel, mais manquent les capitaux pour acquérir les équipements nécessaires. Ainsi, plusieurs start-ups peuvent partager des infrastructures communes pendant quelques années, jusqu'à leur graduation où elles quitteront ces établissements publics. À titre d'exemple, mentionnons le Centre québécois d'innovation en biotechnologie (CQIB) situé dans la Cité de la Biotech du Montréal métropolitain et reconnu en tant que chef de file mondial en matière de démarrage d'entreprises dans les domaines des sciences de la vie et des technologies de la santé. En France, il existe 23 incubateurs publics créés principalement par les établissements d'enseignement supérieur et les organismes de recherche dans le cadre des dispositions de la loi sur l'innovation et la recherche de 1999. La Chine aussi a des mégas parcs scientifiques (technopoles ou pôles de technologie), dont celui de Souzhou, qui est très réputé.

1. Voir l'article de Hiltzik paru dans le Los Angeles Times du 28 décembre 1988.

Plusieurs pays en développement ont réussi leur intégration dans le commerce international des biens de haute technologie comme le secteur aéronautique dans le cas du Brésil, les services informatiques et la médecine dans le cas de l'Inde. Leur percée découle d'une prise de conscience de la logique sous-tendant le commerce international : l'essentiel du commerce international implique des pays riches qui échangent des biens semblables, mais qui présentent des caractéristiques différentes. Cette observation faite par Krugman (1979) est à l'origine de ce qu'on appelle la « nouvelle théorie » du commerce international qui remet en cause l'idée selon laquelle les pays riches devraient vendre aux pays pauvres des biens manufacturés et acheter de ces derniers des matières premières dont ils sont dotés. La réussite de pays comme le Brésil et l'Inde s'explique largement par le fait qu'ils font concurrence à l'Europe et aux États-Unis sur leurs propres marchés pour des produits haut de gamme ainsi que les services (Krugman et Obstfeld, 2009).

Cependant, qui dit haute technologie dit aussi main-d'œuvre hautement qualifiée. À l'heure actuelle, la RDC n'en dispose pas en quantité suffisante, en raison du désinvestissement dans le système éducatif, qui est la clé de voute du processus d'industrialisation. À court terme, le Congo peut compter sur sa diaspora intellectuelle. En effet, les Congolais se recrutent dans tous les domaines de haut savoir, qu'il s'agisse de la médecine et des biotechnologies, le nucléaire, l'aéronautique et bien d'autres encore.[1] La question pertinente est la suivante : est-ce qu'à l'instar de la Chine, la RDC peut mettre sur pied une politique de rapatriement des cerveaux pour développer des secteurs stratégiques ? À ce sujet, notons que la Chine organise chaque année des missions scientifiques à travers le monde pour rapatrier les chercheurs chinois en Chine continentale, en leur garantissant un financement à vie pour leurs activités de recherche.[2]

6. Relever le défi des ressources humaines : des politiques de main-d'œuvre et une culture d'entreprenariat

Le succès de la stratégie d'industrialisation du gouvernement doit s'appuyer sur une main-d'œuvre suffisante et adéquatement qualifiée, mais aussi sur des entrepreneurs locaux. Ce pari n'est pas gagné d'avance compte tenu de la faiblesse du système d'éducation congolais, d'une part, et du sous-financement des institutions d'enseignement supérieur, d'autre part. Ces dernières réalisent, par ailleurs, très peu de recherche de haut calibre.

L'exemple du Brésil, de l'Inde ou encore de la Chine montre comment ces économies émergentes se sont tisser une place de choix dans l'économie mondiale, grâce aux investissements en capital physique, mais aussi en capital humain.[3] Ce dernier est du reste le véritable moteur de l'innovation et de la transformation économique. Le déficit

1. Voir, par exemple, le site de l'Organisation des professionnels congolais du Canada (OPCC) : http://opcc-canada.org/category/revue-de-presse/

2. Voir magazine Regard No 1, « Pharmaceutique et biotechnologies : le Québec toujours dans la course? » sous la direction de Jean-Marc Kilolo Malambwe (2008).

3. Environ la moitié des étudiants chinois obtiennent un grade universitaire en sciences, c'est à peine le cas d'un cinquième des étudiants africains (CEA, 2011). Cette comparaison ne tient toutefois pas compte de la qualité de la formation qui serait à l'avantage de la Chine.

du savoir-faire technologique des pays africains en général, et de la RDC en particulier, est probablement un facteur explicatif important du cantonnement de ces derniers dans un rôle de fournisseurs de matières premières aux pays du Nord.

Plusieurs études empiriques, dont celle de Glaser et Kerr (2009), montrent bien que la présence d'une main-d'œuvre qualifiée explique pourquoi la création d'entreprises est plus forte dans certaines régions que dans d'autres. On peut en déduire, pour la RDC, que l'attraction des investissements directs étrangers (IDEs) est tributaire de la main-d'œuvre locale, capable d'assurer la conduite des opérations.

Depuis les travaux de Spence (1973), prix Nobel 2001, on sait que la scolarité d'un individu sert de signal aux employeurs potentiels quant aux qualifications et à la capacité de travail de ce dernier[1]. Il nous semble que cette théorie du signal s'applique aussi à l'échelle d'un pays : en effet, le fait qu'un pays dispose d'une masse critique de travailleurs qualifiés dans un domaine particulier renvoie un signal aux entreprises selon lequel ledit pays peut combler leurs besoins en main-d'œuvre. Les pouvoirs publics congolais devraient donc accorder une attention spéciale à renforcer l'éducation publique, ce qui devrait aussi encourager les investissements étrangers, puisque les entreprises étrangères auraient l'assurance de trouver les travailleurs qualifiés dont elles ont besoin.

Il importe que le signal soit crédible, c.-à-d. que le diplôme soit reconnu par les employeurs locaux, ce qui n'est pas nécessairement le cas aujourd'hui. En effet, il est plus probable pour un chercheur d'emploi congolais formé à l'étranger d'obtenir un emploi dans le secteur privé que son homologue diplômé au pays, puisque l'employeur s'attend à ce qu'il soit plus productif que ce dernier.

Un récent rapport du FMI (IMF, 2013) dresse un faible bilan du système éducatif congolais: il souligne l'absence de programmes de formation l'enseignement technique et professionnel, ainsi que l'inadéquation entre les cours dispensés et les besoins du marché du travail. Par ailleurs, les installations et les équipements existants sont vétustes et insuffisants. Enfin, le personnel enseignant est vieillissant. En outre, la perception sociale de l'enseignement professionnel est négative, l'opinion générale considérant que ces filières sont en fait l'exutoire des étudiants inaptes aux études universitaires. Le rapport note une détérioration de l'enseignement supérieur et constate que la ville-province de Kinshasa et la province du Katanga accueillent plus de la moitié des étudiants et accaparent les quatre cinquièmes des postes officiels d'enseignement au Congo. Enfin, ledit rapport note la faiblesse de la recherche scientifique, ce qui n'est pas étonnant compte tenu de la vétusté des équipements et du faible nombre de scientifiques reconnus sur le plan international œuvrant sur le territoire national.

Plusieurs pays africains ont déjà amorcé la construction d'une main-d'œuvre qualifiée en établissant des alliances avec des institutions de réputation internatio-

1. Dans modèle de « job search », le signal est l'information donnée (diplôme) par un émetteur (le candidat) qui aide le récepteur (l'employeur potentiel) à prendre une décision (embaucher ou pas). Il est important que le signal soit crédible aux yeux du récepteur.

nale : c'est le cas du Rwanda. Conscient du rôle de l'éducation, le Rwanda voisin a réussi à attirer l'université américaine Carnegie-Melon qui offre deux programmes de maîtrise (technologie d'information d'une part, et génie électrique et informatique, d'autre part). Il s'agit du premier établissement d'enseignement américain de haut rang en Afrique.[1] Par ailleurs, ce pays a reçu à au moins deux reprises, le très célèbre professeur de stratégie, Michael Porter, qui a donné aux moins de conférences sur les grappes industrielles au Rwanda et leur place stratégique en Afrique.[2] Il a même publié dans la très prestigieuse *Harvard Business Review* une étude sur la transformation économique du Rwanda, reprise dans ses notes de cours à la Harvard Business School.[3] Il est évident que cela sert au marketing politique du Rwanda pour attirer des investissements étrangers.[4] En misant sur le développement des technologies de l'information et de la communication (TIC) dans les années 2000, la Tunisie a su convaincre plusieurs compagnies étrangères d'externaliser des services (« outsourcing »), ce qui a généré des milliers d'emplois dans les services comptables et surtout dans les centres d'appels. L'exemple tunisien illustre bien le positionnement stratégique « avantage cout de main d'œuvre – main d'œuvre qualifiée » dans un domaine précis (TIC).

Compte tenu des contraintes à court terme pesant sur le système éducatif, le Congo peut recourir à sa diaspora en mettant sur pied des programmes de rapatriement des cerveaux, comme le fait la Chine. Ainsi, la diaspora professionnelle et scientifique serait un apport précieux à la « révolution de la modernité » initiée par le gouvernement actuel.

En résumé, la formation de la main-d'œuvre devrait être un des piliers de la nouvelle politique industrielle de la RDC : il s'agit, entre autres, d'offrir des formations spécialisées, axées sur le développement des compétences.

Cette politique de promotion de la main-d'œuvre qualifiée, ne devrait pas concerner uniquement des professionnels et chercheurs hautement qualifiés, mais également les techniciens dans des métiers spécialisés. Prenons l'exemple du textile : cette industrie requiert du travail minutieux à la chaine qui nécessite une main d'œuvre qualifiée, capable de répondre aux exigences des compagnies multinationales chefs de fil du secteur. A Kinshasa, par exemple, on voit un peu partout des tailleurs de prêt-à-porter qui ont un savoir-faire, mais qui travaillent avec des équipements parfois vétustes. Ces travailleurs constituent donc un bassin de main-d'œuvre pour l'industrie textile moderne (couture) que souhaite promouvoir l'état congolais dans sa stratégie pour l'émergence économique; on peut penser que travailler avec des équipements haut de gamme accroitrait la productivité de ces travailleurs.

On peut facilement imaginer la création d'écoles de tailleurs de diamants à

1. Voir le site Internet http://www.cmu.edu/rwanda/

2. Les travaux de Michael Porter font autorité partout dans le monde en stratégie. C'est lui qui a forgé le terme « chaine de valeur ». Il est considéré comme un des plus grands chercheurs en stratégie.

3. Porter, Michael E., and Michael Patrick McCreless. "Rwanda: National Economic Transformation (TN)." Harvard Business School Teaching Note 708-437, July 2007.

4. Par ailleurs, le Rwanda s'est adjoint les services de l'ancien premier ministre britannique, Tony Blair, comme conseiller spécial du président de la République; ce qui permet d'accroitre le réseau d'influence du pays tant dans les milieux politiques qu'économiques internationaux. Ce type d'actions devrait inspirer les décideurs congolais.

Tshikapa, réputée pour le commerce et l'extraction du diamant de joaillerie en RDC. Ce type d'initiatives permettrait de faire de cette ville la plaque tournante du diamant, à l'instar d'Anvers, ce qui engendrerait des retombées énormes.

Parmi les filières prioritaires du projet industriel congolais figure le secteur des bâtiments et matériaux de construction pour la reconstruction du pays. Sur les chantiers de construction, ce ne sont bien évidemment pas les ingénieurs qui construisent les routes ou qui réalisent des grands travaux, mais plutôt des ouvriers qualifiés, sous la supervision des contremaîtres, capables de comprendre des spécifications techniques et de les respecter. Ceci suppose le développement des corps et métiers du secteur de la construction. À ce sujet, il convient de noter que beaucoup de grands travaux réalisés au Congo après l'indépendance l'ont été avec le concours de la main-d'œuvre étrangère : il s'agit par exemple, des édifices comme le palais du peuple, le stade des martyrs; encore aujourd'hui, les travailleurs chinois sont fortement impliqués dans la réfection des infrastructures routières et autres dans le cadre des cinq chantiers.

En plus de la nécessité des travailleurs adéquatement qualifiés, il convient d'avoir une masse critique d'entrepreneurs qui créent de la richesse en concrétisant leurs projets d'affaires. Une façon de soutenir l'esprit d'entreprise consiste à mettre sur pied des programmes de formation à l'entreprenariat, au démarrage d'entreprise ou encore un service d'aide aux jeunes entrepreneurs pour bâtir un plan d'affaires. Ces programmes devraient être accessibles à tous sous certaines conditions. La formation peut prendre la forme de séminaires ou de déjeuners-conférence ou des entrepreneurs à succès partagent leur expérience. Il peut également s'agir de système de mentorat ou de maillage. L'état devrait travailler de concert avec des organisations telles que la Fédération des entreprises du Congo (FEC), les chambres de commerce et autres regroupements d'entreprise pour définir les besoins de formation et les autres besoins des entreprises dans les différents secteurs jugés prioritaires.

Une bonne connexion entre les pouvoirs publics et les regroupements d'entreprises permet de traduire concrètement la vision stratégique en actions concrètes avec des retombées économiques mesurables. Par ailleurs, elle permet aux instances étatiques de mieux représenter les intérêts des milieux d'affaires locaux dans des instances internationales telles que l'OMC et les autres institutions supranationales régionales (COMESA, SADC, etc.), en vue de conquérir des parts de marché.[1] Il importe de souligner le fait qu'une stratégie industrielle n'est pas une œuvre de laboratoire, mais elle suppose l'implication de toutes les parties prenantes (état, entreprises et milieux de la recherche, pour ne citer que ceux-là).

1. Les gouvernements négocient les accords commerciaux en fonction des intérêts de leurs firmes domestiques, lesquelles sont souvent constituées en lobbies. Ainsi, le lobby « a » du pays « A » va faire pression son gouvernement pour négocier un meilleur accès au marché du pays « B » qui, lui-même, subit des pressions du lobby « b » qui vise à obtenir des concessions commerciales dans le pays « A ». En fait, les firmes sont mieux à même d'identifier les entraves au commerce auxquelles elles font face que les gouvernements à qui elles relaient l'information. Cependant, ces mêmes lobbies peuvent faire pression sur leurs gouvernements respectifs pour limiter la concurrence étrangère sur le marché domestique (voir par exemple, Bagwell et Staiger, 2010; Maggi et Rodríguez-Clare).

En somme, l'émergence de la RDC requiert une planification de la main-d'œuvre dans différents domaines jugés prioritaires. Il s'agit tant de l'enseignement régulier (primaire, secondaire et supérieur) que des métiers dont l'économie congolaise a besoin. Rappelons que la localisation géographique des activités économiques dépend des atouts et compétences locales, notamment la compétence et le cout de la main-d'œuvre. Par ailleurs, les institutions publiques devraient mettre sur pied des mécanismes de soutien et de formation d'une base entrepreneuriale solide.

7. Asseoir une administration efficace capable d'appuyer la stratégie d'émergence

L'expérience des tigres est-asiatiques montre que le succès des politiques industrielles dépend de la surveillance des indicateurs de performance, qui devraient conditionner l'octroi des mesures incitatives aux firmes locales. Autrement dit, l'état ne doit pas offrir un bar ouvert aux entreprises, mais doit plutôt se montrer sélectif pour réussir sa politique. Lorsque les résultats ne sont pas probants, l'état devrait cesser de soutenir les entreprises inefficaces. La gestion des incitations suppose la mise sur pied des bases de données gérées par des centres de services aux entreprises par des technocrates qui évaluent les performances afin de réduire les risques d'échec et aussi rectifier le tir lorsque le besoin se fait sentir.

Il s'agit véritablement d'un exercice de pilotage de la politique industrielle. En effet, il convient de distinguer la stratégie de développement, définie par le gouvernement, de sa mise en œuvre par les fonctionnaires de l'état (des cadres opératifs et tactiques). Afin de maximiser les chances de succès de la nouvelle politique industrielle, il convient de communiquer la vision de la politique industrielle aux agents de l'état. Autrement dit, la mise en place de la stratégie ne devrait pas être le fait des membres de cabinets ministériels, mais bien de fonctionnaires formés et mandatés agissant selon des directives précises. Cette disposition contribuerait à assainir le climat des affaires, dans la mesure où l'application des règles du jeu ne dépendrait plus des gouvernements, mais des institutions administratives.

Un constat amer aujourd'hui, c'est que les opérateurs économiques doivent remplir de multiples formalités auprès de divers ministères afin d'avoir pignon sur rue. En 2014, le Congo se classe en 183e position sur 189 dans le classement de Doing Business.[1] Selon ce dernier, les difficultés les plus notables dans l'environnement des affaires concernent la création d'entreprises. Ce qui n'est pas surprenant, puisque, dans plusieurs cas, l'obtention des permis d'exercice est conditionnée par la signature des ministres, alors que ces actes administratifs sont généralement posés par des fonctionnaires de l'état dans les pays industrialisés. En effet, l'implication du gouvernement ne s'observe que dans des cas très limités : par exemple, lorsqu'il s'agit d'investissements étrangers dans des secteurs stratégiques, vis-à-vis desquels le pays ne souhaite pas perdre le contrôle aux mains des intérêts étrangers, ou lorsque que l'investissement est susceptible de modifier substantiellement la structure

1. Source : http://francais.doingbusiness.org/rankings.

du marché dans un secteur donné. L'intervention de l'état est également justifiée lorsque l'investissement est supposé avoir des impacts économiques, sociaux et environnementaux majeurs dans une région ou dans l'ensemble du pays.

À titre d'exemple, plusieurs compagnies américaines et canadiennes ont fait pression sur les gouvernements des deux pays pour bloquer l'acquisition de la compagnie pétrolière canadienne Nexen par la société d'état chinoise CNOOC pour 15 milliards $US. Pour se réaliser, cette transaction devait obtenir l'aval préalable du ministre de l'industrie. Ce dernier a dû s'assurer que « l'investissement est favorable aux Canadiens, à la compétitivité canadienne sur les marchés mondiaux, aux créations d'emplois et au maintien de la concurrence. » (Samet, 2012).

Ce type d'évaluation repose justement sur l'expertise de fonctionnaires dans les domaines concernés et qui peuvent procéder à des études d'impacts. Dans le cas canadien, en effet, le fait que les experts soient des agents de la fonction publique réduit leur dépendance vis-à-vis du pouvoir politique. Cette façon de procéder permet d'affiner la politique économique, dans la mesure où les gouvernants bénéficient d'outils d'aide à la décision en vue de résultats efficaces.

Il convient de noter que le gouvernement actuel de la RDC fournit des efforts; ainsi, pour palier la lourdeur administrative, ce dernier a notamment mis sur pied un guichet unique, auquel les entrepreneurs peuvent s'adresser pour obtenir toutes les autorisations nécessaires pour opérer. En marge de ce qui précède, l'état devrait également renforcer les capacités des différentes entités de contrôle. Concernant l'agroindustriel, par exemple, on devrait avoir en RDC, comme dans les pays développés comme les États-Unis ou le Canada, un organisme qui certifie que la production agroalimentaire est propre à la consommation. Dans le cas américain (Food and drugs administration, FDA) ou canadien (Santé Canada), l'organisme en question qui régule la vente des médicaments sur le marché. L'idée est de protéger la santé du public ; bien évidemment, l'avis émis par ces organismes est basé sur l'expertise interne du personnel scientifique qui y travaille. En RDC, l'Office congolais de contrôle (OCC) assure diverses missions de contrôle, notamment : le contrôle de qualité des marchandises et produits, le contrôle de prix ainsi que la production des statistiques sur le commerce extérieur et la production nationale (PIB).[1] Il ressort de l'examen des mandats de l'OCC que ces derniers vont bien au-delà des attributions généralement dévolues à un organisme de contrôle; par ailleurs, certaines missions empiètent sur les prérogatives dévolues aux organismes statistiques, en particulier sur la production de données sur le commerce et le PIB.

Conclusion

L'objectif de cet article était de présenter les défis que pose l'émergence de l'économie congolaise et de proposer quelques réformes qui devraient faire partie de la nouvelle stratégie industrielle du Congo. En s'appuyant sur le potentiel agricole et minier, l'état peut développer une agro-industrie floris-

1. Voir site Internet de l'OCC : http://www.occ-rdc.cd/article2.html.

sante et une industrie de transformation de minerais capables d'absorber l'abondante main-d'œuvre. Ces deux créneaux font d'ailleurs partie des choix arrêtés par le Congo qui vise à entrer dans le groupe des pays émergents.

Toutefois, plusieurs obstacles de taille devront être surmontés. Même si la RDC présenterait un avantage coût par rapport à sa main-d'œuvre, cette dernière n'est généralement pas adéquatement formée. De plus, l'inadéquation des infrastructures (électricité, installations aéroportuaires, routes, etc.) réduit la productivité du travail et par le fait même, le rendement des investissements. Par ailleurs, le pays a un déficit d'entrepreneurs.

Dans le cadre des cinq chantiers de la république, la réhabilitation et la construction des infrastructures a déjà débuté à travers le pays. Toutefois, il reste beaucoup de chemin à faire en ce qui a trait à l'amélioration du système éducatif et à la formation des entrepreneurs qui sont autant d'impératifs pour soutenir la nouvelle politique industrielle.

Compte tenu des contraintes à court terme, le pays peut compter sur sa diaspora. Là encore, le gouvernement devrait faire prendre d'ingéniosité pour valoriser les compétences intellectuelles, parfois inexploitées à l'étranger, ainsi que le savoir-faire entrepreneurial.

Références bibliographiques

BAfD, OCDE, PNUD (2014), « Les Les chaînes de valeur mondiales et l'industrialisation de l'Afrique, » *Perspectives économiques en Afrique 2014*, www.africaneconomicoutlook.org/fr/thematique.

Bagwell. R. and Robert W. Staiger (2010), « The World Trade Organization: Theory and Practice, » *Annual Review of Economics*, 2, 223-256.

Banque Mondiale (2011), « Optimisation du phénomène migratoire pour l'Afrique. Envois de fonds, compétences et investissements, » Washington, 217 pages.

Basu, A. et K. Srinivasan (2002), « Foreign direct investment in Africa – some case studies », document de travail, vol. 2/61, Fonds monétaire international, Washington DC, www.imf.org/external/pubs/ft/wp/2002/wp0261.pdf.

BIAC, rapport annuel 2010, https://www.biac.cd/doc/rapport_2010.pdf.

Economic Commission for Africa (ECA, 2011), « Industrial Policies for the Structural Transformation of African Economies: Options and Best Practices », Policy Research Paper No 2.

Glaeser, Edward L. and William R. Kerr (2009,), « Local Industrial Conditions and Entrepreneurship: How Much of the Spatial Distribution Can We Explain? » *Journal of Economics & Management Strategy*, 18 (3), pp. 623–663.

Hausmann, R., Hwang, J. and Rodrik, D. (2007). What you export matters. Journal of Economic Growth. 12 (1): 1–25.

International Monetary Fund (2013), « Democratic Republic of the Congo: Poverty Reduction Strategy Paper », IMF Country Report No. 13/226.

Lukambil, Alfred (2014), « Lancement du parc agro-industriel de Bukanga Lonzo Cap sur le ventre du Congolais », accès en ligne http://www.7sur7.cd, le 24/08/2014.

Maggi G. and A. Rodriguez-Clare (2007), « A political economy theory of trade agreements », *American Economic Review* 97(4), 1374-1406.

Martineau, Patrick (2003), « La route commerciale du coltan congolais : une enquête », Note de recherche du GRAMA, mai, 41 pages.

Norro, Michel (1998), « Économies africaines: analyse économique de l'Afrique subsaharienne », De Boeck Université, 307 pages.

Pharmabio Développement (2008), « Pharmaceutique et biotechnologies : le Québec toujours dans la course? » magazine *Regard sur les industries des produits pharmaceutiques et des biotechnologies*, sous la direction de Jean-Marc Kilolo Malambwe.

Porter, Michael E. (1998). « Clusters and the new economics of competition », *Harvard Business Review*, November-December, pp. 77-90.

Porter, Michael E., and Michael Patrick McCreless (2007). « Rwanda: National Economic Transformation (TN). » Harvard Business School Teaching Note 708-437, July 2007.

Primature (2014), « Inauguration par Joseph Kabila des travaux du Parc agro-industriel de Bukanga-Lonzo L'industrie agricole congolaise se met en place » en ligne le 16 juillet 2014, accessible sur https://www.primature.cd/public/.

Samet, Gérard (2012), « La vente de Nexen aux Chinois bloquée par les Américains », Canal argent, les Affaires, en ligne le 30 juillet 2012. http://argent.canoe.ca/nouvelles/affaires/nexen-chinois-americains-30072012.

Sarel, Michael (1997), « Growth in East Asia What We Can and What We Cannot Infer », IMF, Economic Issues, No 1.

Spar, Debora (1998), « Attracting High Technology Investment: Intel's Costa Rican Plant, » FIAS Occasional Paper 11. Washington D.C.: World Bank.

World Bank (2001), World Development Indicators (WBI, 2011), online access at http://data.worldbank.org/indicator.

WTO, 2011, Trade Policy Review, TPR, No WT/TPR/S/240/Rev.1

Note biographique

Après avoir débuté sa carrière dans le secteur bancaire canadien, Jean-Marc Kilolo Malambwe exerce la profession d'économiste au Canada. Ses récents travaux portent sur l'immigration, la qualité de l'emploi ainsi que la surqualification. Son intérêt pour les questions d'économie internationale et du développement l'ont conduit à présenter ses recherches à l'IJAS tenu à Harvard, aux HEC-Montréal, l'UQAM et à l'École Polytechnique de Paris, notamment. M. Kilolo Malambwe a appris l'économie à l'université catholique de Louvain. Durant ses études, il a été président de l'Union des Étudiants congolais de Louvain (UECL). Il détient également une maîtrise en sciences économiques de l'Université de Montréal, en plus d'un MBA en Management Consulting de l'UQAM. Il a récemment complété sa thèse de doctorat en sciences économiques à l'École Polytechnique de Paris.

Les zones économiques spéciales en République démocratique du Congo

Serge Songolo Aruna*, Auguy Bolanda Menga** & Eliane Manyonga Majambo***

Résumé

Les Zones Économiques Spéciales (ZES) constituent un moteur important de développement économique appliqué dans plusieurs pays. La République Démocratique du Congo (RDC), un pays post-conflit relativement vaste, envisage d'en promouvoir la politique afin (i) de rééquilibrer le développement du pays, (ii) de redynamiser la politique d'industrialisation du pays, (iii) d'attirer des capitaux nationaux et étrangers, et des technologies avancées, (iv) de promouvoir la création d'emplois et, (v) de faciliter l'intégration de l'économie congolaise dans la dynamique régionale et internationale des échanges. Une loi a été promulguée pour encadrer le régime de ces zones. Ce papier étudie l'opportunité d'implanter des ZES en RDC et conclut que les caractéristiques socio-économiques actuelles du pays permettent leur création progressive en tenant compte du potentiel de chaque région d'accueil. Les avantages leur accordés devront être calibrés. Une mission particulière d'import-substitution et d'impact substantiel sur l'économie nationale devra aussi leur être assignée. En dépit de l'évolution socio-économique des récentes années, les contraintes institutionnelles

* Assistant à la Faculté des sciences économiques et de gestion de l'Université de Goma

** Coordonnateur de la Cellule d'Appui aux Zones Economiques Spéciales (CAZES)

*** Assistante à la Faculté des sciences économiques et de gestion de l'Université de Kinshasa

ainsi que le mauvais état des infrastructures demeurent de potentiels obstacles au succès des ZES en RDC.

ABSTRACT

Special Economic Zones (SEZs) constitute engines of economic development applied in several countries. The Democratic Republic of Congo (DRC), a vast post-conflict country strives to create some SEZs (i) to balance the development of the country, (ii) to make dynamic the industrialization policy of the country, (iii) to attract national and foreign funds easily, and of the advanced technologies, (iv) to promote job creation and, (v) to facilitate the integration of the Congolese economy in the regional and international exchanges. Thus, a law has been promulgated. This paper studies the importance of implementing this program and concludes that the present socioeconomic features of the country permit their progressive creation, while taking into account the potential of every region. The advantages granted to them should be calibrated. A particular mission of industrialization by import substitution and substantial impact on the national economy should also be assigned to every SEZ. Despite some improvements, the institutional constraints and the inadequacy of infrastructures remain potential obstacles to the success of the SEZs in DRC.

REMERCIEMENTS
Nos remerciements s'adressent à André Nyembwe Musungaie et à Jean-Marc Kilolo Malambwe, qui ont lu et commenté les versions antérieures de ce papier. Toute erreur qui persiste relève, toutefois, de l'entière responsabilité des auteurs.

Mots clés
République Démocratique du Congo ; Zone Economique Spéciale ; Emergence ; *Benchmarking*.

1. INTRODUCTION

La plupart des pays du monde – quelles que soient leurs idéologies politiques dominantes – ambitionnent d'être suffisamment attractifs pour les investissements étrangers en quantité et qualité voulues. A cette fin, des pays « développés », mais aussi ceux dits « émergents » et ceux « en voie de développement » adoptent, depuis, des mesures qui visent l'atteinte des quatre objectifs traditionnellement reconnus à toute politique économique, que sont (i) la croissance économique, (ii) le plein emploi, (iii) la stabilité des prix et (iv) l'équilibre extérieur[1]. Plusieurs pays ont, depuis des décennies, intégré la créa-

1.Arnaud DIEMER (sans date), Economie générale, cours inédit à l'IUFM Auvergne, lu le 05 juillet 2014 sur <http://www.oeconomica.net/private/cours/economiegenerale/CAPET/12.politiqueeconomique.pdf>

tion de « zones économiques spéciales » (ZES) dans leurs politiques de développement. Parmi eux, certains « tigres » et « dragons » asiatiques avec, au premier plan, la Chine. Les bénéfices directs de la création de ZES sur leurs territoires ont été l'accroissement sensible des revenus de change et des investissements directs étrangers, la création d'emplois, l'augmentation des revenus pour les gouvernements, et la hausse des exportations. Globalement, ces pays ont aussi bénéficié indirectement de l'acquisition de compétences, de l'expérimentation de réformes économiques, de transferts de technologies, de la diversification des exportations, de l'amélioration de l'efficience des firmes exportatrices, et d'un signal fort (d'application de réformes dans ces pays) à destination du monde. D'autres pays ont plutôt adopté, pour leur développement, la stratégie de pôles de croissance.

La RDC est un pays « post-conflit », grand comme l'Europe occidentale avec une superficie d'environ 2.345.409 km², à cheval sur l'équateur, au centre du continent africain pour plus de 9.000 km de frontières et – à peine – 40 km de littoral sur son flanc-Ouest. Avec une population estimée à 67,51 millions d'habitants en 2013[1], 80 millions d'hectares de terres arables et réputé « scandale géologique » pour son immense potentiel minier, le pays souffre, pourtant, d'un cadre légal peu fiable et du manque d'infrastructures de transport et de communication développées pouvant faciliter les échanges socio-économiques.

Après des décennies de conflits, la RDC s'est lancée, depuis 2007 dans un processus d'amélioration de la gouvernance économique et ambitionne de devenir une économie émergente à l'horizon 2030. Pour atteindre cet objectif, elle se doit d'enregistrer des taux de croissance à deux chiffres sur plusieurs décennies[2] et envisage de promouvoir, entre autres moyens, la création de ZES à l'horizon 2015 dans l'objectif de promouvoir le développement de son tissu industriel. Une loi a été promulguée à cet effet[3] qui traduit la vision de la RDC dans ce domaine, et une Cellule d'Appui aux Zones Economiques Spéciales (CAZES)[4] a été créée.

Il est question, dans ce papier, de savoir si la République Démocratique du Congo est prête à abriter et à développer efficacement des ZES sur son territoire au regard de ses caractéristiques socio-économiques actuelles. La section 2 de cet article présente la politique de ZES (ses facteurs de succès, ses avantages et ses inconvénients) et la stratégie de pôles de croissance, et reprend l'expérience de plusieurs pays en matière de ZES. La section 3 discute de l'opportunité de la création de ZES en RDC.

2. Zones économiques spéciales et pôles de croissance

Une ZES est une enclave située dans une zone bien définie dans laquelle les

1.Banque mondiale (sans date), « République démocratique du Congo », lu le 13 juillet 2014 sur <http://donnees.banquemondiale.org/fr/country/drc>

2. Cabinet du Premier Ministre (mai 2012), «Programme d'action du Gouvernement 2012 – 2016 », lu le 25 mai 2015 sur <file:///C:/Users/HP/Downloads/Programme%20du%20gouvernement%20mai%202012.pdf>

3. Journal Officiel de la République Démocratique du Congo (25 juillet 2014), « Loi n° 14/022 du 07 juillet 2014 fixant le régime des Zones Economiques Spéciales en République Démocratique du Congo »

4. La CAZES a été créée le 08 février 2010 et son site internet est le www.cazesrdc.net.

lois économiques sont plus libérales, et donc plus avantageuses pour les entreprises, que celles pratiquées dans le reste du pays. Ces dernières peuvent ainsi s'y installer à bon compte, produire et exporter sans pesanteurs bureaucratiques grâce à certaines mesures mises en place par les autorités du pays.[1] Les ZES regroupent des entreprises interconnectées qui sont en concurrence tout en coopérant. Il en existe quatre grands profils : des ZES multi-produits intégrées avec une infrastructure complexe sur une étendue relativement vaste ; des ZES regroupant des entreprises d'une même industrie sur une vaste étendue ; des ZES regroupant des entreprises à productions similaires ; et des ZES regroupant des entreprises de services.

Depuis les années 50, beaucoup de pays à travers le monde ont adopté le développement des zones économiques comme stratégie de croissance. Tandis que des pays tels que les Etats-Unis et la France avaient procédé à la création de regroupements industriels (*Industrial Clusters*), les ZES, elles, s'étaient particulièrement répandues dans les pays en développement. Leur étude peut conduire à un étalonnage (*benchmarking*) intéressant avec, comme modèles, les cas chinois et indien, deux pays émergents de premier plan.

Connues sous d'autres formes dans d'autres pays et régions du monde (*Maquiladoras* en Amérique latine, *Export Processing Zones (EPZ)* en Asie), les ZES sont des zones franches. Elles ont été réinventées sous cette forme en Chine (à travers la *China's policy of Special Economic Zone* de 1979), un pays à idéologie communiste qui souhaitait attirer des investissements directs étrangers (IDE) dans ses zones « libéralisées ». Après le décès de Mao TSE-TUNG en 1976, le pays est ainsi progressivement passé d'une économie socialiste et fermée à une économie de marché.[2] La première ZES fut créée en 1980 – sous le gouvernement de Deng XIAOPING – à Shenzhen, dans la province de Guangdong, à proximité des villes de Hong-Kong et Macao, et non loin de l'île de Taiwan. Shenzhen est aujourd'hui la ZES qui enregistre le plus grand succès. Cette ville, qui n'était qu'un petit village, est devenue une grande agglomération avec le niveau de revenu le plus élevé de la Chine.[3] Dans ce pays, le terme « ZES » renvoie normalement à sept zones spécifiques s'étendant sur de larges étendues : Shenzhen, Zhuhai, Shantou, Xiamen, Hainan, Shanghai Pudong New Area et Tianjin Binhai New Area. Celles-ci sont qualifiées de « spéciales » à cause des lois plus libérales y appliquées.[4] Les autres zones économiques sont de quatre types : des zones de développement technologique et économique (qui sont des ZES à tailles réduites), des zones de développement industriel *high-tech* (dé-

1.Vitraulle MBOUNGOU (24 septembre 2012), « Les zones économiques spéciales : un modèle de réussite ? », lu le 05 juillet 2014 sur <http://www.afriqueexpansion.com/les-zones-economiques-speciales-/5215-les-zones-economiques-speciales-un-modele-de-reussite.html>

2.Vitraulle MBOUNGOU (25 septembre 2012), « Les zones économiques spéciales : le success story chinois », lu le 05 juillet 2014 sur <http://www.afriqueexpansion.com/les-zones-economiques-speciales-/5229-les-zones-economiques-speciales--le-success-story-chinois.html>

3.Xiaozi LIU, Gerhard K. HEILIG, Junmiao CHEN, Mikko HEINO (2007), « Interactions between economic growth and environmental quality in Shenzhen, China's first special economic zone », Ecological Economics 6, pp. 559-570

4.Chang Woon NAM, Doina Maria RADULESCU (2005), « Do Corporate Tax Concessions Really Matter for the Success of Free Economic Zones? », Economics of Planning 37, pp. 99-123

veloppées dans le but de promouvoir la commercialisation de la recherche et du développement), des zones de libre échange (qui devaient permettre à la Chine d'expérimenter le libre échange avant son accession à l'OMC en ciblant les exportations, le commerce international et la logistique) et des zones franches d'exportation (ou *EPZ*, créées pour développer les industries exportatrices et améliorer les gains d'échange avec l'étranger).[1]

Les ZES chinoises ont permis à ce pays d'intégrer l'économie mondiale sans compromettre son idéologie politique.[2] Le franc succès qu'ont connu les ZES chinoises a, depuis, engendré des vagues d'émulation à travers le monde. Les *EPZ* indiennes s'étaient ainsi muées en ZES en 2005, à la suite de la *SEZs Act*.[3] La présence de ZES dans les économies chinoise et indienne (alors en plein processus de libéralisation) avait influé positivement sur l'accroissement du niveau des IDE et celui des exportations qui, à leur tour, avaient induit une augmentation du rythme de la croissance économique.[4] Plus de 3000 ZES ont, à ce jour, été créées ou sont en projet dans plus de cent pays à travers le monde.[5] Le succès de la recette chinoise repose, en grande partie, sur certains préalables : le fait que le pays possède une population de plus d'un milliard d'individus, une abondance de capitaux internationaux provenant de sa diaspora et des lois et normes du travail très aléatoires.[6] La politique de ZES a aussi connu du succès dans d'autres pays, à l'exemple de l'Ile Maurice qui avait misé sur des réformes économiques permettant aux zones créées de s'imbriquer dans une politique industrielle courageuse.

Dans le cadre de sa stratégie « *Going Global* » (concept indiquant la « direction » de la Chine vers le monde extérieur), la Chine envisageait d'exporter son expérience, en soutenant la création de ZES dans d'autres pays. L'objectif était de trouver de nouveaux marchés pour les produits chinois, de rendre plus visibles les marques chinoises, d'augmenter les investissements chinois à l'étranger et de faciliter les exportations vers l'Europe et l'Amérique du Nord en évitant certaines barrières imposées aux exportations provenant de l'empire du milieu. Un autre objectif, plus idéologique, était de transférer aux autres pays en développement un des éléments à succès de la Chine contemporaine. La phase expérimentale de ce programme avait commencé en 1998.[7] En Afrique, six pays

1.Douglas Zhihua ZENG (mars 2011), « How do Special Economic Zones and Industrial Clusters drive China's rapid development? », Policy Research Working Paper 5583, Banque mondiale

2.Malini L. TANTRI (2013), « Trajectories of China's Integration with the World Economy through SEZs: A Study of Shenzhen SEZ », China Report 49, pp. 227-250

3.N. VISWANADHAM (décembre 2006), « Design of Special Economic Zones as Economic Engines of Growth », Thought Leadership White Papers, pp. 93-115

4.Chee Kian LEONG (septembre 2013), « Special economic zones and growth in China and India: an empirical investigation », International Economics and Economic Policy 10, pp. 549-567

5.N. VISWANADHAM (décembre 2006), « Design of Special Economic Zones as Economic Engines of Growth », Thought Leadership White Papers, pp. 93-115

6.Jean-Nicolas SAUCIER (28 septembre 2012), « Les zones économiques spéciales : tremplin ou servitude ? », lu le 05 juillet 2014 sur <http://www.afriqueexpansion.com/les-zones-economiques-speciales-/5265-les-zones-economiques-speciales--tremplin-ou-servitude-.html>

7.Deborah BRAUTIGAM, Xiaoyang TANG (décembre 2011), « China's Investment in Special Economic Zones in Africa », sous la direction de Thomas FAROLE et Gokhan AKINCI dans « Special Economic Zones : Progress, Emerging Challenges, and Future Directions », Directions in Development Trade, Banque mondiale, pp. 69-100

avaient été retenus à l'issue d'un processus d'appel d'offres : l'Égypte, l'Éthiopie, l'Algérie, l'Ile Maurice, le Nigéria et la Zambie. Quelques divergences de vue entre la Chine et certains de ces pays (notamment l'Egypte et l'Ethiopie) témoignent, toutefois, des limites qu'il y a eu au transfert de l'expérience de la Chine au-delà de ses frontières. Les divergences concernaient l'aménagement et l'investissement dans les ZES à créer, deux composantes des projets que certains pays africains, notamment l'Egypte, ne souhaitaient pas confier à une seule entité – contrairement au souhait de la Chine – avec, en toile de fond, l'objectif de récupérer à terme les infrastructures créées.[1]

Toute création de ZES doit être motivée et tenir compte, en particulier, des caractéristiques et des besoins de la région destinée à les accueillir. L'objectif, à terme, est d'atteindre un certain niveau de développement économique dans la région d'accueil et, ensuite, un effet d'entraînement dans le reste du pays.[2] C'est en ceci que la stratégie de pôles de croissance et la politique de ZES convergent. En effet, quoique la localisation de certaines ZES reflète parfois des préoccupations plus politiques qu'économiques, beaucoup d'entre elles ont été créées par les gouvernements pour agir comme de véritables pôles de croissance.[3] Un pôle de croissance est destiné à un processus de propagation dans l'espace de l'essor engendré par une agglomération d'entreprises motrices et dynamiques où l'investissement a des effets d'entraînement importants sur l'économie régionale. *Les pôles de croissance sont, toutefois, différents des ZES en ce sens qu'au lieu de mettre l'accent sur les mesures de compétitivité de l'offre visant à surmonter les obstacles à l'investissement privé, les pôles de croissance combinent généralement les investissements publics et privés et sont destinés à être bâtis autour d'une ressource préexistante.*[4]

L'effet d'entraînement du développement des ZES sur le reste de l'économie n'est pas toujours automatique. Il revient ainsi à chaque Etat de créer ce lien, particulièrement en développant les infrastructures et en disposant d'une législation volontariste, dans l'objectif d'accroitre la production et de hausser le niveau des entreprises locales qui vendent aux ZES des biens et des services. Le choix des régions destinées à accueillir ces zones doit aussi tenir compte du besoin de développer ces régions ou de palier à une faiblesse économique précise. Ainsi, certains pays développent des ZES dans le souci de diversifier leurs économies dépendantes d'un secteur donné (tels que l'Ile Maurice avec la filière sucrière). D'autres l'ont fait pour faciliter la création d'emplois afin de résorber un chômage devenu quasi-structurel (à l'exemple de l'Ile Maurice, de Madagascar). D'autres encore, à l'exemple de la Chine et de l'Inde, l'ont fait pour attirer des IDE et de la

1.Deborah BRAUTIGAM, Xiaoyang TANG (2014), « "Going Global in Groups" : Structural Transformation and China's Special Economic Zones Overseas », World Development Vol. 63, pp. 78-91

2.N. VISWANADHAM (décembre 2006), « Design of Special Economic Zones as Economic Engines of Growth », Thought Leadership White Papers, pp. 93-115

3.Thomas FAROLE, Gokhan AKINCI (2011), « Special Economic Zones : Progress, Emerging Challenges, and Future Directions », Directions in Development Trade, Banque mondiale

4.BURKINA FASO (sans date), « Le Pôle de Croissance de Samendeni », lu le 16 mai 2015 sur <http://alpha.burkinafasoindia.org/documents/Samendeni%20FINAL%20French.pdf>

TABLEAU N°1
Quelques avantages de la politique de ZES

Bénéfices directs	**Bénéfices Indirects**
Revenus de change	Acquisition de compétences
Investissements directs étrangers	Expérimentation de réformes économiques
Création d'emplois	Transferts de technologie
Revenus pour le gouvernement	Diversification des exportations
Hausse des exportations	Amélioration de l'efficience des firmes exportatrices
-	Signal à l'international (des réformes dans le pays)

Source : Douglas Zhihua ZENG (mars 2011), « How do Special Economic Zones and Industrial Clusters drive China's rapid development? », Policy Research Working Paper 5583, Banque mondiale

technologie destinée à être diffusée, en suite, au reste de l'économie.[1]

Le tableau ci-dessus résume les avantages possibles pour les pays en développement qui adoptent la politique de ZES.

Le succès des ZES dépend de plusieurs facteurs internes et externes au pays concerné, et peuvent varier d'un pays à un autre. Généralement, les facteurs de succès des ZES sont (i) un engagement fort pour la réforme et le pragmatisme des hauts dirigeants, (ii) des politiques préférentielles et de l'autonomie institutionnelle, (iii) un soutien fort et une participation active des gouvernements, (iv) l'apprentissage de la technologie, la culture de l'innovation, la modernisation, et des liens étroits avec l'économie nationale, (v) des objectifs clairs, des repères et une concurrence intense entre entreprises résidant dans les ZES, (vi) les avantages géographiques liés aux sites, et (vii) un approvisionnement adéquat en énergie. Ces leviers permettent aux entreprises de voir leurs coûts d'investissement, de financement et d'exploitation réduits considérablement avec, par exemple, un système d'aides directes à l'installation comme l'instauration d'une prime à l'investissement ou la fourniture de terrains et de locaux à prix réduits.[2] Les autres facteurs de succès sont les avantages accordés à ces zones, notamment (i) des exonérations d'impôts sur une période donnée ; (ii) des exonérations de droits de douane pour les marchandises achetées à des fins d'utilisation par le résident de la zone spéciale ou (iii) une garantie

1.N. VISWANADHAM (décembre 2006), « Design of Special Economic Zones as Economic Engines of Growth », Thought Leadership White Papers, pp. 93-115

2.Vitraulle MBOUNGOU (24 septembre 2012), « Les zones économiques spéciales : un modèle de réussite ? », lu le 05 juillet 2014 sur <http://www.afriqueexpansion.com/les-zones-economiques-speciales-/5215-les-zones-economiques-speciales-un-modele-de-reussite.html>

de la protection contre un changement de la législation fiscale défavorable au résident de la ZES.[1]

Quatre principales composantes rendent les ZES compétitives : la technologie (dans les domaines de l'information et de la logistique), la gestion des différentes ressources disponibles (ressources humaines, naturelles, financières), l'innovation et le degré d'intégration dans l'économie de la région où la ZES est établie. Les ZES devraient ainsi être perçues comme un ensemble de compétences dérivées des relations entre plusieurs réseaux d'affaires (firmes, centres de recherche, institutions locales)[2] dont la mise en œuvre ne doit pas faire l'objet d'une politique isolée mais être intégrée dans une vision globale de développement.

Les ZES jouissent de plusieurs avantages pour qu'elles soient efficaces quoique ces seuls avantages accordés aux entreprises résidentes ne suffisent pas pour en garantir le succès. La promotion des investissements dans un pays conduit à la non taxation des bénéfices d'entreprises, à la prise de certaines mesures de dépréciation monétaire généreuse, à des décisions de subventions aux coûts d'investissement, et à d'autres avantages fiscaux. Les incitations ont un rôle à jouer mais elles doivent être limitées et contrôlées[3], surtout en matière fiscale. Sous certaines conditions favorables, l'établissement de ZES accompagné d'une politique fiscale appropriée (une imposition optimale[4]) peut conduire à une augmentation des entrées fiscales du pays qui peuvent, à leur tour, être injectées dans le financement des infrastructures ou dans la production de biens publics.[5] En effet, en cas de dégrèvement fiscaux, les recettes fiscales peuvent être réduites dans un premier temps. Mais ces conditions peuvent attirer des investissements qui, à leur tour, peuvent conduire à une augmentation des entrées fiscales. C'est l'effet de Laffer.[6] La considération du « cas par cas » dans les avantages accordés à chaque ZES est ainsi importante.

Pour motiver les entreprises à investir dans les zones créées, la Chine avait mis en place différentes politiques préférentielles pour ses ZES, incluant des terres à bas prix, des exonérations fiscales, des facilitations douanières, la possibilité de rapatrier les profits et les capitaux investis, des exonérations sur l'importation de matières brutes et intermédiaires destinées à être incorporés

1.Centre de Commerce et d'Industrie Européen (5 juin 2012), « Les Zones Economiques Spéciales », lu le 05 juillet 2014 sur <http://www.c-cie.eu/index.php?article22/les-zones-economiques-speciales>

2.Konstantinos J. HAZAKIS (2013), « Key Conditions for the Effectiveness of Special Economic Zones in Regional Development: Opportunities and Challenges for the Thrace Region », sous la direction de Pantelis SKLIAS et Nikolaos TZIFAKIS dans « Greece's Horizons: Reflecting on the Country's Assets and Capabilities », The Konstantinos Karamanlis Institute for Democracy Series on European and International Affairs, Centre for European Studies Publications, pp. 235-247

3.Thomas FAROLE (2011), « Special Economic Zones in Africa : Comparing Performance and Learning from Global Experience », Directions in Development Trade, Banque mondiale

4.Plusieurs travaux scientifiques ont essayé de traiter de la question de la fiscalité optimale, particulièrement celle appliquée aux sociétés.

5.Albert G. SCHWEINBERGER (2003), « Special Economic Zones in Developing and/or Transition Economies: a Policy Proposal », Review of International Economics 11, pp. 619-629

6.Vadim ARKIN, Alexander SLASTNIKOV, Svetlana ARKINA (2007), « Investment Timing Problem Under Tax Allowances: The Case of Special Economic Zones », sous la direction de Jörg KALCSICS et Stefan NICKEL dans « Operations Research Proceedings Volume 2007, 2008 », The Annual International Conference of the German Operations Research Society, pp. 173-178

dans les produits à exporter, des exonérations à l'exportation des produits, une licence limitée permettant de vendre sur le marché domestique, etc. Des politiques favorables avaient aussi été mises en place pour attirer une main-d'œuvre qualifiée (y compris la diaspora) portant sur des facilités d'installation, un fonds pour la recherche, des allocations pour l'éducation des enfants, etc. En plus, les ZES avaient bénéficié d'une plus grande autonomie politique et économique. Ils avaient l'autorité de développer des lois municipales et de régulation en se basant sur les lois nationales, incluant certaines taxes et structures locales, et d'administrer ces zones. A Shenzhen, le gouvernement était très pragmatique, et ses politiques innovantes étaient efficaces. La ZES de Shenzhen obtint, en 1992, le pouvoir de légiférer.[1]

Les aspects négatifs des ZES chinoises et indiennes sont les inégalités dans le développement entre provinces, les terres arables perdues, les spéculations foncières, les violences dans le milieu professionnel, le fait que les firmes présentes dans les zones économiques n'investissent pas beaucoup dans la qualité et basent leur concurrence sur le prix, et le fait que, pour certaines organisations telles que l'OIT (Organisation Internationale du Travail) et la CNUCED (Conférence des Nations Unies sur le Commerce et le Développement), l'anticipation des bénéfices n'a pas mis au premier plan des priorités le développement des capacités de la force de travail à part dans les industries de pointe où la routine n'est pas de mise. Ces aspects ont poussé certains académiciens et leaders, chinois notamment, à demander leur démantèlement pur et simple.[2] La forte industrialisation des ZES a aussi un impact globalement négatif sur l'environnement. Une étude a ainsi démontré que l'impact sur l'environnement a été négatif dans la ZES de Shenzhen, en dépit de son succès retentissant.[3] Sur un autre chapitre, en ce qui concerne les ZES elles-mêmes, leur création et leur développement peuvent engendrer des phénomènes de migration internes des régions où les investissements dans les ZES sont faibles vers les régions où les investissements dans les ZES sont plus importants et où sont créés beaucoup plus d'emplois.[4] Ces phénomènes peuvent créer, à leur tour, d'autres défis socio-économiques importants, tels que ceux liés à l'intégration socio-économique des immigrés, la criminalité, etc.

La négligence de l'importante question foncière et des éventuelles dépossessions de terres qui s'en suivent peut conduire à des « guerres de terre ».[5] En effet, la tendance a souvent été – dans les pays en développement – de transformer des terres initialement consacrées à la production agricole pour l'implantation de ZES, aggravant par conséquent des situations de sécurité et d'autosuffisance alimentaires souvent précaires.

1.Douglas Zhihua ZENG (mars 2011), « How do Special Economic Zones and Industrial Clusters drive China's rapid development? », Policy Research Working Paper 5583, Banque mondiale

2.Shankar GOPALAKRISHNAN (2007), « Negative Aspects of Special Economic Zones in China », Economic and Political Weekly Vol. 42, No. 17, pp. 1492-1494

3.Xiaozi LIU, Gerhard K. HEILIG, Junmiao CHEN, Mikko HEINO (2007), « Interactions between economic growth and environmental quality in Shenzhen, China's first special economic zone », Ecological Economics 6, pp. 559-570

4.Scott R. SANDERS, David L. BROWN (novembre 2011), « The Migratory Response of Labor to Special Economic, Zones in the Philippines, 1995-2005 », Population Research **and** Policy Review 31, pp. 141-164

5.Michael LEVIEN (2013), « Regimes of Dispossession: From Steel Towns to Special Economic Zones », Development and Change 44, pp. 381-407

En Inde, où l'expérience de zones économiques n'avait pas rencontré autant de succès qu'en Chine, les compagnies étrangères disposaient parfois des pleins pouvoirs. Ces entreprises pouvaient aller jusqu'à déposséder les paysans de leurs terres, sans contrainte aucune, causant des crises sociales. Pourtant, en ce qui concerne les terres, un arbitrage efficient entre les droits fonciers et la croissance économique voudrait que les terres affectées au développement industriel soient celles à faible productivité agricole. De fait, les coûts d'opportunité sont énormes en cas de dépossession de terres tant pour les paysans dépossédés que pour le pays qui perd, entre temps, en productions agricoles.[1] Des études ont démontré que les objectifs assignés aux ZES en termes d'augmentation des revenus moyens et du niveau d'emploi peuvent être atteints en promouvant simultanément les ZES et le secteur agricole par des investissements substantiels conséquents.[2] La dimension foncière avait ainsi plombé les résultats de la stratégie de développement de l'Inde par la création de zones économiques, mise en place depuis les années 60. Aujourd'hui encore, d'autres lois foncières telles que les limites (plafonnements) dans l'acquisition de terres en milieux urbains et les clauses d'utilisation de la terre dans le contexte de ZES constituent le problème primaire pour le développement du secteur privé dans ses ZES.[3] Pour pallier à cette situation, l'aménagement se fait soit par le gouvernement indien seul, soit par les privés ensemble avec le gouvernement dans le cadre de partenariats publics-privés, ce dernier étant fortement impliqué dans le rassemblement de terres.[4]

Il est globalement admis que l'Afrique possède un avantage comparatif dans le domaine des ressources naturelles. Mais le *scanner* économique de l'Afrique met en exergue ce besoin réel de développer son tissu industriel, plus créateur d'emplois que le secteur de la distribution qui concerne, à titre d'exemple, 90% des entreprises de l'Afrique francophone.[5] En RDC, 43% du PIB de 2012 revenait au secteur primaire, 33% au secteur tertiaire et 24% « seulement » au secteur secondaire.[6] En dépit de la faible industrialisation des pays africains, les succès des zones économiques créées sur le continent ont été limités, à l'exception notable des pays tels que l'Ile Maurice et Madagascar. L'expérience de l'Ile Maurice repose sur des réformes économiques et politiques idoines. À l'origine, s'inspirant du modèle des pays d'Asie du Sud-Est et ne voulant plus se contenter des industries d'import-substitution, une ZES y fut établie en 1971 pour absorber

1.Ramachandra BHATTA (2013), « Tradeoffs between Land Rights and Economic Growth: A Case Study of Coastal Karnataka », Journal of Land and Rural Studies 1, pp. 229-243

2.Sarbajit CHAUDHURI, Shigemi YABUUCHI (2010), « Formation of special economic zone, liberalized FDI policy and agricultural productivity », International Review of Economics and Finance 19, pp. 779-788

3.Triyakshana SESHADRI (août 2012), « An Analysis of the Feasibility of Private Land Assembly for Special Economic Zones in India », Urban Studies 49, pp. 2285-2300

4.Triyakshana SESHADRI (août 2012), « An Analysis of the Feasibility of Private Land Assembly for Special Economic Zones in India », Urban Studies 49, pp. 2285-2300

5.Ministère de la Modernisation des Secteurs Publics, Centre Africain de Formation et de Recherche Administratives pour le Développement, Fondation Hanns Seidel, Conférence panafricaine des Ministres, Rabat, 12-14 décembre 2011, Firmin KINZOUNZA, « Les chainons manquants de l'émergence économique en Afrique : le benchmarking des pays émergents d'Asie »

6.Jeune Afrique (sans date), « Repères économiques », lu le 13 juillet 2014 sur <http://www.jeuneafrique.com/Reperes-economiques-pays_79_RD Congo>

le surplus de main-d'œuvre. Elle avait attiré du capital venant de Hong-Kong et de la Chine, mais aussi des exploitants locaux de sucre qui voulaient diversifier leurs sources de revenu. Enfin, une partie du revenu de l'impôt supplémentaire avait été utilisée pour augmenter les dépenses sociales de 6% du PIB à 10% du PIB. A Madagascar, les zones économiques employaient de manière prédominante de jeunes femmes, ouvrières semi-qualifiées. Elles gagnaient considérablement plus que leurs *alter egos* dans le secteur informel et avaient un salaire équivalant à celui des hommes.[1]

De nombreux pays africains ont adopté la création de ZES comme stratégie économique de développement. Le Gabon l'a fait en 2009 avec la ZES de Nkok montée en partenariat public-privé.[2] D'autres pays d'Afrique subsaharienne ont aussi des projets dans ce domaine. Parmi eux, la République du Congo et la République Démocratique du Congo.

3. Les ZES en RDC : état des lieux et perspectives

La vision congolaise en matière de ZES est traduite par la Loi n° 14/022 du 07 juillet 2014 fixant le régime des Zones Economiques Spéciales en République Démocratique du Congo, texte conçu et promulgué dans l'objectif (i) de rééquilibrer le développement du pays, (ii) de redynamiser la politique d'industrialisation du pays, (iii) d'attirer facilement des capitaux nationaux et étrangers, et des technologies avancées du fait des avantages y associés, (iv) de promouvoir la création d'emplois et, (v) de faciliter l'intégration de l'économie congolaise dans la dynamique régionale et internationale des échanges. La valeur ajoutée aux productions congolaises devra avoir une incidence sur le niveau de vie des populations congolaises. A l'horizon 2015, le Gouvernement congolais projette la création des premières ZES et cette expérience nouvelle – qui est intégrée dans le grand projet « pôle de croissance » de la Banque mondiale[3] et qui vise les marchés national, régional et international – concernera :

- le Centre du pays : c'est l'axe Ilebo-Tshikapa-Kananga-Mbuji-Mayi qui est visé et la ZES à y créer portera sur la logistique de transport et des industries agro-alimentaires au Kasaï-Occidental et au Kasaï-Oriental ;
- le Sud du pays avec l'axe Kolwezi-Likasi-Lubumbashi-Sakania : la ZES à y créer devra permettre le développement des industries lourdes et manufacturières axées sur les minerais du Katanga ;
- l'Est du pays avec l'axe Uvira-Bukavu-Goma-Butembo-Beni-Bunia, où est prévue l'installation d'industries manufacturières et agro-alimentaires au Nord-Kivu et au Sud-Kivu ;
- le Nord-Ouest sur l'axe Kisangani-Bumba-Mbandaka afin de déve-

1.Thomas FAROLE, Gokhan AKINCI (2011), « Special Economic Zones : Progress, Emerging Challenges, and Future Directions », Directions in Development Trade, Banque mondiale

2.Léopold NSEKE (28 septembre 2012), « Les zones économiques spéciales : Qui s'investit ? », lu le 05 juillet 2014 sur <http://www.afriqueexpansion.com/les-zones-economiques-speciales-/5257-les-zones-economiques-speciales--qui-sinvestit-.html>

3.Pathou Kinzala NKUKA (06 février 2013), « Le site de Maluku choisi pour être une zone économique pilote en RDC », lu le 05 juillet 2014 sur <http://www.digitalcongo.net/article/89605>

lopper les industries du bois et de l'agriculture en Province Orientale et à l'Equateur ;

- l'Ouest du pays avec l'axe Kinshasa-Matadi-Inga-Boma-Banana, où la ZES à y créer devra contribuer au développement des activités stratégiques concentrées sur l'hydroélectricité, le pétrole et la bauxite, et sur les industries manufacturières autour des ports maritimes de Matadi et Boma.

Pour cette dernière région, les travaux préliminaires devant aboutir à l'implantation d'une ZES pilote à Maluku, près de Kinshasa, ont été amorcés (le Décret n° 12/021 du 16 juillet 2012, porte création d'une Zone Economique Spéciale à Maluku). Son site est proche de l'aéroport international de N'djili, à proximité du fleuve Congo (Pool Malebo) et de la route nationale n°1.

Le choix de tous ces axes se base sur plusieurs critères. Les plus importantes régions du pays sont concernées, regroupant les principales villes et cités (à l'exception de Bandundu, Kikwit et Kindu et de leurs zones environnantes) sur les plans démographique et économique. L'objectif est de développer l'industrie axée soit sur des secteurs d'activités économiques déjà bien implantées (le Sud avec l'exploitation minière, l'Est avec l'exploitation minière et l'agriculture industrielle, le Nord-Ouest avec l'exploitation forestière, et l'Ouest du pays avec les activités industrielles et portuaires), soit sur des secteurs d'activités économiques peu développés dans une région (c'est le cas du Centre du pays dont l'économie était, jadis, fortement dépendante de l'exploitation du diamant industriel), avec l'agriculture au premier plan. Celle-ci occupe, en effet, une place importante dans l'économie des deux Kivu. Les économies de la Province Orientale et de la Province de l'Equateur dépendent aussi sensiblement de l'agriculture, de même que de l'exploitation forestière. L'hydroélectricité, le pétrole et la bauxite sont produits au Bas-Congo qui compte les ports maritimes de Matadi, Boma et Banana. L'économie de la Province du Katanga est fortement axée sur l'industrie extractive des minerais. Dans les provinces du Kasaï-Occidental et du Kasaï-Oriental, le choix des filières de la logistique de transport et de l'industrie agro-alimentaire a pour objectif de désenclaver le centre du pays, de développer l'agriculture et de faire de cette région où la sécurité et l'autosuffisance alimentaires n'avaient pas priorité sur l'exploitation minière (actuellement dans le déclin), un grenier agricole.

Sur le plan géographique, tous les axes concernés disposent de dotations factorielles. La non-prise en compte de ces facteurs géographiques avait conduit à l'échec de la Société Sidérurgique de Maluku (SOSIDER). En effet, le projet de cette aciérie – qui devait mettre à profit la disponibilité en énergie électrique provenant des barrages d'Inga – avait été mal conçu dès le départ du fait qu'il n'y avait pas de source sûre de matières premières localement. La SOSIDER devait plutôt recycler les mitrailles pour produire.

Le type de ZES le plus apparenté aux projets du Gouvernement congolais est celui de « Zone de Libre Echange », à l'exception de la ZES à développer au Sud qui s'apparente plutôt à une « Zone Franche d'Exportation ». Il convient, toutefois, d'apporter une nuance qui découle bien de « l'exception » congolaise. La RDC occupe une position stratégique au centre de l'Afrique et possède une longue frontière terrestre partagée avec neuf pays. Mais, en dépit du fait que son solde commercial est positif depuis 2009 et que ses déficits courants sont principalement et de plus en plus financés par l'IDE[1], le pays reste largement sous-industrialisé. L'évolution positive du solde commercial est fortement corrélée à la hausse des exportations des produits miniers. A travers ses ZES et dans un premier temps, la RDC ne devrait pas seulement chercher à devenir globalement « exportatrice nette » mais à ne plus être « importatrice nette » dans certains secteurs stratégiques en s'appuyant sur son marché intérieur, moins dépendant de la qualité de ses relations bilatérales et multilatérales. Quoique l'essentiel des axes choisis soient localisés près de ses frontières, leurs productions devraient, en premier, viser l'import-substitution (tant des inputs que des outputs), particulièrement dans le secteur agro-alimentaire où la RDC importe encore pour plus de un milliard USD par an. L'agriculture est un secteur à forte intensité de main-d'œuvre qui peut assurer au pays la sécurité et l'autosuffisance alimentaires tout en permettant de sortir une partie de la population de l'extrême pauvreté. Le développement de l'industrie agro-alimentaire est stratégique. Mais globalement, la consommation des biens et services produits localement est un sujet de fierté. Les ZES congolaises (en général) pourraient, à terme, considérablement exporter une partie de leurs productions (au niveau sous-régional en premier, parce que sous-industrialisé) et permettre l'accroissement des revenus de change.

En RDC, le régime des ZES est fixé par une loi qui exprime la vision du pays dans ce domaine dans l'objectif de maintenir la croissance économique à un rythme soutenu et d'atteindre, à terme, l'émergence et le développement. Cette loi ne concerne pas uniquement les projets de ZES cités plus haut mais aussi tous les projets qui peuvent être initiés par des aménageurs nationaux ou étrangers. Ces projets devront obéir à des critères liés au site, à l'aménagement et à l'environnement et préciser leur contribution au développement économique national et à la création d'emplois. La Loi prévoit que les projets soumis reçoivent le même traitement, quelle que soit la nationalité de l'aménageur qui assume les risques du projet en termes de placement en capital, qui a la zone en concession et qui en fait la promotion. Aussi, seuls les projets initiés soit entièrement par les promoteurs privés nationaux ou étrangers, soit encore par des partenariats publics-privés, peuvent être agréés au sein des ZES, ce qui concoure au bon climat des affaires.

En somme, cette Loi prévoit certaines politiques préférentielles : (i) la simplification des procédures administratives, notamment en matière fiscale (sans pour autant porter préjudice aux dispositions de la Loi relative aux finances publiques), (ii) la possibilité pour les gouvernements provinciaux d'accorder certains avantages et incitatifs dont la nature n'est pas précisée, (iii) la possibilité pour les entreprises de rapatrier dans leurs pays d'origine les retours financiers découlant de leurs investissements, (iv) le renforce-

1.Fonds Monétaire International (octobre 2014), « Rapport n° 14/301, Consultations de 2014 au titre de l'article IV - rapport des services du FMI ; communiqué de presse ; et déclaration de l'administrateur pour la République Démocratique du Congo »

ment des mécanismes de résolution des différends liés aux investissements, (v) le calibrage des avantages fiscaux à accorder aux entreprises établies dans une ZES et (vi) la représentation de l'Etat congolais par un Etablissement public à caractère administratif et technique en charge de l'administration des ZES qui servira d'interface aux opérateurs établis dans les ZES. En outre, pour les ZES que le Gouvernement entend développer, il est garanti aux entreprises qui s'y établiront (i) l'applicabilité automatique du Code des investissements de la RDC, (ii) des concessions foncières disponibles et transparentes et (iii) l'accès à toute heure aux infrastructures de ces zones.[1]

Par contre, la Loi renvoie aux lois existantes en matière de gestion des ressources humaines, d'octroi de titres de séjour et de permis de travail aux expatriés, et en matière foncière. Elle reste muette en ce qui concerne particulièrement l'amortissement comptable des immobilisations. Des précisions sur ces derniers points sont, toutefois, importantes et la Loi fixant régime des ZES est, partant, appelée à « évoluer » avec le temps et avec l'expérience issue de la mise en place des premières zones.

En matière fiscale, chaque projet de ZES en RDC bénéficiera d'une étude préliminaire et chaque contrat d'aménagement entre l'Etablissement public en charge de l'administration de toutes les ZES congolaises (qui sera créée) et l'aménageur choisi fixera les avantages fiscaux, parafiscaux et douaniers dont jouissent les entreprises établies dans une ZES. Les Ministres ayant l'industrie et les finances dans leurs attributions présenteront au Parlement (à chaque session ordinaire), les contrats d'aménagement signés ainsi que les avantages accordés. Un régime particulier de paiement des taxes et des frais administratifs sera établi dans les ZES par un Arrêté du Ministre ayant les finances dans ses attributions. Les provinces concernées peuvent aussi offrir des avantages fiscaux par des édits. Tout l'enjeu, dans ce domaine, consistera donc à bien étoffer et calibrer ces avantages fiscaux suivant les caractéristiques socio-économiques des activités à développer quoique, de manière précise, la Loi oblige l'administration fiscale et douanière au sein des ZES de prévoir des procédures de contrôle simplifiées pour les marchandises émanant ou à destination des ZES, de n'exiger aucune caution douanière pour les marchandises émanant ou à destination des ZES ou y entreposées, et de n'exiger aucune caution pour les appels des décisions fiscales au sein des ZES.

En sus de la politique fiscale, les raisons économiques et politiques influent sur les décisions d'investissement et certaines peuvent particulièrement dissuader les investisseurs : marché potentiel limité, longue situation de détérioration économique, faible compétitivité des zones économiques existantes face aux zones franches d'autres pays, interférences politiques, faible décentralisation dans l'établissement de politiques économiques, relations internationales médiocres avec certaines nations stratégiques, etc. Une zone serait difficilement en mesure de protéger les investisseurs du climat des affaires qui les entoure, particulièrement si elle ne sait pas se

1.Banque mondiale (sans date), « Appel Aux Investisseurs Intéressés Par Le Développement De Leurs Activités Économiques Dans La Zone Économique Spéciale Proposée À Maluku, Province De Kinshasa », lu le 13 juillet 2014 sur <http://www.banquemondiale.org/projects/procurement/noticeoverview?lang=fr&id=OP00017135&>

libérer de l'influence de l'Etat. Ce fut le cas de la Corée du Nord.[1] L'échec de sa politique de ZES était dû au fait que, tout en étant communiste comme la Chine, le pays n'avait pas su fournir autant d'efforts d'ouverture au monde extérieur que cette dernière.[2] Un mauvais climat des affaires pourrait ainsi pousser certains pays à compenser avec de larges avantages fiscaux, un choix coûteux et peu sûr.[3]

La RDC affiche, depuis 2012, des taux d'inflation relativement faibles, preuve d'une stabilité macroéconomique appréciable. Le taux d'inflation est passé de 53,4% en 2009[4] à 1,03% en 2014.[5] La monnaie nationale, le Franc congolais, connaît une stabilité face aux devises étrangères même si une telle politique n'est pas de nature à doper les exportations. La stabilité observée permettra d'éviter que l'octroi de différents avantages fiscaux ne produise les incitations voulues aux investisseurs.[6] En effet, quand le taux d'inflation est particulièrement élevé, l'hyperinflation fait alors office d'une taxe (inflationniste) et annihile les effets positifs attendus d'une politique d'incitations fiscales. Le défi pour le pays est de garder ce cap au-delà du changement de décideurs politiques.

La RDC est aussi un pays post-conflit où la question sécuritaire se pose encore dans certaines régions, particulièrement dans l'ancien Kivu. Des études poussées sont attendues pour comprendre le rôle des ZES dans un environnement post-conflit. Toutefois, il s'avère que si un secteur privé dynamique avait existé avant le conflit et que des investissements sont prioritairement affectés aux infrastructures, les zones économiques peuvent avoir un effet catalyseur important. Dans le cas contraire et si l'Etat est faible (ou fort mais prédateur), les ZES seraient moins efficaces. Les ZES sont ainsi généralement plus efficaces dans les pays avec des Etats forts et non prédateurs[7], ce qui n'est pas le cas de la RDC qui présente les caractéristiques d'un Etat faible encore en quête d'autorité. Avant la guerre civile, le secteur privé n'était pas assez développé et la détérioration de l'économie congolaise aurait connu un tournant avec la politique dite de « zaïrianisation » de 1974.[8]

Actuellement, peu d'entreprises privées dynamiques du secteur secondaire existent en RDC, et les entreprises établies dans les ZES congolaises ne pourront pas se passer de l'importation de certains intrants. La promotion d'un secteur privé national entreprenant et compétitif est donc une nécessité. Les

1.Chang Woon NAM, Doina Maria RADULESCU (2005), « Do Corporate Tax Concessions Really Matter for the Success of Free Economic Zones? », Economics of Planning 37, pp. 99-123

2.Young NAMKOONG (2003), « North Korea's Policy of Sinuiju Special Economic Zone: Implications and Prospects », Asian Survey Vol. 32, No. 11, pp. 1026-1045

3.Thomas FAROLE (2011), « Special Economic Zones in Africa : Comparing Performance and Learning from Global Experience », Directions in Development Trade, Banque mondiale

4.Banque mondiale (sans date), « République démocratique du Congo », lu le 13 juillet 2014 sur <http://donnees.banquemondiale.org/fr/country/drc>

5.Banque Centrale du Congo (février 2015), « Rapport sur la politique monétaire en 2014 », N°009

6.Chang Woon NAM, Doina Maria RADULESCU (2005), « Do Corporate Tax Concessions Really Matter for the Success of Free Economic Zones? », Economics of Planning 37, pp. 99-123

7.Thomas FAROLE (2011), « Special Economic Zones in Africa : Comparing Performance and Learning from Global Experience », Directions in Development Trade, Banque mondiale

8.Renaud TOWE (19 août 2012), « La zaïrianisation de Mobutu, de l'homme au demi-dieu », lu le 13 mars 2015 sur <http://www.afrik.com/article26594.html>

ZES ne doivent pas, en effet, s'apparenter à des îlots dans un large océan de marasme économique. Des mesures telles que la promotion de banques d'investissement et de la microfinance, la promotion de l'entrepreneuriat des jeunes, une véritable promotion de l'industrie, la création d'une bourse congolaise de valeurs mobilières, et la promotion d'un label de qualité (le « *made in* RDC ») peuvent, à terme, permettre aux congolais de véritablement « contrôler leur économie ».

Après une longue période de détérioration économique, plusieurs réformes sont entreprises dans le pays depuis une décennie même si le climat des affaires est encore réputé peu incitatif (184e pays/189 avec 40,60% selon le Rapport *Doing Business* 2015[1] et un indice Coface D du risque associé au pays en 2015[2]). Le pays connaît toujours des situations d'interférences politiques dans le milieu des affaires qui contribuent déjà aux contre-performances du Fisc national. Aussi, le processus de décentralisation stagne quoique légalement prévu. Quelques évolutions positives sont, cependant, enregistrées et les récentes politiques macroéconomiques sont encourageantes, ce que renseignent les notations de la RDC par MOODY'S (B3 en septembre 2013[3]) et STANDARD & POORS (B à court terme et B- à long terme, en février 2014) accompagnées de perspectives stables.[4] Dans la perspective de la poursuite des reformes – qui constituent un préalable au succès des ZES – et en dépit d'un faible niveau relatif des investissements (domestiques, en particulier, qui ne représentent que 28,621% du PIB[5]), il demeure judicieux pour les ZES de bien sélectionner des niches de compétitivité ou des activités à fort rentabilité qui peuvent attirer les investisseurs potentiels.

La protection juridique des investissements, la promotion du secteur privé et de la concurrence améliorent le climat des affaires. La Loi fixant le régime des ZES en RDC prévoit que tout investisseur, quelle que soit sa nationalité, jouisse des mêmes droits et soit soumis aux mêmes obligations dans l'exercice de ses activités et qu'en cas de différend, à défaut de solution à l'amiable, l'arbitrage soit privilégié. Les décisions de l'Etablissement public en charge de l'administration des ZES pourront aussi faire l'objet de recours administratifs conformément au droit commun. Quant aux contentieux fiscaux et douaniers, ils se traiteront conformément à la Loi fiscale et au Code douanier. La Loi établit la concurrence entre entreprises au sein d'une ZES qui peuvent entreprendre toute activité économique qui n'est pas interdite par la législation congolaise et

1.Banque mondiale (sans date), « Facilité des affaires, Congo, République Démocratique du », lu le12 janvier 2015 sur <http://francais.doingbusiness.org/reports/global-reports/doing-business-2015>

2.Compagnie Française d'Assurance pour le Commerce Extérieur (sans date), « Congo, République Démocratique du », lu le 20 avril 2015 sur <http://www.coface.com/fr/Etudes-economiques-et-risque-pays/Congo-Republique-democratique-du>

3.MOODY'S (6 septembre 2013), « Rating Action: Moody's assigns B3 ratings to the Democratic Republic of the Congo, stable outlook », lu le 25 mai 2015 sur < https://www.moodys.com/research/Moodys-assigns-B3-ratings-to-the-Democratic-Republic-of-the--PR_281558>

4.Omer MBADI (16 décembre 2013), « S&P maintient la note du Cameroun à B et attribue la note B- à la RD Congo », lu le 13 juillet 2014 sur <http://economie.jeuneafrique.com/regions/afrique-subsaharienne/20966-sap-maintien-la-note-du-cameroun-a-b-et-attribue-b-a-la-rd-congo.html>

5.Jeune Afrique (sans date), « Repères économiques », lu le 13 juillet 2014 sur <http://www.jeuneafrique.com/Reperes-economiques-pays_79_RD Congo>

étendre leurs champs d'activités. En ce qui concerne certains types d'investissements (même dans l'aménagement de zones économiques), les politiques actuelles de plusieurs gouvernements consistent en un certain désengagement. L'objectif est d'éviter le surendettement public et d'orienter les budgets publics vers les secteurs régaliens ou d'autres à forte connotation sociale tels que l'éducation et la santé. Ces gouvernements privilégient alors les partenariats publics-privés. La RDC s'engage peu à peu sur cette voie et devra se doter d'une loi pouvant encadrer ce type de contrats.

Malgré une population évaluée à 67,51 millions d'habitants, le marché intérieur congolais est faible, puisque cette population est en majorité pauvre (63% de la population[1]) et son pouvoir d'achat est faible. Le PIB annuel *per capita*, en parité de pouvoir d'achat (PPA), était de 747 USD en 2013.[2] En outre, certaines habitudes de consommation ne sont pas encore développées pour des biens pourtant produits localement (le café, par exemple). Quelle incidence sur l'efficacité des ZES congolaises ? Dans les pays à petits marchés, les ZES performantes ont eu tendance, dans un premier temps, à profiter de la localisation, des avantages commerciaux, des choix permettant la création d'emplois à grande échelle et à supporter la transition d'un secteur de ressources naturelles vers un secteur industriel embryonnaire. Certains de ces pays se sont aussi servis de zones économiques pour passer d'un secteur industriel à emplois intensifs à un secteur industriel de haute technologie. Les ZES de la RDC devront miser sur la localisation et se concentrer sur des activités permettant la création d'emplois à grande échelle (le secteur agro-alimentaire, l'agro-industrie, les mines, le tourisme, etc.) tout en préparant le pays à passer d'un secteur de ressources naturelles vers celui de l'industrie *high-tech*. Corolairement, le marché intérieur congolais constituera un atout pour les investisseurs si les productions des ZES correspondent au faible pouvoir d'achat de la population. Ces entreprises pourraient ainsi compter sur des débouchés internes, pourvu que les infrastructures de transport soient développées. Elles pourront aussi compter sur des débouchés externes pour leurs produits industriels et de l'agriculture industrielle. De manière générale, les ZES africaines peuvent se concentrer et se spécialiser dans les activités liées aux ressources naturelles (où les pays hôtes ont souvent un avantage comparatif) et être intégrées dans une stratégie de croissance plus large touchant les secteurs commercial et industriel.[3]

La localisation stratégique et une connexion multimodale avec les marchés potentiels sont d'autres facteurs importants du succès d'une ZES. Les projets sélectionnés devraient correspondre à l'environnement géographique et économique des ZES, avec avantage pour les projets à caractère complémentaire[4] (l'industrie agro-alimentaire, par

1.Banque mondiale (sans date), « République démocratique du Congo – Vue d'ensemble », lu le 10 mars 2015 sur <http://www.banquemondiale.org/fr/country/drc/overview>

2.Banque mondiale (sans date), « République démocratique du Congo », lu le 13 juillet 2014 sur <http://donnees.banquemondiale.org/fr/country/drc>

3.Thomas FAROLE (2011), « Special Economic Zones in Africa : Comparing Performance and Learning from Global Experience », Directions in Development Trade, Banque mondiale

4.N. VISWANADHAM (décembre 2006), « Design of Special Economic Zones as Economic Engines of Growth », Thought Leadership White Papers, pp. 93-115

exemple). Les cinq premiers projets de ZES correspondent aux spécificités économiques régionales, à côté des principaux ports de la RDC (Matadi, Boma, Uvira, Kisangani, Mbandaka et Kinshasa), et dans des régions traversées par les routes d'intérêt national, à proximité des principales agglomérations du pays. L'accès aux intrants sera facile pour le secteur industriel. Il demeure, néanmoins, un risque élevé en ce qui concerne l'application de certaines lois[1], les approvisionnements en pièces de rechange et en énergie, et en ce qui concerne l'état des infrastructures encore faiblement développées. Dans ce dernier domaine, une étude menée aux Philippines sur une période de 12 ans a montré qu'au niveau international en général, et qu'au niveau régional, en particulier, les IDE sont plus orientés vers les zones disposant d'infrastructures de qualité.[2] Dans la recherche des IDE, en cas de concurrence entre les ZES des pays en développement, celles développées en RDC ne partent pas favorites. Les infrastructures congolaises constituent une grande faiblesse pour un pays relativement vaste.

En plus des politiques d'incitations économiques, du climat des affaires, de la localisation et de l'aménagement, le succès des zones économiques dépend aussi de leur gestion et de leur « design », selon qu'elles sont développées par le secteur public ou par des privés. En dépit de l'absence d'analyses poussées sur une éventuelle meilleure performance des ZES privées, les données existantes ont montré que celles-ci sont moins coûteuses à développer et à gérer, et engrangeraient de bien meilleurs résultats économiques. En convertissant les *EPZ* en ZES, l'Inde avait pour objectif de faciliter l'aménagement privé de grandes villes industrielles. De l'expérience internationale, le modèle de ZES suggéré serait celui qui[3] :

- assure que le régime est flexible, permettant autant les activités industrielles que commerciales ;
- en promeut le développement privé au lieu d'un développement public ;
- permet l'établissement, au sein de la même zone économique, des entreprises bénéficiant de son régime et celles bénéficiant d'autres régimes.

Les projets à caractère complémentaire sont à privilégier parce qu'ils peuvent créer une interaction significative, que

1.De façon particulière, le Code minier jugé trop large en faveur des miniers par la Société civile et la Loi agricole (Loi n° 11/022 portant principes fondamentaux relatifs à l'agriculture du 24 décembre 2011 publiée dans le Journal Officiel du 27 décembre 2011) qu'il serait judicieux de revoir, notamment à ses articles 16 et 21. L'article 16 – qui n'encourage pas les investissements privés agricoles en RDC – stipule que les conditions d'obtention des concessions agricoles sont : (i) être une personne physique de nationalité congolaise ou une personne morale de droit congolais dont les parts sociales ou les actions, selon le cas, sont majoritairement détenues par l'Etat congolais et/ou par les nationaux ; (ii) avoir une résidence, un domicile ou un siège social connu en République Démocratique du Congo ; (iii) présenter la preuve de son inscription au registre de commerce, s'il s'agit d'une personne exerçant le commerce ; (iv) justifier de la capacité financière susceptible de supporter la charge qu'implique la mise en valeur de la concession ; (v) produire une étude d'impact environnemental et social. L'article 21 bloque les investisseurs en cas de cession de leurs concessions, étant entendu que l'investisseur tant étranger que national est libre de changer d'activité à tout moment au point que la cession de son capital ne peut être soumise à une quelconque condition en matière d'éligibilité de nouveaux acquéreurs.

2.Maria Peregrina MAKABENTA (mars 2002), « FDI location and Special Economic Zones in the Philippines », Review of Urban & Regional Development Studies Vol. 14, No. 1, pp. 59-77

3.Thomas FAROLE, Gokhan AKINCI (2011), « Special Economic Zones : Progress, Emerging Challenges, and Future Directions », Directions in Development Trade, Banque mondiale

ce soit dans le cadre de ZES multi-produits intégrées, des ZES regroupant des entreprises d'une même industrie, de ZES regroupant des entreprises à productions similaires ou de ZES regroupant des entreprises de services. Ainsi, par exemple, il faudrait veiller à ne pas « mélanger » certaines industries lourdes avec les industries agro-alimentaires.

La Loi fixant le régime des ZES en RDC donne une place prépondérante au secteur privé dans la création et la marche des ZES quoiqu'il soit prévu la création d'un Etablissement public en charge de l'administration de toutes les ZES. Cette implication du secteur privé pourra être efficace dans le cas où les interférences étatiques, à travers l'Etablissement public en charge de l'administration des ZES, sont réduites au minimum. A ce sujet, la Loi prévoit que les inspections et les contrôles administratifs effectués par les services de l'Etat ne peuvent avoir lieu dans les ZES qu'en coordination avec l'Etablissement public en charge de l'administration des ZES et leurs aménageurs respectifs.

Sur les questions foncières touchant aux ZES, la Loi fixant leur régime prévoit que les plans d'usage du sol, de zonage et d'aménagement des ZES soient définis conformément à la Loi foncière en vigueur en RDC, où l'Etat exerce une souveraineté permanente sur le sol, le sous-sol, les eaux et les forêts, sur les espaces aérien, fluvial, lacustre et maritime congolais ainsi que sur la mer territoriale congolaise et sur le plateau continental.[1] Cette disposition de la Constitution de la RDC n'est pas de nature à encourager les IDE mais donne une bonne marge de manœuvre au Gouvernement dans le cas où l'expropriation est certainement avantageuse. Le défi est donc de trouver le juste milieu, un arbitrage qui permet d'atteindre le développement industriel par les ZES sans léser les activités agricoles et les agriculteurs. En cas de création de la concurrence entre les activités de la ZES et des autochtones, une reconversion professionnelle et/ou un engagement des autochtones dans la ZES sont nécessaires, pourvu que les bénéficiaires adhèrent au projet et ne s'en retrouvent pas économiquement et socialement diminués. Et s'il s'avère avantageux de procéder à des dépossessions de terres, l'indemnisation doit être conséquente.[2] Pour les ZES non centrées sur les activités agricoles, les sites choisis devront être, au mieux, des terrains à faible productivité agricole. Globalement, toutes les ZES congolaises devront obéir aux critères liés au site, à l'aménagement et à l'environnement précisés par la Loi qui fixe leur régime. Les critères liés à l'environnement sont, entre autres, l'existence de plans de prévention et d'atténuation des impacts environnementaux et sociaux, et le respect des normes d'émission de polluant gazeux, liquides et solides dans l'air, dans les eaux et dans les sols.

Parmi les déterminants de la destination des IDE (hormis les IDE eux-mêmes), il y a aussi le coût du travail.[3] En Afrique, il est relevé par les coûts de transaction et des risques encourus.

1.Article 9 de la Constitution de la République Démocratique du Congo promulguée le 18 février 2006

2.CAZES (21 septembre 2013), « Les occupants du site de la ZES de Maluku bientôt indemnisées », lu le 05 juillet 2014 sur <http://www.cazesrdc.net/index/php/a-propos-des-zes>

3.Leonard K. CHENG, Yum K. KWAN (2000), « What are the determinants of the location of foreign direct investment? The Chinese experience », Journal of International Economics 51, pp. 379-400

Aussi, la faible spécialisation d'une grande partie de la main-d'œuvre induit souvent une faible productivité.[1] En RDC, presque tous les types d'industries ne trouveront pas, à leur implantation, suffisamment de personnel local qualifié. L'objectif de création d'emplois directs et indirects risquera alors de ne pas être complètement atteint sauf si une politique de main-d'œuvre est mise en place. Cette politique devrait, dans la foulée, permettre d'attirer la diaspora congolaise (en actionnant, par exemple, le levier fiscal) qui pourrait aussi apporter des capitaux frais au pays. En outre, la Loi fixant le régime des ZES prévoit que les entreprises peuvent recourir aux services du personnel expatrié dont les qualifications et compétences ne sont pas disponibles localement conformément au Code du travail en vigueur en RDC. La Loi lie ainsi le recours au personnel expatrié au seul manque d'un personnel local qualifié. La création d'emplois est, en effet, l'un des objectifs du pays qui voudrait conforter le revenu national en promouvant les ZES. Aussi, les bénéficiaires de ces emplois seraient plus susceptibles de prendre des décisions économiques bénéfiques à toute l'économie nationale. La promotion d'écoles techniques et professionnelles spécialisées par l'Etat est, par conséquent, impérieuse : elles ne représentent que 10% du tissu scolaire et académique congolais.[2] Leur développement présente, pourtant, un double avantage : l'emploi des diplômés nationaux et l'attrait de certains types d'industries spécialisées, desquelles des transferts de technologies associées peuvent être opérés (la RDC peut en exiger des entreprises désireuses de s'implanter dans les ZES à créer).

La RDC, devra-t-elle compter un « grand nombre » de ZES pour son développement ? Plusieurs années de recherche ont montré que les zones économiques jouent un rôle important de catalyseur dans le processus de transition économique. Mais il a été prouvé que l'augmentation du nombre des ZES dans un pays a un effet négligeable sur sa croissance économique.[3] Pour atteindre ses objectifs de développement par la création de ZES, la RDC n'a par conséquent pas besoin de miser sur leur quantité mais sur leur qualité. La plupart des zones économiques africaines n'ont pas, en effet, donné de bénéfices significatifs à ce jour en dépit du fait qu'elles gardent le potentiel d'atteindre les objectifs leurs assignés.[4] Les facteurs de la contre-performance des zones économiques africaines sont essentiellement les déficiences enregistrées en matière d'infrastructures (à l'intérieur et en dehors de ces zones), la faible attention portée aux questions de facilitations commerciales, la faible qualité de la programmation et de la gestion, les challenges de la coordination insti-

1.Thomas FAROLE (2011), « Special Economic Zones in Africa : Comparing Performance and Learning from Global Experience », Directions in Development Trade, Banque mondiale

2.Tshingi KUENO NDOMBASI (sans date), « A la croisée des chemins ou le nouveau défi africain du 21ème siècle », lu le 14 janvier 2015 sur <http://www.congovision.com/images2/A_la_croisee_des_chemins_tshingi.pdf>

3.Chee Kian LEONG (septembre 2013), « Special economic zones and growth in China and India: an empirical investigation », International Economics and Economic Policy 10, pp. 549-567

4.Thomas FAROLE (2011), « Special Economic Zones in Africa : Comparing Performance and Learning from Global Experience », Directions in Development Trade, Banque mondiale

tutionnelle, la politique économique et la compétitivité générale des pays hôtes.

Enfin, pourquoi les zones économiques congolaises seraient-elles qualifiées de « spéciales » ? Parce qu'elles pourraient permettre le développement d'un tissu industriel très pauvre et désarticulé (entre autres pour l'import-substitution) dans un pays « post-conflit » où le climat des affaires est encore peu incitatif, mais qui jouit d'une position géographique stratégique, d'un cadre macroéconomique stabilisé et d'un avantage comparatif dans la production de plusieurs matières premières. Le pays devra aussi continuer à investir dans les infrastructures, particulièrement celles qui sont en connexion directe avec les ZES. La RDC vise l'émergence à l'horizon 2030 et la promotion de ZES est un programme ambitieux. Les défis en matière d'infrastructures de transport et de communication demeurent parmi les plus grands et nécessitent d'importants investissements sur une période relativement longue. La question énergétique demeure aussi s'il faut considérer le déficit que connaît le pays dans ce domaine malgré le faible niveau d'industrialisation actuel. La question réglementaire, elle, avance mais souvent sans célérité dans un monde pourtant globalisé et hautement compétitif.

La création des ZES devra progresser avec la résolution de toutes les faiblesses relevées. Cette résolution peut bien être régionale, particulièrement en ce qui concerne les voies de transport et de communication, et les sources d'énergie. De profondes analyses coûts-avantages devront aussi être faites au préalable afin de se rassurer de l'opportunité économique de la création de chaque ZES et des mesures d'incitation idoines à prendre.

4. Conclusion

Les ZES ont été « inventées » dans la Chine populaire qui est devenue, depuis 2014, la première économie mondiale (si l'on ne prend en compte que les chiffres du PIB publiés par le Fonds Monétaire International en octobre 2014 et exprimés en parité de pouvoir d'achat)[1], place qu'elle occupait déjà avant les « guerres de l'opium » qui la contraignirent à signer des traités inégaux en matière de commerce international avec les pays occidentaux. Les ZES ont aussi constitué une stratégie économique de développement appliquée parfois avec succès dans plusieurs pays. En promulguant une Loi encadrant leur régime, La RDC envisage de promouvoir le développement de ZES sur son territoire. Au vu des éléments développés dans ce papier, leur implantation efficace devra être progressive en tenant compte, essentiellement, des contraintes socio-économiques auxquelles fait face le pays. Ces contraintes, conséquences de plusieurs années de guerre civile et de récession économique et qui disparaissent peu à peu depuis plus d'une décennie, sont de nature institutionnelle, concernent le pouvoir d'achat du marché intérieur et le déficit en infrastructures (énergétiques, de transports et de communication). Ces zones devront aussi revêtir une mission particulière d'import-substitution et d'impact substantiel sur l'économie nationale.

1. Brett ARENDS (04 décembre 2014), « It's official : America is now No. 2 », lu le 10 janvier 2015 sur <http://www.marketwatch.com/story/its-official-america-is-now-no-2-2014-12-04>

Références

Albert G. SCHWEINBERGER, « Special Economic Zones in Developing and/or Transition Economies: a Policy Proposal », Review of International Economics 11, pp. 619-629, 2003

Arnaud DIEMER, Economie générale, cours inédit à l'IUFM Auvergne, <http://www.oeconomica.net/private/cours/economiegenerale/CAPET/12.politiqueeconomique.pdf>, sans date (consulté le 05 juillet 2014)

Banque Centrale du Congo, « Rapport sur la politique monétaire en 2014 », N°009, février 2015

Banque mondiale, « Appel Aux Investisseurs Intéressés Par Le Développement De Leurs Activités Économiques Dans La Zone Économique Spéciale Proposée À Maluku, Province De Kinshasa », <http://www.banquemondiale.org/projects/procurement/noticeoverview?lang=fr&id=OP00017135&>, sans date (consulté le 13 juillet 2014)

Banque mondiale, « Facilité de faire des affaires, Congo, République démocratique du », <http://francais.doingbusiness.org/reports/global-reports/doing-business-2015>, sans date (consulté le 12 janvier 2015)

Banque mondiale, « République démocratique du Congo – Vue d'ensemble », <http://www.banquemondiale.org/fr/country/drc/overview>, sans date (consulté le 10 mars 2015)

Banque mondiale, « République démocratique du Congo », <http://donnees.banquemondiale.org/fr/country/drc>, sans date (consulté le 13 juillet 2014)

Brett ARENDS, « It's official : America is now No. 2 », <http://www.marketwatch.com/story/its-official-america-is-now-no-2-2014-12-04>, 04 décembre 2014 (consulté le 10 janvier 2015)

BURKINA FASO, « Le Pôle de Croissance de Samendeni », <http://alpha.burkinafasoindia.org/documents/Samendeni%20FINAL%20French.pdf>, sans date (consulté le 16 mai 2015)

Cabinet du Premier Ministre, «Programme d'action du Gouvernement 2012 – 2016 », <file:///C:/Users/HP/Downloads/Programme%20du%20gouvernement%20mai%202012.pdf>, mai 2012 (consulté le 25 mai 2015)

CAZES, « Les occupants du site de la ZES de Maluku bientôt indemnisées », <http://www.cazesrdc.net/index/php/a-propos-des-zes>, 21 septembre 2013 (consulté le 05 juillet 2014)

Centre de Commerce et d'Industrie Européen, « Les Zones Economiques Spéciales », <http://www.c-cie.eu/index.php?article22/les-zones-economiques-speciales>, 05 juin 2012 (consulté le 05 juillet 2014)

Chang Woon NAM, Doina Maria RADULESCU, « Do Corporate Tax Concessions Really Matter for the Success of Free Economic Zones? », Economics of Planning 37, pp. 99-123, 2005

Chee Kian LEONG, « Special economic zones and growth in China and India: an empirical investigation », International Economics and Economic Policy 10, pp. 549-567, septembre 2013

Compagnie Française d'Assurance pour le Commerce Extérieur, « Congo, République démocratique du », <http://www.coface.com/fr/Etudes-economiques-et-risque-pays/Congo-Republique-democratique-du>, sans date (consulté le 13 juillet 2014)

Constitution de la République Démocratique du Congo, février 2006

Deborah BRAUTIGAM, Xiaoyang TANG, « "Going Global in Groups": Structural Transformation and China's Special Economic Zones Overseas », World Development Vol. 63, pp. 78-91, 2014

Deborah BRAUTIGAM, Xiaoyang TANG, « China's Investment in Special Economic Zones in Africa », sous la direction de Thomas FAROLE et Gokhan AKINCI dans « Special Economic Zones : Progress, Emerging Challenges, and Future Directions », Directions in Development Trade, Banque mondiale, pp. 69-100, 2011

Douglas Zhihua ZENG, « How do Special Economic Zones and Industrial Clusters drive China's rapid development? », Policy Research Working Paper 5583, Banque mondiale, mars 2011

Fonds Monétaire International, « Rapport nº 14/301, Consultations de 2014 au titre de l'article IV - rapport des services du FMI ; communiqué de presse ; et déclaration de l'administrateur pour la République Démocratique du Congo », octobre 2014

Jean-Nicolas SAUCIER, « Les zones économiques spéciales : tremplin ou servitude ? », <http://www.afriqueexpansion.com/les-zones-economiques-speciales-/5265-les-zones-economiques-speciales--tremplin-ou-servitude-.html>, 28 septembre 2012 (consulté le 05 juillet 2014)

Jeune Afrique, « Repères économiques », <http://www.jeuneafrique.com/Reperes-economiques-pays_79_RD Congo>, sans date (consulté le 13 juillet 2014)

Journal Officiel de la République Démocratique du Congo, « Loi n° 14/022 du 07 juillet 2014 fixant le régime des Zones Economiques Spéciales en République Démocratique du Congo », 25 juillet 2014

Journal Officiel de la République Démocratique du Congo, « Loi n° 11/022 du 24 décembre 2011 portant principes fondamentaux relatifs à l'agriculture », 27 décembre 2011

Konstantinos J. HAZAKIS, « Key Conditions for the Effectiveness of Special Economic Zones in Regional Development: Opportunities and Challenges for the Thrace Region », sous la direction de Pantelis SKLIAS et Nikolaos TZIFAKIS dans « Greece's Horizons: Reflecting on the Country's Assets and Capabilities », The Konstantinos Karamanlis Institute for Democracy Series on European and International Affairs, Centre for European Studies Publications, pp. 235-247, 2013

Leonard K. CHENG, Yum K. KWAN, « What are the determinants of the location of foreign direct investment? The Chinese experience », Journal of International Economics 51, pp. 379-400, 2000

Léopold NSEKE, « Les zones économiques spéciales : Qui s'investit ? », <http://www.afriqueexpansion.com/les-zones-economiques-speciales-/5257-les-zones-economiques-speciales--qui-sinvestit-.html>, 28 septembre 2012 (consulté le 05 juillet 2014)

Malini L. TANTRI, « Trajectories of China's Integration with the World Economy through SEZs: A Study of Shenzhen SEZ », China Report 49, pp. 227-250, 2013

Maria Peregrina MAKABENTA, « FDI location and Special Economic Zones in the Philippines », Review of Urban & Regional Development Studies Vol. 14, No. 1, pp. 59-77, mars 2002

Michael LEVIEN, « Regimes of Dispossession: From Steel Towns to Special Economic Zones », Development and Change 44, pp. 381-407, 2013

Ministère de la Modernisation des Secteurs Publics du Maroc, Centre Africain de Formation et de Recherche Administratives pour le Développement, Fondation Hanns Seidel, Conférence panafricaine des Ministres, Rabat, 12-14 décembre 2011, Firmin KINZOUNZA, « Les chainons manquants de l'émergence économique en Afrique : le benchmarking des pays émergents d'Asie »

MOODY'S, « Rating Action: Moody's assigns B3 ratings to the Democratic Republic of the Congo, stable outlook », <https://www.moodys.com/research/Moodys-assigns-B3-ratings-to-the-Democratic-Republic-of-the--PR_281558>, 6 septembre 2013 (consulté le 25 mai 2015)

N. VISWANADHAM, « Design of Special Economic Zones as Economic Engines of Growth », Thought Leadership White Papers, pp. 93-115, décembre 2006

Omer MBADI, « S&P maintient la note du Cameroun à B et attribue la note B- à la RD Congo », <http://economie.jeuneafrique.com/regions/afrique-subsaharienne/20966-sap-maintien-la-note-du-cameroun-a-b-et-attribue-b-a-la-rd-congo.html>, 16 décembre 2013 (consulté le 13 juillet 2014) CHERCHER MOODYS ET STANDARD AND POORS

Pathou Kinzala NKUKA, « Le site de Maluku choisi pour être une zone économique pilote en RDC », <http://www.digitalcongo.net/article/89605>, 06 février 2013 (consulté le 05 juillet 2014)

Radio Okapi, « Le Sénat de la RDC a voté la création de zones économiques spéciales à travers le pays », <http://radiookapi.net/actualite/2013/05/14/le-senat-de-la-rdc-vote-la-creation-de-zones-economiques-speciales-travers-le-pays/>, 14 mai 2013 (consulté le13 juillet 2014)

Ramachandra BHATTA, « Tradeoffs between Land Rights and Economic Growth: A Case Study of Coastal Karnataka », Journal of Land and Rural Studies 1, pp. 229-243, 2013

Renaud TOWE, « La zaïrianisation de Mobutu, de l'homme au demi-dieu » <http://www.afrik.com/article26594.html>, 19 août 2012 (consulté le 13 mars 2015)

Sarbajit CHAUDHURI, Shigemi YABUUCHI, « Formation of special economic zone, liberalized FDI policy and agricultural productivity », International Review of Economics and Finance 19, pp. 779-788, 2010

Scott R. SANDERS, David L. BROWN, « The Migratory Response of Labor to Special Economic, Zones in the Philippines, 1995-2005 », Population Research **and** Policy Review 31, pp. 141-164, novembre 2011

Shankar GOPALAKRISHNAN, « Negative Aspects of Special Economic Zones in China », Economic and Political Weekly Vol. 42, No. 17, pp. 1492-1494, 2007

Thomas FAROLE, « Special Economic Zones in Africa : Comparing Performance and Learning from Global Experience », Directions in Development Trade, Banque mondiale, 2011

Thomas FAROLE, Gokhan AKINCI, « Special Economic Zones : Progress, Emerging Challenges, and Future

Directions », Directions in Development Trade, Banque mondiale, 2011

Triyakshana SESHADRI, « An Analysis of the Feasibility of Private Land Assembly for Special Economic Zones in India », Urban Studies 49, pp. 2285-2300, août 2012

Tshingi KUENO NDOMBASI, « A la croisée des chemins ou le nouveau défi africain du 21ème siècle », <http://www.congovision.com/images2/A_la_croisee_des_chemins_tshingi.pdf>, sans date (consulté le 14 janvier 2015)

Vadim ARKIN, Alexander SLASTNIKOV, Svetlana ARKINA, « Investment Timing Problem Under Tax Allowances: The Case of Special Economic Zones », sous la direction de Jörg KALCSICS et Stefan NICKEL dans « Operations Research Proceedings Volume 2007, 2008 », The Annual International Conference of the German Operations Research Society, pp. 173-178, 2007

Vitraulle MBOUNGOU, « Les zones économiques spéciales : le success story chinois », <http://www.afriqueexpansion.com/les-zones-economiques-speciales-/5229-les-zones-economiques-speciales--le-success-story-chinois.html>, 25 septembre 2012 (consulté le 05 juillet 2014)

Vitraulle MBOUNGOU, « Les zones économiques spéciales : un modèle de réussite ? », <http://www.afriqueexpansion.com/les-zones-economiques-speciales-/5215-les-zones-economiques-speciales-un-modele-de-reussite.html>, 24 septembre 2012 (consulté le 05 juillet 2014)

Xiaozi LIU, Gerhard K. HEILIG, Junmiao CHEN, Mikko HEINO, « Interactions between economic growth and environmental quality in Shenzhen, China's first special economic zone », Ecological Economics 6, pp. 559-570, 2007

Young NAMKOONG, « North Korea's Policy of Sinuiju Special Economic Zone: Implications and Prospects », Asian Survey Vol. 32, No. 11, pp. 1026-1045, 1992

Le rôle stratégique du secteur énergétique dans la transformation économique de la RDC

Jean-Marc Kilolo Malambwe*

Introduction

La République démocratique du Congo (RDC) a un potentiel énergétique énorme : elle peut alimenter en électricité les trois quarts du continent africain (Esseqqat, 2011). Pourtant, à peine 15 % de la population congolaise estimée à 64 millions de personnes a accès à l'électricité.[1] Selon un document du European Union Energy Initiative (EUEI, 2011), l'absence de politique énergétique et l'obsolescence du système d'alimentation électrique occasionnent de graves problèmes d'approvisionnement en électricité dont pâtissent les consommateurs ; tant les ménages que les entreprises sont désormais accoutumés au phénomène du « délestage ».

Cette situation qui perdure depuis des lustres constitue une hypothèque sur la transformation économique de la RDC. En effet, cela nuit non seulement à la fourniture des services publics les plus élémentaires, tels que la santé et l'éducation, mais cela paralyse aussi l'activité économique dans son ensemble.

À ce propos, plusieurs études empiriques montrent que la consommation d'électricité stimule le développement économique, et inversement (Ferguson, Wilkinson et Hill, 2000; Huang, 1990; Morimoto et Hope, 2001; Yang, 2000). Selon d'autres recherches, la disponibilité des ressources énergétiques d'un pays attire les investissements directs étran-

*. L'auteur tient à remercier M. André Nyembwe pour ses précieux commentaires sur la version antérieure de cet article.

1. Ces chiffres sont tirés du World Development Indicators, accessible en ligne. Le pourcentage relatif à l'accès à l'électricité se rapporte à l'année 2010, tandis que l'estimation de la population est faite pour 2011.

gers (IDEs) et ce faisant, supporte le processus d'industrialisation et le transfert de technologie (Tang, 2009).

Dans cet article, nous examinons ces hypothèses dans le cas du Congo. En un premier temps, nous intéressons au lien entre la consommation d'électricité – qui, du reste, est la principale source d'énergie – et la croissance économique. Cette investigation empirique repose à la fois sur une analyse graphique et un modèle de régression. En un deuxième temps, nous faisons la même analyse pour ce qui est du lien entre la consommation d'électricité et l'IDE.

Dans les deux cas, une comparaison est faite entre la RDC, d'une part, et la Chine et l'Inde, d'autre part, en vue de dégager des leçons de l'expérience internationale. Il ressort de l'analyse que la consommation d'électricité par habitant est un déterminant important tant de la croissance économique que de l'IDE. Ces résultats poussent à croire que le succès des politiques industrielles du gouvernement est en partie tributaire de la fourniture énergétique aux entreprises et aux ménages.

L'évolution du secteur énergétique et du PIB depuis 1971

En observant l'évolution de la consommation énergétique en République Démocratique du Congo depuis 1971, on s'aperçoit qu'en moyenne les Congolais consomment moins d'électricité en 2011 qu'il y a 40 ans. Par ailleurs, malgré un revirement de tendance amorcée au début des années 2000, Le PIB per capita affiche une tendance baissière (voir figure 1. A).

La situation décrite ci-dessus est atypique, puisqu'à l'échelle mondiale, tant la consommation mondiale d'électricité par tête que le PIB per capita tendent à augmenter à travers le temps (voir figure 1. B). Cette dernière observation conforte les théories économiques selon lesquelles la consommation d'énergie soutient la croissance économique. Ce qui suggère donc que l'existence d'infrastructures électriques, mais surtout leur consommation dans l'économie domestique, est un facteur de développement économique.[1]

Ce lien est d'ailleurs très intuitif : les industries ont besoin d'énergie pour fonctionner. En outre, la performance d'un travailleur dépend de sa force de travail, mais aussi et surtout de son capital humain et de sa santé. Or, ces deux facteurs qui sont déterminants pour la croissance économique d'un pays sont également énergivores. Pensons un peu au système éducatif et à celui de la santé : les centres hospitaliers autant que les institutions d'enseignement ont besoin d'énergie pour opérer différents équipements.

Une comparaison entre la RDC et certains pays du BICS[2]est très éloquente : on constate à partir du tableau 1 qu'en 1971, le PIB per capita du Congo-Kinshasa (799,6 $) était largement plus élevé que celui de la Chine (150,5 $) ou celui de l'Inde (271,6 $).[3] Ainsi, le niveau de vie du Congolais moyen d'il y a 40 ans était au moins 5 fois supérieur à celui de son homologue chinois et trois plus important que celui de l'indien moyen. Au cours de la même année, le Congo-

1. Il semble plus juste de s'intéresser à la consommation plutôt qu'à la production, puisque cette dernière peut être exportée.

2. BICS : Brésil, Inde, Chine et Afrique du Sud. La Russie n'est pas incluse, compte tenu du manque de données

3. Ces chiffres sont exprimés en dollars constants de 2005, ce qui permet d'éliminer l'effet de l'inflation.

FIGURE 1

Évolution de la consommation d'électricité et du PIB en RDC et dans le monde

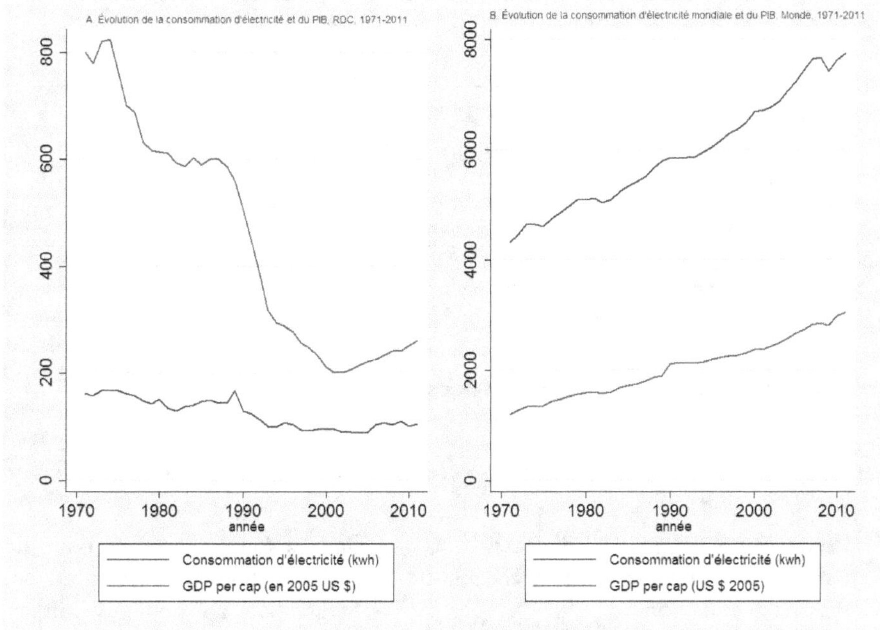

Source: World Development Indicators, en ligne

lais avait un meilleur accès à l'électricité que ses pairs chinois et indiens. En effet, les consommations par tête étaient respectivement de 162,3 kWh, 151,2 kWh et 97,8 kWh.

Que s'est-il passé en l'espace de deux générations ? On note d'une part, un recul du niveau de vie des Congolais d'environ 67 %, lequel contraste avec le gain réalisé par les Chinois (+ 1974 %) et les Indiens (300 %). Par conséquent, le PIB per capita congolais représente moins de 10 % de celui du chinois et à peine le quart de son homologue indien. D'autre part, la consommation moyenne d'électricité par habitant au Congo est passée de 162,3 kWh à 105,3 kWh; ce recul est probablement la conséquence de la vétusté des équipements, mais aussi du manque d'investissements dans la capacité de production pour satisfaire une population plus nombreuse et une économie plus complexe dont les besoins en énergie sont plus importants qu'il y a 40 ans. Autrement dit, ce recul reflète non seulement une demande industrielle accrue, mais aussi et surtout, une demande de consommation des ménages plus élevée.[1]Revenant à la Chine et à

1. En 1971, la population rd-congolaise est estimée à environ 20 millions habitants; 40 ans plus tard, elle s'élève à

TABLEAU 1

Évolution de la consommation électrique par tête et du PIB, RDC et pays du BRICS, 1971 et 2011

	PIB per capita (constant 2005 US$)			Consommation d'électricité par habitant (kWh per capita)	
	1971	2011		1971	2011
RDC	799,6	261,9		162,3	105,3
Brésil	2577,3	5721,3		455,5	2438,0
India	271,6	1086,0		97,8	684,1
Chine	150,5	3122,0		151,2	3298,0
Afrique du Sud	4872,8	5821,0		2246,1	4603,9

Source: World Bank Indicators, en ligne

l'Inde, la consommation d'électricité a, au contraire, augmenté respectivement de 2081 % et de 600 %.

De ce qui précède, on peut penser que l'amélioration de l'approvisionnement en électricité en Chine et en Inde, qui sont des modèles de croissance pour les pays pauvres, a joué un rôle majeur dans leur développement économique. On utilise souvent l'expression « usine du monde » pour parler de la Chine; or une usine ne peut fonctionner sans électricité. Comme nous le verrons ci-dessous, la politique énergétique à elle seule ne suffit pas; il faut l'accompagner d'une politique de main-d'œuvre ainsi que d'autres mesures accommodantes pour aboutir à une croissance économique soutenue et à une véritable transformation économique telle que l'ont connue ces deux pays.

près de 64 millions d'âmes. Ainsi, en deux générations, la population a crû de 211 %.

Dans la section suivante, nous présentons une analyse graphique et un modèle de régression ad hoc qui confirment l'effet positif de la consommation énergétique sur la croissance économique en RDC.

Lien entre consommation d'énergie et croissance économique

Les études recensées établissent un lien positif entre la consommation d'énergie et la croissance économique pour un ensemble de pays ou pour un pays donné. L'objectif de cette section est de montrer que cette relation est aussi vraie pour l'économie congolaise. À l'aide de la figure 1 A., on a pu se rendre compte que le PIB per capita a suivi la même évolution que celle de la consommation d'électricité. La figure 2 ci-dessus suggère de manière plus explicite le lien positif entre le PIB per capita et

FIGURE 2

Lien entre PIB per capita et la consommation d'électricité, RDC, 1971-2011

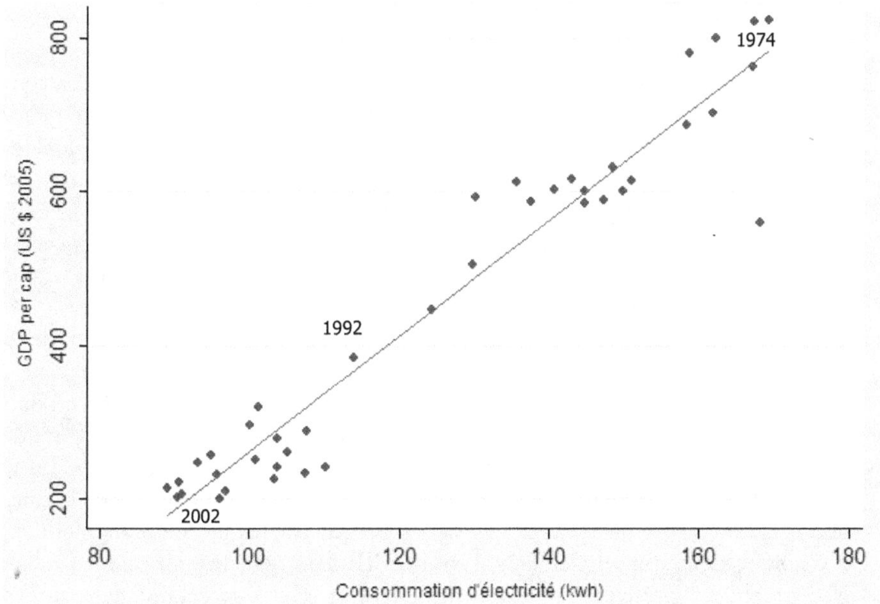

Source : World Development Indicators, en ligne.

la consommation d'électricité en RDC durant la période 1971-2011.

Chaque point sur la figure 2 correspond à une année donnée. On y voit que les années durant lesquelles la consommation d'électricité par habitant a été la plus forte correspondent au moment où le pays a eu le PIB par tête le plus élevé et inversement. Sur cette figure, trois années méritent une attention particulière. La première, c'est 1974, année au cours de laquelle l'on observe le niveau de consommation d'électricité le plus élevé de la période et concomitamment, le record du PIB par tête. À partir de cette année, on observe une chute quasicontinue de ces deux indicateurs. Il faut noter que 1974 correspond aussi au moment de la zaïrianisation, mais aussi à l'effondrement des prix des matières premières exportées par le Congo. Cette mauvaise conjoncture n'est pas sans conséquence sur l'évolution de ces indicateurs. Malgré la tendance baissière notée au cours de la période, deux évènements politiques vont accentuer la chute de la consommation d'électricité ainsi que celle du PIB par tête. Il s'agit des pillages de 1992 et de la guerre de l'est de la RDC en 2002. Sur la figure 2, l'année 1992 apparaît comme un point isolé des autres, ce qui indique une rupture avant et après cette année. Enfin, on note que la première moitié des années 2000 marquée par la guerre à l'est du pays correspond à la période où la RDC enregistre à la fois la consommation électrique la plus faible et un niveau plancher du PIB par tête.

Ces observations indiquent que la baisse d'activité économique implique une faible demande d'électricité et donc une consommation moins importante. On observe aussi un recul de la production d'électricité par tête entre 1971 et 2011. Cette dernière passe de 172,4 kwh à 123,3 kwh. Ceci suggère bien la double causalité entre l'activité économique et la consommation d'électricité; plusieurs travaux empiriques sur le sujet vont dans ce sens (voir notamment Omri et Kahouli, 2014).

Quoique riche d'enseignements, l'analyse graphique présentée ci-dessus ne permet pas de quantifier l'impact de la consommation d'énergie sur la croissance économique. Dans ce qui suit, nous développons un simple modèle d'analyse multivariée qui permet de capturer l'effet marginal de différentes variables explicatives. Le modèle de base (modèle 1 dans le tableau 2 ci-dessous) est semblable à celui de Yang (2000), dans laquelle nous tentons d'expliquer le taux de croissance du PIB per capita à l'année *t* par sa valeur au cours de l'année précédente ainsi que par le taux de croissance de la consommation d'énergie électrique par tête $\Delta\%ELECT_{t-1}$. Mathématiquement, cela s'écrit comme suit :

$$\Delta\%PIB\ cap_t = a + b\ \Delta\%PIB\ cap(t-1) + c\ \Delta\%ELECT_{t-1} + u_t \quad (1)$$

Dans cette équation (1), u_t, représente le terme d'erreur qui tient compte de l'omission d'autres facteurs explicatifs de la croissance du PIB et des erreurs de mesure des variables incluses dans le modèle.

L'inclusion de la variable retardée dans l'équation 1 permet de tenir compte des conditions initiales; cette pratique est très courante dans les modèles empiriques de croissance. En outre, toutes les variables sont exprimées en taux de croissance plutôt qu'en niveau; cette procédure permet de rendre ces variables stationnaires.[1]

Avant d'estimer le modèle de base décrit ci-dessus, nous faisons une estimation du modèle bivarié correspondant à la figure 2 que nous appelons modèle 1 dans le tableau 2 (colonne 1). L'estimation indique qu'une hausse de la consommation électrique de 1 % augmenterait le PIB d'un tiers de pour cent.

Cet effet est certainement surévalué puisque la croissance du PIB dépend de plusieurs autres facteurs; on s'aperçoit en effet que la prise en compte des conditions initiales réduit sensiblement l'impact de la consommation électrique. En effet, le modèle 2 indique que la croissance enregistrée au cours de la période précédente a un effet environ trois et demi supérieur à celui de la consommation d'électricité (colonne 2 du tableau 2). Par ailleurs, l'ajout de cette variable améliore le pouvoir explicatif du modèle : le coefficient de détermination ajusté (R^2) passe de 0,170 à 0,531.

1. L'analyse des séries chronologies montre que ces dernières affichent souvent une tendance (à la hausse ou à la baisse), laquelle peut biaiser les résultats. Pour éliminer la tendance, les économètres transforment généralement les séries en différences premières après les avoir mises sous forme logarithmique. Omri et Kahouli(2014) montrent qu'exprimer les variables sous forme de taux croissance permet aussi de les rendre stationnaire.

TABLEAU 2

Effets de la consommation d'électricité sur la croissance économique, 1971-2011*

	RDC								Chine et Inde	
Variables indépendantes	**Modèle 1**		**Modèle 2 (de base)**		**Modèle 3**		**Modèle 4**		**Modèle 5**	
PIB per capita			0,649	***	0,537	***	0,633	***	0,175	*
			(0,119)		(0,119)		(0,123)		(0,102)	
Électricité	0,337	***	0,184	**	0,220	**	0,162	*	0,432	***
	(0,112)		(0,090)		(0,085)		(0,096)		(0,047)	
IDE					0.490	**	0.0001		0.689	***
					(0.190)		(0,0005)		(0.237)	
FBCF							0,001			
							(0,001)			
Population							0,015			
							(0,019)			
Constant	-0,232	***	-0,007		-0,017	**	-0,271		0.011	
	(0,08)		(0,007)		(0,007)		(0,335)		(0.007)	
R2	0,191		0,556		0,627		0,579		0,522	
R2 ajusté	0,170		0,531		0,595		0,515		0.502	
Nombre d'observations	40		39		39		39		78	

Notes: Les erreurs standards sont indiquées entre parenthèses

* Coefficient significatif au seuil de 1%

** Coefficient significatif au seuil de 5%.

*** Coefficient significatif au seuil de 10%.

* Pour certaines années, les observations sur l'IDE et la consommation électrique sont manquantes pour l'Inde et la Chine. Nous avons imputé une valeur très proche de zéro (0.001), conserver la taille de l'échantillon sans influencer les résultats du modèle.

Pour tester la stabilité des effets estimés et leur robustesse, on introduit successivement une variable dans les estimations présentées dans les colonnes précédentes. Dans le modèle 3, on a introduit la variable IDE, qui est le ratio de l'investissement direct étranger sur le PIB. Le coefficient de cette variable vient au second rang, après celui de Δ%PIB cap_{t-1}. Cette dernière variable voit son coefficient diminuer au profit de la consommation d'électricité. On s'aperçoit en outre que ce modèle est plus performant, le R^2 s'élevant 0,595.

Pour mesurer la robustesse de nos résultats, nous ajoutons deux variables qui mesurent les déterminants traditionnels de la croissance, à savoir le facteur travail (faute de donnée appropriée, nous employons le logarithme naturel de la population comme proxy) ainsi que le facteur capital (mesuré ici par la variation du ratio de la formation brute du capital fixe sur le PIB; nous la dénommons FBCF). Ces deux facteurs ont un effet positif, mais non significatif sur la croissance dans le modèle 4. Ce résultat est probablement le reflet de l'étroitesse du marché du travail au Congo, d'une part, et de la faiblesse du ratio du capital sur le PIB, d'autre part. Concernant ce dernier, il se situe en moyenne à 11 % entre 1971 et 2009. Depuis 2010, il est supérieur à 20 % en raison de l'afflux des capitaux étrangers (IDE), en particulier dans le secteur niveau. En Inde et en Chine, ce ratio s'élève respectivement à 46 % et 32 % en 2011. En intégrant la FBCF, la variable IDE devient non significative, ce qui témoigne probablement du fait que l'IDE est une composante essentielle de la FBCF.

Toutefois, tant l'effet de la consommation d'électricité que celui de la croissance en période t-1 demeurent robustes à l'inclusion de ces variables. Ainsi, ce qui ressort fortement dans notre exercice analytique, c'est que la consommation d'électricité est un facteur déterminant de la croissance économique.

En appliquant le modèle 3 à la Chine et l'Inde (colonne 5)[1], on s'aperçoit que l'IDE et la consommation d'énergie électrique stimulent la croissance plus que le PIB per capita. L'IDE s'avère le déterminant le plus important de la croissance économique. Son coefficient est plus d'une fois et demie plus élevé que celui de la variable mesurant la consommation électricité. Ce modèle, assez simple, décrit une réalité majeure du développement économique des deux plus grandes économies émergentes : la transformation économique de la Chine et de l'Inde s'explique largement par l'IDE, et non par le dynamisme des entreprises locales.

La question qu'il faut dès lors se poser est celle de savoir ce qui attire les entreprises multinationales (EMN) en Chine et en Inde. Selon la théorie économique, une EMN peut desservir un marché étranger de deux façons : soit en y exportant ses produits, soit en y établissant une filiale (IDE). Bien évidemment, le choix entre ces deux options repose essentiellement sur la rentabilité. En particulier, la décision d'investir en établissant une filiale dépend des coûts de production, de la taille de la demande et du potentiel du marché étranger.

Même si à la fin des années 1970,ces deux pays ne représentaient pas des marchés importants, des EMN ont fait le choix de s'y établir en raison du coût de main-d'œuvre et des politiques industrielles attrayantes, notamment en mettant sur pieds des zones économiques spéciales (ZES).[2,3] À travers une politique de main-d'œuvre, la Chine a su lever une armée de travailleurs qualifiés prêts à répondre à la demande de ces EMN.[4]

Concernant son secteur énergétique, la Commission internationale des grands barrages recense 23 842 grands barrages en Chine, ce qui représente environ 40 % des barrages de la planète; ainsi, avec une production de 721 térawatts heure (TWh) en 2010,la Chine est le premier producteur mondial d'énergie hydroélectrique.

1. Nous avons préféré le modèle 3 aux autres parce que c'est celui qui présente le R^2le plus élevé et donc, le meilleur ajustement linéaire selon ce critère.

2. Le lecteur intéressé par l'impartition des activités économiques peut consulter l'article de Helpman, Melitz et Rubinstein (2004) paru dans l'*American Economic Review*.

3. Voir l'article sur les zones économiques spéciales en RDC dans ce le présent volume pour plus d'informations.

4. Pour plus détails, voir l'article sur les « Défis de la transformation économique de la RDC ». Dans ce même volume.

Ce qui démontre bien la capacité énergétique de ce pays et son rôle dans le développement de l'attraction des IDEs. Pour devenir l'usine du monde, la Chine s'est dotée d'une grande capacité énergétique qui permet justement à l'usine de fonctionner à plein régime.

L'analyse multivariée présentée ci-dessus corrobore l'idée selon laquelle le secteur de l'énergie est un facteur important pour la croissance. Dans la section suivante, nous étudions son rôle pour attirer les IDEs.

Le secteur de l'énergie, un stimulus pour l'IDE

L'attraction des IDEs a joué un rôle important dans la croissance des pays asiatiques, particulièrement en Chine. On note d'ailleurs que dans les 1990, la Chine recevait à elle seule près de la moitié des IDEs des pays en développement; qui plus est, elle était la 2e destination mondiale des IDEs, après les États-Unis (Huang, 2001 ; OCDE, 2000).

La capacité énergétique du pays a certainement joué un rôle clé dans l'attraction des IDEs, tel que le suggère la figure 3. En effet, tant pour la Chine que pour l'Inde, on observe une relation positive entre d'une part, l'IDE (mesurée en terme de part du PIB courant), et d'autre part, la consommation électrique par tête.

Par contre, dans le cas du Congo, on n'observe aucune relation. À la différence des deux pays mentionnés ci-haut, la figure 3 indique que le ratio IDE/PIB gravite autour de zéro en RDC. On constate aussi que, avant 1998, le ratio IDE/PIB est systématiquement inférieur à 1 %; certaines années, il est même négatif. Depuis 2001, ce ratio est toujours supérieur à 1 % et atteint même 12,7 % en 2010, un record historique. L'année 2009, marquée par la récession, fait exception : en effet, l'IDE est négatif (– 1,5 %).

Le revirement de situation observé au début des années 2000 est probablement le reflet de la demande mondiale pour les matières premières; en effet, l'essentiel de l'IDE au Congo profite au secteur primaire, qui est traditionnellement très volatile. Il faut noter que ce revirement des IDEs coïncide aussi avec la remontée de la croissance.

Les estimations présentées dans le tableau 3 appuient les conclusions tirées de la figure 3. En effet, contre toute attente, le modèle 1 montre que la consommation d'électricité en RDC a un effet négatif (et non significatif) sur l'IDE. En rajoutant d'autres variables (modèle 2), on s'aperçoit que l'effet est toujours négatif. Ce résultat est plutôt surprenant, puisqu'on s'attendait à un effet positif, comme c'est généralement le cas pour d'autres pays ou des panels (données sur différents pays couvrant plusieurs années).Afin d'évaluer la robustesse de ce résultat, nous procédons à un test de causalité de Granger; ce dernier indique bien que la consommation d'électricité est un facteur causal de l'IDE en RDC.

Lorsqu'on fait ces mêmes régressions avec les données de la Chine et de l'Inde, on s'aperçoit que la consommation d'électricité a un effet positif et très significatif sur l'IDE (voir tableau 3).[1]

1. Le test de Granger indique un lien de causalité uniquement dans le cas de l'Inde.

FIGURE 2

Lien entre IDE et consommation d'électricité, Chine, Inde et RDC

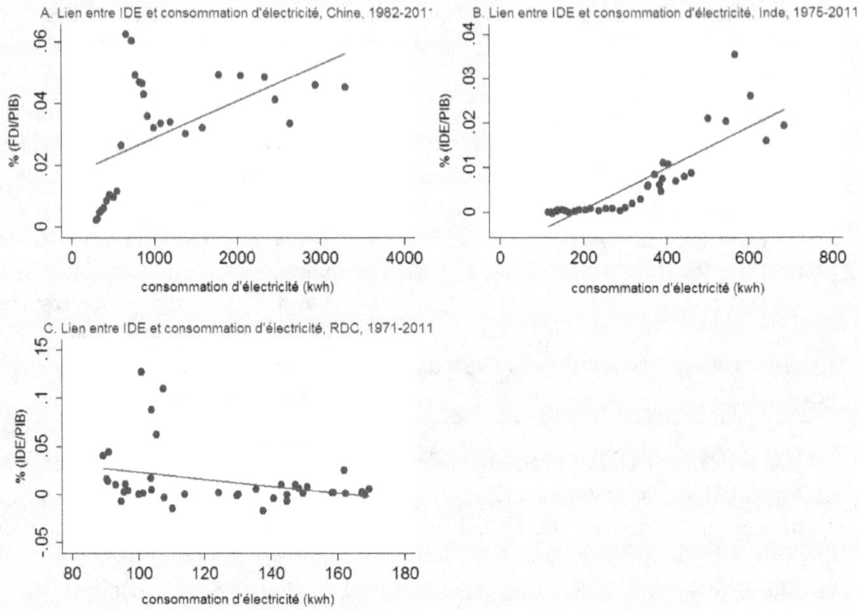

Source : World Development Indicators, en ligne.

Ces résultats ont des fortes implications en termes de politique économique : en raison de sa faible capacité énergétique, la RDC n'a pas su attirer suffisamment d'entreprises multinationales (EMN) sur son territoire pour y établir des industries créatrices d'emplois contrairement à la Chine et à l'Inde.

La nouvelle politique industrielle du gouvernement qui consiste à créer des parcs industriels, notamment les parcs agroindustriels, devrait être accompagnée d'une politique énergétique visant à garantir aux investisseurs étrangers et nationaux une bonne fourniture en électricité. Ce qui permettrait de réaliser leurs opérations.

La mise en valeur du potentiel hydroélectrique de la RDC pourrait répondre à cette préoccupation. Selon une note de la Banque Mondiale (2014), le potentiel hydroélectrique de la RDC est évalué à 100 GW, le troisième plus grand au monde derrière la Chine et la Russie. Selon un rapport de l'UNEP sur le Congo (2013), ce pays pourrait alimenter toute l'Afrique subsaharienne en électricité.

Pour valoriser ce potentiel, le gouvernent entend construire un autre barrage sur le site d'Inga (Inga 3).

TABLEAU 3

Effets de la consommation d'électricité sur l'IDE, 1971-2011*

	RDC				Chine et Inde			
Variables indépendantes	**Modèle 1**		**Modèle 2**		**Modèle 1**		**Modèle 2**	
PIB per capita			5,39e109	***			-1,52e10-10	
			(1,83e109)				(04,28e10-10)	
Électricité	-4,68e10-8		-2,69e109	**	6,64e10-11	***	8,69e10-10	*
	(2,36e10-8)		(1,35e109)		(-1,66e10-10)		(4,69e10-10)	
IDE (t-1)			0,292	*			1,181	***
			(0,156)				(0.031)	
Constant	2,36e10-8	**	2,99e10-8		-1,66e10-10		-4,24e10-9	
	(9,79e107)		(1,08e10-8)		(1,24e10-10)		(2,88e10-9)	
R2	0,0028		0,319		0,171		0,960	
R2 ajusté	-0,0234		0,262		0,161		0,958	
Nombre d'observations	40		40		80		80	

Notes : Les erreurs standards sont indiquées entre parenthèses

* Coefficient significatif au seuil de 1%

** Coefficient significatif au seuil de 5%.

*** Coefficient significatif au seuil de 10%.

* Pour certaines années, les observations sur l'IDE et la consommation électrique sont manquantes pour l'Inde et la Chine. Nous avons imputé une valeur très proche de zéro (0.001), conserver la taille de l'échantillon sans influencer les résultats du modèle.

Doté d'une capacité de 40 GW, le site hydroélectrique du Grand Inga sera le plus grand du monde et probablement la source d'énergie la moins chère du continent africain. Son coût de production serait d'environ 0,03 dollar/kWh.

Le défi pour réaliser ce projet, c'est sa viabilité économique. Si l'engagement de l'Afrique du Sud d'acheter plus de la moitié de l'électricité produite par le barrage résout ce problème, il n'en demeure pas moins qu'il faut mettre l'énergie produite au service de l'économie nationale qui, jusqu'ici, ne bénéficie que de 2 % de l'immense potentiel hydroélectrique du pays.[1]

Comme nous l'avons montré, le développement économique passe par l'accès à l'énergie pour les consommateurs (ménages, entreprises et administrations publiques). Le piège à éviter, c'est de renforcer la position d'état-rentier qui vend ses matières premières et son énergie au profit du reste du monde, mais au

1. Voir « Inga 3 au service de l'Afrique : défis et perspectives », présentation à la 2ème édition de la Conférence minière de la RDC à Goma par le Ministre des Ressources Hydrauliques et Électricité en mars 2014.

détriment du développement local. La perspective du gouvernement devrait être de créer, à l'aide d'une politique énergétique, un environnement propice aux investissements étrangers. Ces derniers sont le moyen par excellence pour un transfert de technologie, tel que l'ont connu la Chine et l'Inde qui ont remonté la chaîne de valeur, en diversifiant l'activité économique et en conquérant des domaines de haut savoir.

Conclusion

Dans cet article, nous avons tenté de montrer l'importance du secteur énergétique pour la croissance économique et l'attraction des investissements directs étrangers (IDE). Recourant à l'analyse graphique et multivariée, nous avons montré que la consommation d'électricité est un déterminant majeur de la croissance économique. Ce résultat empirique a été prouvé dans le cas du Congo, mais aussi pour la Chine et l'Inde.

En plus de l'énergie, l'analyse multivariée met en évidence l'importance de l'IDE dans la croissance économique observée tant en RDC, d'une part, qu'en Chine et en Inde sur la période 1971-2011.

Alors que le secteur énergétique a favorisé l'investissement direct étranger en Chine et en Inde, il semble jouer un rôle plutôt modeste en RDC. En fait, l'analyse économétrique présentée dans cet article montre que la consommation énergétique n'a pas contribué à attirer l'IDE. Il y a lieu de croire que la faible capacité énergétique du pays n'encourage pas les firmes multinationales à s'y établir.

Ainsi, la mise sur pied d'une politique énergétique contribuerait à créer des conditions favorables pour attirer les investisseurs étrangers, comme la Chine a su la faire. La construction du complexe du Grand Inga, qui sera fort probablement le site hydroélectrique le plus grand du monde,serait une action dans la bonne direction. Toutefois, le préalable est de dédier une bonne partie de cette énergie à l'alimentation de futures industries locales, quoique la viabilité économique de cet immense projet de génie dicte une exportation vers d'autres pays africains. Le risque, c'est évidemment le maintien d'un système d'état rentier, fournisseur de matières premières et d'énergie au reste du monde.

À l'heure actuelle où l'Union Européenne, la Chine et l'Inde déploient une diplomatie des matières premières, notamment l'accès à l'énergie, il est plus que temps pour la RDC d'établir une politique énergétique qui soutienne sa transformation économique telle que prônée par les décideurs publics.

Compte tenu du manque d'infrastructures de base, en l'occurrence les routes, et de l'immensité du territoire, le coût de l'offre de l'électricité à partir des sources traditionnelles (hydroélectricité) sur toute l'étendue du pays pourrait s'avérer prohibitif. C'est pourquoi il convient d'intégrer dans la nouvelle politique énergétique du pays les énergies renouvelables comme solution de rechange pour l'électrification de l'arrière-pays.

Bibliographie

Banque Mondiale (2014), « Projet d'assistance technique au développement du projet Inga 3 basse chute et de centrales hydroélectriques de moyenne puissance», mis en ligne le 20 mars 2014, site www.worldbank.org.

EU Energy Initiative Partnership Dialogue Facility (EREI PDF, 2011), «Energy Policy Support to the Democratic Republic of the Congo», November 2011.

Ferguson, R., Wilkinson, W. et Hill, R. (2000),«Electricity use and economic development »,*Energy Policy*, 28, 923-934.

Morimoto and C. Hope (2001), « The impact of electricity supply on economic growth in Sri Lanka», The Judge Institute of Management StudiesWP 24/2001.

Esseqqat, Henri (2011), « Les Énergies Renouvelables en République Démocratique du Congo, »document du PNUE.

Grenier, Emmanuel (2014), « Chine : accélération de la construction de barrages hydroélectriques », International Commission on Large Dams, le 12 Février 2014

http://www.icold-cigb.org/share/article/354/chine-acceleration-de-la-construction-de-barrages-hydroelectriques.

Huang, Yasheng (2001), « The Role of Foreign-Invested Enterprises in the Chinese Economy: An Institutional Foundation Approach, » in *China, the United States and the Global Economy*, (Santa Monica, CA: Rand Corporation, 2001).

International Commission on Large Dams, « Number of Dams by Country Members », accès sur http://www.icold-cigb.org/GB/World_register/general_synthesis.asp?IDA=206, le 17-03-2015.

Lucas, Robert E. Jr., «Why Doesn't Capital Flow from Rich to Poor Countries? », *American Economic Review*, 80 (2).

Omria, Aniset Bassem Kahoulib (2014), « Causal relationships between energy consumption, foreign direct investment and economic growth: Fresh evidence from dynamic simultaneous-equations models», *Energy Policy*, 67, 913–922.

OCDE (2000), «Main determinants and impacts of foreign direct investment on China's economy», Directorate For Financial, Fiscal And Enterprise Affairs, Working Papers On International Investment, Number 2000/4.

Tang, C.F. (2009), «Electricity consumption, income, foreign direct investment, and population in Malaysia: new evidence from multivariate framework analysis», *Journal of Economic Studies* 36,371–382.

Yang, H-Y (2000) «A note on the causal relationship between energy and GDP in Taiwan », *Energy Economics* 22, 309-317.

Annexe

Le test de Dickey-Fuller augmenté montre que les séries suivantes sont stationnaires pour la RDC

$$x_t = \boxtimes + \boxtimes x_{t-1} + \boxtimes t + \Delta x_{t-1} + u_t$$

TABLEAU 4
Test de Dickey-Fuller augmenté

Z(t)	Test stat	1 % critical value	5% critical value	10% critical value
Électricité	-4,790	-4,260	-3,548	-3,209
IDE	-4,818	-4,260	-3,548	-3,209
Population	-6,618	-4,251	-3,544	-3,206
FBCF	-5,789	-4,260	-3,548	-3,209
Nombre d'observations	38	38	38	39

En effet, on s'aperçoit que la statistique Z(t) pour chaque variable est, en valeur absolue, supérieure à la valeur critique pour chaque seuil (1%, 5%, 10%).

Gouvernance mondiale et émergence*

Bertrand Ateba**

Les pays tiers-mondistes, en proie à une pauvreté galopante, rêvent tous d'émergence. Dans le contexte africain, nombreux sont ceux qui ont déjà arrêté l'horizon probable de la survenance de cette lueur salvatrice[1]. Entre pessimisme et espoir, les populations attendent patiemment l'amélioration de leurs conditions de vie. Dans cette quête d'un mieux vivre et d'un mieux être, l'apport des acteurs externes est abondamment sollicité, d'autant plus que la mondialisation impose de composer avec tous les autres acteurs de la société internationale. L'émergence se présente comme la valorisation de tous les atouts possibles à la disposition d'un Etat, pour atteindre des résultats économiques susceptibles de relever le niveau de vie de ses citoyens par la mise en place d'infrastructures dans divers domaines, un meilleur traitement salarial des fonctionnaires, bref, la réduction du coût assez élevé de la vie en zone urbaine comme en zone rurale.

Les Etats vivants dans une société anarchique dans laquelle règne la loi du plus fort, il est évident que cette envie d'émergence est gravement compromise s'il n'y a pas un minimum d'organisation au sein de la communauté internationale. On se rend compte aussi à l'évidence, combien gouvernance mondiale

* Cet article est la version améliorée d'une communication présentée lors du Colloque International pluridisciplinaire sur le thème : « Quelles trajectoires vers une émergence à visage humain de l'Afrique ? » organisé par l'Université Catholique Saint Jérôme de Douala au Cameroun du 08 au 10 janvier 2014.

** Sinologue. Ph.D. en Science Politique de l'Université de Pékin, chargé de Cours à La F.S.J.P. de l'Université de Douala. ateba03@gmail.com.

1. Le Cameroun par exemple a fixé son cap pour 2035.

et émergence sont intimement associées. Au sens de Pierre de Senarclens, « dans l'univers hétérogène et peu structuré de la politique internationale, le concept de gouvernance peut exprimer l'ensemble des structures institutionnelles et des pratiques contribuant au maintien d'un certain ordre »[1]. En effet, La gouvernance mondiale renvoie aux mécanismes de régulation de la société internationale, dont la vie tourne autour du diptyque paix et guerre[2]. L'absence d'une autorité supérieure aux Etats disposant du recours légitime à la force, capable de défendre la justice et le droit, d'arbitrer les conflits entre Etats et de contraindre ces derniers à respecter ses sentences judiciaires, rend difficile la pacification de cet espace commun de vie aux acteurs des relations internationales. La bonne gouvernance mondiale est pourtant un important catalyseur de l'émergence, de la stabilité et du développement économico-social des Etats tiers-mondistes. La coopération et la solidarité internationales sont d'application difficile en l'absence de mécanismes efficaces de régulation internationale. La gouvernance mondiale peut-elle être mise à contribution pour provoquer ou accélérer l'émergence de pays économiquement faibles ? Cet article constate d'une part que la gouvernance mondiale est en crise, ce qui compromet sérieusement les efforts nationaux déployés par les Etats en vue de leur émergence (1), et d'autre part en s'appuyant sur le cas de la République Populaire de Chine, que l'émergence d'un Etat peut poser des problèmes à la gouvernance mondiale, par la contestation de l'ordre établi (2).

1. Une gouvernance mondiale en crise

Oran Young affirme que les acteurs de la scène internationale agissent de manière prévisible en suivant des mécanismes de régulation formels et informels, malgré l'absence de pouvoir de coercition légitime. Il considère que les institutions, les normes et les procédures qui permettent aux gens d'exprimer leurs aspirations et de lutter pour leurs intérêts dans un contexte relativement prévisible et équitable constituent les fondements de la bonne gouvernance[3]. Pourtant, la société internationale demeure difficile à pacifier (1.1), et cela met à mal l'émergence de l'Etat qui sur le plan international, devrait reposer sur la coopération et la solidarité internationales (1.2).

1.1. La difficile pacification de la société internationale

Les premiers efforts de pacification et de mise en ordre de la société internationale datent du 17e siècle. En effet tel qu'on le constate dans les travaux des auteurs comme Hugo Grotius, Samuel Pufendorf, Jeremy Bentham, Emmanuel Kant ou l'Abbé de Saint Pierre, il se dessine dès le 17e siècle, un courant de pensée exprimant la volonté de ses auteurs de promouvoir des institutions et des normes qui obligeraient les Etats à sortir de l'état de nature. En 1939, un historien britannique faisant l'analyse de la faillite

1. Pierre de Senarclens, *La mondialisation: théories, enjeux et débats*, 2e édition, Armand Colin 2001. p. 56.

2. Voir Raymond Aron, *Paix et guerre entre les nations.* Paris Calmann-Lévy, 1962.

3. Oran Young, *International governance. Protecting the environment in a stateless society.* Ithaca, Cornell University Press. 1994. p.7.

de la Société des nations (SDN) écrivait fort à propos que « la science de la politique internationale trouve son origine dans le désir passionné de prévenir la guerre »[1]. Malheureusement, on constate l'échec des tentatives d'organisation de la société internationale, société, dans laquelle le rapport de forces est instable et fluctuant.

1.1.1. Échec des tentatives d'organisation de la société internationale

Selon James Rosenau, la société internationale comprend un niveau croissant d'institutionnalisation et d'innombrables mécanismes de régulation, tout en étant dépourvue d'instance supranationale. Il y voit un exemple typique de « gouvernance sans gouvernement », à savoir un système de gestion orienté par des valeurs et des entreprises communes[2]. Cette belle description contraste pourtant avec la réalité d'une société internationale dont la pacification connait d'énormes difficultés. La mise en place de la Société des Nations (SDN) au sortir de la première guerre mondiale en 1919, n'a pas empêché la survenance d'une deuxième en 1939. Prenant acte des erreurs et des errements de cette institution internationale, une autre fut mise en place en 1945. Si elle a pu au moins éviter une troisième guerre mondiale, elle n'a pas réussi jusqu'aujourd'hui à instaurer une paix durable entre les acteurs de la scène internationale. Malgré les progrès du droit international public depuis la fin du 19e siècle, ses dispositions et ses prescriptions motivées par des idéaux pacifiques, se sont heurtées au sempiternel problème d'absence d'une force contraignante capable de veiller efficacement à leur application. Jusqu'aujourd'hui, les rapports de pouvoir et d'hégémonie président au maintien de la paix et aux échanges économiques au sein de la société internationale.

La pacification de la société internationale est encore rendue plus difficile après la deuxième guerre mondiale et surtout au début de la grande rivalité idéologique entre les deux superpuissances. Cette période est celle au cours de laquelle les conceptions juridiques mises en place et les projets de sécurité collective sont dénoncés comme utopiques. Ils cèdent ainsi le pas à des approches théoriques inspirées de Thucydide, Carl Von Clausewitz, Thomas Hobbes, Nicholas Machiavel et de la Realpolitik allemande qui s'imposent sous la dénomination de « réalisme ». Le réalisme insiste sur la dimension essentiellement conflictuelle de la politique internationale. D'après ce courant de pensée, le principe de souveraineté étatique oblige les Etats à une politique de puissance. En l'absence d'une autorité légitime capable d'arbitrer leurs conflits d'intérêts, les Etats doivent mobiliser leurs propres ressources politiques et stratégiques pour assurer leur sécurité, pour réaliser leurs ambitions politiques et pour atteindre leurs objectifs économiques. La paix dans un tel contexte est souvent celle des puissants qui imposent leur volonté aux autres. Ce fut le cas au lendemain de la seconde guerre mondiale, avec la paix des vainqueurs. Lorsque les Etats puissants ne s'accordent plus sur leurs

1. Edward Hallett Carr, The Twenty Years' Crisis. An introduction to the study of international Relations. London. Macmillan &Co Ltd, 1962. p.8.

2. James Rosenau, "Governance, Order and Change in World Politics" in James Rosenau and E.O. Czempel, *Governance without Government: Order and Change in World Politics.* Cambridge University Press 1992. pp 3-4.

intérêts, la paix repose alors sur l'équilibre de la puissance, comme pendant la guerre froide. Les Etats étant guidés dans leurs actions par leurs seuls intérêts, la pacification de la société internationale devient problématique, du fait de la difficulté à harmoniser ou à concilier les intérêts divergents de ses membres. En outre la puissance des Etats est tellement fluctuante qu'on assiste fréquemment à la montée en puissance des uns comme au déclin des autres.

1.1.2 Une société internationale en constante mutation

La société internationale appelle constamment une reconsidération des indicateurs de la puissance des Etats. Nous sommes dans une société qui n'est pas statique. La redéfinition du système international se fait en fonction de la distribution de la puissance, c'est-à-dire la capacité des Etats à imposer leur volonté aux autres. Les éléments de puissance sont inscrits dans plusieurs registres : la cohésion nationale, l'efficacité des forces de défense, la taille de la population, la solidité d'une monnaie, la qualité des services de renseignements, les avancées technologiques, la prospérité économique, la qualité du leadership, le nationalisme etc. Tous ces atouts ont été bouleversés, à des degrés divers, par les évènements majeurs qui sont survenus dans la société internationale depuis la première guerre mondiale. De fait, la redistribution de la puissance résulte de l'impact de la guerre sur ces différents atouts. Que ce soit la première guerre mondiale, la deuxième ou la guerre froide, il y a toujours eu des changements qui affectent la sécurité internationale. Au lendemain de la première guerre mondiale, certaines grandes puissances d'avant-guerre s'effondrent : l'Empire Ottoman, l'Autriche-Hongrie, l'Empire Tsariste et l'Allemagne. Parmi les vainqueurs, le coût de la guerre diminue la puissance de certains Etats : inflation, anémie démographique, divisions politiques, destruction du potentiel industriel, etc. Ce sont les armées victorieuses qui assurent la puissance. Trois faits essentiels sont à noter dans les relations internationales :

- La puissance économique américaine se démarque ;
- La mise à l'écart de l'Allemagne du cercle des grandes puissances ;
- La redéfinition du système international demeure tributaire du jeu classique des puissances.

Pour remettre de l'ordre sur la scène internationale, le wilsonisme[1] a tenté de proposer une coopération internationale par le biais de la Société des Nations (SDN) et reposant sur les mécanismes de la sécurité collective. Ces principes ont été développés dans son programme en quatorze points, annoncé en janvier 1918. Les tentatives hégémoniques d'une puissance seraient circonscrites non plus par l'alliance de deux ou trois autres grandes puissances, mais par une

1. Néologisme forgé à partir du nom du Président des Etats Unis de 1913 à 1921 Woodrow Wilson. Il s'agit d'une conception idéaliste cherchant à établir la paix internationale par l'autodétermination des peuples et par la mise en place d'un système de sécurité collective fondé sur le droit et le dialogue entre les nations. La pensée de Woodrow Wilson en matière de relations internationales, s'inscrit dans la tradition des projets de paix de l'Abbé de Saint Pierre et d'Emmanuel Kant. Wilson ambitionnait de réconcilier morale et politique, en exportant à l'échelle mondiale le modèle de démocratie américaine. Il contribua de manière significative à la création d'une instance de coopération internationale qui devint la Société des Nations (SDN).

coalition universelle des nations qui ramènerait l'agresseur à la raison selon les principes inscrits dans la coutume et les traités internationaux. Mais face à la bonne volonté des uns et des autres pèsent le poids des intérêts nationaux, la méfiance et surtout la volonté d'imposer une paix des vainqueurs. L'arrivée au pouvoir en Europe de Mussolini puis d'Hitler et le renforcement au Japon des courants militaristes, remettent en cause l'ordre établi. L'esprit de revanche, le nationalisme et le désir d'impérialisme remettent la guerre au goût du jour.

A la défaite des forces de l'Axe vaincues par les puissances alliées, se pose à nouveau la problématique du rétablissement de la paix et de la sécurité internationales. L'Organisation des Nations Unies nait des cendres de la SDN et s'érige en outil prometteur en matière de maintien de la paix. Contrairement à la SDN, elle n'est pas liée au règlement de la paix, elle bannit tout recours à la force et même à la menace du recours à la force sauf en cas de légitime défense. Le Conseil de sécurité est doté de pouvoirs réels, notamment dans le domaine militaire et, enfin, la participation des grandes puissances est assurée grâce au droit de veto. La guerre froide est venue jeter un coup de froid à cette ambiance messianique en prenant en otage la sécurité collective enlevant à l'organisation mondiale la responsabilité principale en matière de paix et de sécurité internationales. C'était désormais aux deux blocs antagonistes d'imposer une paix par l'équilibre de la terreur. Avec l'effondrement de l'Union Soviétique et la fin de la guerre froide, on assiste à une paix hégémonique imposée par l'unilatéralisme américain. La nature des menaces à la paix et à la sécurité internationales a aussi changé. Pendant la guerre froide, les menaces étaient beaucoup plus militaires. Dans le monde post-guerre froide, les plus grandes menaces identifiées sont non-militaires. Il s'agit plus du fossé grandissant entre les riches et les pauvres, de la dégradation de l'environnement, de l'hyper-terrorisme, du sida et des trafics de tous genres.

Même s'il est vrai que les institutions internationales sont de plus en plus nombreuses et diversifiées en ce qui concerne les problèmes auxquels elles font face, il reste que celles-ci sont dominées par le rapport de force existant entre leurs membres. En attendant d'autres développements qui viendront à nouveau changer ce rapport de force, la réalité des relations internationales reste la précarité, l'imprévisibilité et l'instabilité.

1.2. La mise à mal de la coopération et de la solidarité internationales

L'émergence à laquelle aspire la plupart des pays tiers-mondistes sera difficilement réalisable sans le concours de la communauté internationale, et notamment les pays développés et les institutions financières internationales. Par la mise en œuvre de la coopération et de la solidarité internationales, des moyens financiers, des expertises de hauts niveaux en association avec les efforts individuels des Etats, raccourciraient à coup sûr les délais arrêtés pour la réalisation de l'émergence. Malheureusement, le difficile transfert de technologie et les illusions de l'aide au développement s'érigent en barrières difficilement franchissables[1].

1. Les notions de transfert de technologie et d'aide au développement dans notre analyse participent d'une solidarité agissante de la communauté internationale et

1.2.1. Un difficile transfert de technologie

Les menaces pesant sur l'évolution de la société internationale découlent de facteurs qui ne concernent pas uniquement les affaires militaires, mais qui sont inhérentes, plus fondamentalement, aux problèmes économiques, sociaux et écologiques. L'ONU a multiplié au cours des dernières décennies de grandes conférences[1], mais aucune sur la question cruciale du transfert de technologie. Les économies des pays en voie de développement sont par définition dépendantes des contraintes extérieures. Elles ont un grand besoin de capitaux étrangers pour financer leur industrialisation, leur politique publique, leur déficit commercial. Elles sont tributaires de la fluctuation des prix de leurs matières premières sur les marchés mondiaux, des transferts de technologie par le biais des entreprises multinationales ou de l'aide publique au développement. Une solution au problème du sous-développement est apparue dans le transfert international de technologie, qui combine à la fois assistance, formation, coopération, et parfois aide financière.

Le transfert de technologies représente désormais une part importante des échanges entre les pays industrialisés et les pays en voie de développement. Les formes en sont multiples, ressortissent au domaine public ou privé, et interviennent au niveau national ou international: associations coopératives de recherche et de développement entre sociétés ayant souvent un caractère transnational, relations entre centres de recherche, universités, etc., accords de coopération gouvernementale, action des différentes organisations internationales, etc. Souvent l'Etat intervient en aidant les transféreurs nationaux par l'octroi de crédits et d'assurances contre les défaillances des pays récepteurs.

Pourtant, les pays industrialisés ont du mal à opérer le transfert de technologie nécessaire à la mise en place d'une véritable politique d'industrialisation dans les pays tiers-mondistes en quête d'émergence.

Le transfert de technologies qui s'effectue sous de multiples formes, représente désormais une part importante des échanges entre les pays industrialisés et les pays en développement et de ce fait doit connaître une certaine régulation internationale, dans le respect des intérêts des parties en présence. Le lien entre capacités technologiques et développement économique et social fait du transfert une part importante de l'aide publique au développement. L'inégalité des situations et l'hétérogénéité des pays que recouvre le concept de pays en voie de développement imposent une approche diversifiée. Le nouveau contexte mondial, une économie mondiale de plus en plus interdépendante et la fin des oppositions idéologiques donnent un nouvel éclairage au rôle des organisations internationales dans la question du transfert et une intervention plus présente de celles-ci est possible et souhaitable. Seule une action concertée et multilatérale peut efficacement garan-

dont l'idéal est que les pays développés et les institutions internationales concourent à un début d'industrialisation des pays tiers-mondistes par leur mise en œuvre. Même si cela semble utopique, c'est l'idée que nous développons ici, tout en relevant les obstacles qui empêchent cette politique qui aurait pu être salutaire, de remplir la mission de sa raison d'être.

1. Sur la nutrition (Rome, 1992), sur l'environnement (Rio, 1992), sur les droits de l'homme (Vienne, 1993), sur la population et le développement (Le Caire 1994), sur le développement social (Copenhague, 1995), sur les femmes (Beijing, 1995) ou sur l'habitat (Istanbul, 1996).

tir l'utilité et le bon usage des transferts, aider à combler les retards dans le développement, contribuer à sauver les pays en faillite, et éviter le gaspillage et la dispersion des efforts. Malgré un courant de pensée hostile au transfert, perçu comme une dépendance, et au fait de copier sans autres aménagements les techniques occidentales, le transfert de technologie reste un moyen primordial d'aide aux pays en développement. Son défaut ou ses insuffisances contribuent aux retards dans le développement et à la pauvreté. Une des principales tâches des organisations internationales et la plus urgente, serait d'aboutir enfin à l'élaboration d'un code de conduite international, contenant des normes communes et des critères applicables aux transferts de technologie ainsi que des procédures de contrôle fiables, négociés dans le respect des intérêts des pays en présence.

1.2.2. Les illusions de l'aide au développement

Des mots comme « aide » et « assistance au développement » ont des connotations humanitaires et charitables. L'ensemble de l'aide au développement dans le monde est fractionné en un nombre déroutant d'activités sans lien entre elles et qui se recoupent souvent. Trois principales raisons sont à l' origine du phénomène d'aide au développement :

- La préoccupation générale du bien être des pays pauvres, par la recherche de la croissance économique et du développement ;
- La peur réciproque de l'influence internationale des Etats Unis d' Amérique et de l'Union Soviétique ;
- La politique impérialiste de l'Europe.

Selon Tibor Mende, « l'aide étrangère ressemble à un artichaut. Quand il est en fleur, il est assez plaisant par la forme et la couleur. Avec le temps il devient une plante piquante dont une petite partie seulement est mangeable. Estimé par les spécialistes, il a également ses enthousiastes. On dit même que l'un de ses composants a des effets bénéfiques contre certaines maladies. Mais pour juger de sa valeur véritable, il faut enlever une à une ses innombrables feuilles. Beaucoup doivent être jetées. D'autres contiennent la substance nutritive à laquelle il doit sa réputation. A l'intérieur, profondément, on arrive au cœur qui, convenablement préparé et assaisonné, fournit une récompense savoureuse pour celui qui fait l'effort d'enlever patiemment les feuilles plus ou moins sans valeur qui le cachaient. Pour aller au cœur de ce que l'on appelle couramment l'aide aux pays sous-développés, il est peut être préférable de s'y prendre de la même façon »[1]. L'aide étrangère au développement apparaît comme une douche écossaise, c'est-à-dire bonne et mauvaise. Bonne, parce que fournie sans contraintes, ni manipulations, et utilisée à bon escient par les récipiendaires, elle peut révéler sa vertu, à savoir un important ingrédient concourant au développement des pays pauvres. Mauvaise, parce que accompagnée de conditions et cachant des velléités impérialistes, ou mal utilisée par les pays bénéficiaires, elle perd sa raison d'être et même sa valeur.

La valeur réelle de l'aide varie selon les termes et les conditions des prêts qui la composent ; selon la proportion des

1. Tibor Mende, *De l'aide à la recolonisation*, Éditions du Seuil 1975. p. 69.

dons (c'est-à-dire non remboursables) ; selon qu'elle doit ou non être dépensée dans le pays donateur (aide liée ou non liée) sans parler des diverses restrictions et obligations politiques ou autres, non quantifiables, qui lui sont attachées. Chaque donateur applique son propre mélange de ces ingrédients. Au plus fort de la guerre froide, on pouvait déceler l'influence décisive des politiques de puissance dans le déploiement de l'aide extérieure des deux superpuissances. L'aide était accompagnée d'une influence traduisible en allégeance politique. L'idéal pour le donateur est que les dépendances économique et politique soient entremêlées car ce n'est qu'ensemble qu'elles produisent une situation complète d'Etat-client. La menace de sanctions économiques est une garantie supplémentaire de docilité politique. Aujourd'hui, l'aide fait toujours problème malgré l'évolution de la société internationale. Un effort mérite d'être fait tant du côté des donateurs que de celui des bénéficiaires. L'aide doit être exempte de conditionnalités, elle ne doit pas être liée. Dans les pays récipiendaires, elle doit effectivement servir la cause du développement, au lieu d'être utilisée pour l'achat d'armes destinées au maintien au pouvoir d'hommes dépourvus de toute légitimité. Le rêve d'émergence des pays tiers-mondistes se réalisera avec l'ajustement des pratiques liées à l'offre d'aide et à son usage vertueux dans ces pays engagés dans une course pour le mieux être et le mieux vivre de leurs populations, l'émergence visant avant tout l'être humain.

L'aide unilatérale ou multilatérale et le transfert de technologie sont difficilement détachables des considérations de Realpolitik[1] et apparaissent souvent, comme le moyen pour les pays développés d'accéder aux marchés et aux matières premières des pays qu'ils prétendent aider. Il appartient aux pays demandeurs d'aide et de transfert de technologies de comprendre que les donateurs ne peuvent que mettre ces instruments au service de leurs intérêts. Le vieil adage de relations internationales selon lequel « les Etats n'ont pas d'amis, mais des intérêts »[2], trouve tout son sens ici. Pour atteindre l'émergence, les pays tiers-mondistes devraient abandonner la politique de la main tendue, pour plutôt conquérir le transfert de technologie en misant sur l'efficience économique. La meilleure disposition à prendre dans cette optique serait alors l'investissement accru dans la recherche et le développement, gages pertinents de la croissance à long terme. Bien de pays se sont inscrits dans cette logique, et aujourd'hui, le monde entier admire leurs performances économiques[3].

Émergence et gouvernance mondiale peuvent aussi faire l'objet d'une analyse toute particulière. En effet, dans le cadre de l'émergence de la République Populaire de Chine, tout laisse croire que l'émergence de cet Etat pose un problème à la gouvernance mondiale.

1. Terme d'origine allemande qui désigne toute politique étrangère privilégiant l'analyse des rapports de forces et la protection des intérêts nationaux, sur l'éthique, la morale ou des principes idéologiques. Il s'agit pour les hommes d'Etat, de faire prévaloir le calcul et le pragmatisme sur les choix motivés par des principes, des valeurs ou des considérations religieuses.

2. Lire par exemple Raymond Aron, op. cit.

3. La République Populaire de Chine est un exemple pertinent. Elle est aujourd'hui la deuxième économie mondiale, après les Etats Unis d'Amérique, en termes de dépenses en recherche et développement.

2. Émergence contre gouvernance mondiale : l'exemple de la République populaire de Chine

Avant d'évoquer la problématique de l'émergence de la Chine (2.2), il convient d'analyser les ressorts fondamentaux de son émergence (2.1).

2.1. Les piliers de l'émergence de la Chine

La politique d'ouverture au monde extérieur et le refus du diktat occidental constituent les principaux ingrédients de l'émergence de la Chine.

2.1.1. La politique d'ouverture au monde extérieur

La Chine a plongé dans l'anarchie au moment de la rencontre avec l'Occident et la modernité. La dernière dynastie au pouvoir s'est effondrée en 1911 dans une révolution qui aurait dû donner naissance à un régime libéral, mais qui n'a débouché que sur la division, la loi des seigneurs de guerre, puis la guerre civile et l'occupation japonaise. La guerre civile qui oppose les nationalistes de Tchiang Kai Tcheck aux communistes de Mao Zedong s'achève sans vainqueur ni vaincu, le premier s'étant refugié à l'ile de Formose où il crée la République de Chine, et le second fondant la République Populaire de Chine sur la place Tiananmen à Pékin le 1er octobre 1949. Les campagnes politiques de Mao Zedong tournent au désastre. Du « grand bond en avant » ayant abouti à une famine sans précédent dans le pays, à la « grande révolution culturelle prolétarienne » qui a été son chant de cygne, en passant par « la campagne des cent fleurs » qui a vu la répression de l'intelligentsia chinoise, la Chine est à genoux dans tous les domaines au moment où décède Mao en septembre 1976.

Après une brève querelle de succession, Deng Xiaoping s'impose de manière indiscutable comme le nouveau maitre de la Chine. Il engage alors d'importantes réformes connues sous l'appellation de « politique d'ouverture au monde extérieur ». Il était question de concilier la domination du Parti communiste avec une économie mixte de plus en plus ouverte aux pratiques du capitalisme. Pour cela, la Chine avait besoin de renouer avec le monde libéral, d'accepter les investissements étrangers et de s'engager sur une voie modérée propre à assurer la stabilité. Sur le plan international, La Chine réajusta sa politique extérieure qui devint indépendante et pragmatique et non plus idéologique[1]. La normalisation avec les Etats Unis fut scellée par l'établissement formel des relations diplomatiques le 1er janvier 1979, à la suite d'un rapprochement amorcé par la visite sécrète à Pékin en 1972 de Henry Kissinger, alors Secrétaire d'Etat américain et la visite officielle du président Nixon la même année. A la suite de cette normalisation sino-américaine, c'est tout le bloc capitaliste qui emboita le pas aux Etats Unis d'Amérique, par le rétablissement ou l'établissement des relations diplomatiques avec le nouveau gouvernement de Pékin. La création de zones économiques ouvertes aux investissements étrangers, le transfert de technologie, et la formation de cadres chinois à l'étranger boostèrent l'écono-

1. Pour en savoir plus, lire Bertrand ATEBA "*The Decline of China's Communist Ideology*". Revue de Droit International, de Sciences Diplomatiques et Politiques. Volume 80, No.3 Août-Décembre 2002.

mie chinoise qui connut une croissance impressionnante qui a transformé ce géant économique que le reste du monde admire et craint. L'ouverture à l'investissement étranger permet à la Chine l'acquisition de nouvelles technologies, ainsi que d'un savoir-faire managérial qui faisait alors défaut dans le pays. Ainsi, en 1979, quatre Zones Economiques Spéciales (ZES) s'ouvrent à Shenzhen, Shantou, Zhuhai et Xiamen. Ces ZES bénéficient d'un régime juridique et fiscal particulièrement attractif pour les entreprises étrangères.

La célèbre formule de Deng Xiaoping selon laquelle « qu'importe que le chat soit blanc ou noir, pourvu qu'il attrape les souris », signalait désormais le réalisme dans les choix économiques de la République Populaire de Chine. Dans les projets ambitieux pour le décollage économique de la Chine, se trouve également « la politique des quatre modernisations » à savoir : l'agriculture, l'industrie, la science et la technologie, et la défense nationale. en 1976, à la mort de Mao, l'agriculture occupe encore 75% des actifs chinois : l'agriculture chinoise, peu modernisée, reste peu productive. La Chine de Mao, qui voulait supplanter l'URSS, connait aussi d'énormes retards en matière d'industrie sur son voisin soviétique. Sur un plan scientifique, le retard de la Chine s'explique par une imperméabilité forte au monde extérieur et notamment à l'Occident. Des universités et un équipement peu modernes ralentissent aussi le développement d'une culture scientifique et technologique chinoises. A partir de 1984, le mouvement de libéralisation s'amplifie. Le but est d'accroître la productivité, créer des emplois, améliorer le niveau de vie des habitants, moderniser l'appareil productif en ayant recours à l'importation de technologies. Pour cela, la Chine assouplie le fonctionnement de son économie, généralise le système de responsabilité des agents économiques et développe les secteurs coopératifs et privés.

2.1.2. Le refus du diktat occidental

Contrairement aux pays africains qui subissent le diktat occidental dans de nombreux aspects de leurs choix autant politiques qu'économiques, la Chine tient tête aux occidentaux poursuivant ses réformes dans la voie qu'elle-même a tracée. Les critiques du monde occidental sur l'absence de libéralisation et le non-respect des droits de l'homme, n'ébranlent pas la sérénité des dirigeants chinois. Au début des années 1990, à travers le discours de François Mitterrand à La baule et les conditionnalités imposées par les institutions financières internationales, la démocratie était présentée aux africains comme l'unique voie vers un véritable développement. Beaucoup de pays s'y sont engagés avec des fortunes diverses. La croissance économique et l'émergence de la Chine sans une application de cette démocratie occidentale jette un coup de froid à cette prescription occidentale. On se demande bien si cet enseignement est une spécificité africaine. Sinon, comment expliquer l'émergence de la Chine en dehors de toute démocratie occidentale ? Les chinois considèrent la démocratie et les droits de l'homme tels que pensés par l'Occident, comme une diversion.

Pour les chinois, les droits de l'homme sont d'abord des droits économiques et sociaux. Il s'agit de l'amélioration des conditions de vie des populations en assurant le droit à un emploi et à un logement décents, le droit à la santé, le droit à l'éducation etc. Les droits civiques et politiques sont secondaires. De ce point de vue, il n'ya pas un autre gouvernement qui œuvre à la promotion des droits de ses citoyens comme le gouvernement chinois. D'ailleurs, la légitimité du Parti Communiste Chinois est une « légitimité par les résultats économiques », ainsi que le constate un politologue américain[1]. En effet, La croissance assure la base du pacte social intérieur qui, bon an mal an, garantit la pérennité du régime.

Face aux critiques américaines sur l'absence de libéralisation et le mépris des droits de l'homme en Chine, les chinois rétorquent que « les américains croient que quand la lune est ronde pour eux, elle l'est pour tout le monde »[2]. En regardant les droits de l'homme et la démocratie en Chine à travers les lentilles occidentales, on arrive très vite à la conclusion que le gouvernement de Pékin ne promeut pas les droits de ses citoyens. Mais en considérant ce que Lee Kwang Yee, ancien Premier Ministre et bâtisseur de Singapour appelle « les valeurs asiatiques »⊠, ou alors en regardant la situation des droits humains en Chine avec les lentilles asiatiques, on comprend aussi que la Chine œuvre activement à la promotion des droits de ses citoyens. Après tout, dictature ou démocratie, la finalité de tout gouvernement est de donner à ses citoyens les meilleures conditions possibles de vie. On peut aussi observer que toute dictature n'est pas mauvaise en soi. Un Etat autoritaire qui met l'accent sur une bonne gestion des ressources financières et humaines de l'Etat, qui fait régner l'ordre et la discipline, qui applique rigoureusement les lois en vigueur, qui combat la corruption et l'enrichissement illicite, qui améliore les conditions de vie de ses populations, est préférable à ces démocraties occidentalisées d'Afrique au sein desquelles règnent tous ces maux et qui n'augurent pas aux africains des lendemains qui chantent.

Comme la Chine, l'émergence des pays africains peut tout aussi se produire en refusant le diktat de l'Occident sur leurs choix politiques, économiques et même socioculturels. Peut être est-il temps de mettre en place une véritable politique de « déconnexion » au sens de Samir Amin[3].

2.2. La problématique de l'émergence de la Chine

C'est un secret de polichinelle que l'émergence de la Chine dérange. On peut observer cela par le fait qu'elle est diversement appréciée, puis par la contestation de l'ordre international actuel par le gouvernement de Pékin.

2.2.1. La contestation de l'ordre international par la Chine

Au moment où la République populaire de Chine est fondée le 1er octobre 1949, la guerre idéologique entre les Etats Unis d'Amérique et l'ex-Union Soviétique battait déjà son plein. La Chine en tant qu'acteur autonome des relations internationales débarque sur une scène internationale divisée en blocs antagonistes. Au nom de sa sécurité, elle

1. Phillips W. Shively, *Power and Choice: An Introduction to Political Science*. 4th edition, New York McGraw-Hill 1995.p.110.

2. Voir *Beijing Review*, 17 February-3 March 1997. p. 8.

3. Samir Amin, *La déconnexion*, Ed. La Découverte 1987.

va errer d'un bloc à l'autre, affrontant même pendant une brève période les deux superpuissances[1]. Ce n'est qu'au début des années 1980 que la Chine entreprend une veritable politique extérieure indépendante. L'ordre international qui après moultes mutations continue de régir le monde aujourd'hui, est celui mis en place au lendemain de la deuxième guerre mondiale par les vainqueurs. La Chine qui n'a pas été associée à la mise en place de ce nouvel ordre international, a toutes les raisons de le contester. Les retombées de la politique d'ouverture au monde extérieur ont conféré à la Chine un nouveau statut au sein de la communauté internationale. La Chine qui s'est hissée au rang de deuxième puissance économique mondiale, revendique aujourd'hui la prise en compte de ses intérêts dans la gestion des affaires internationales. L'histoire de ces cinq cents dernières années nous enseigne que sans économie puissante, il n'est pas de nation écoutée. C'est donc à juste titre que la Chine revendique un écho plus grand à sa voix dans les relations internationales, au nom de sa puissante économie.

Il faudrait préciser que la Chine tout en contestant l'ordre international établi, tout en critiquant l'unilatéralisme américain, ne cherche pas à mettre sur pied un ordre alternatif. Pour Pékin, mieux vaut l'ordre établi même américain, même peu favorable que le chaos, qui contrarierait ses projets de croissance et son ambition mondiale. La Chine tient à préserver l'accalmie internationale qui lui permet de consolider son émergence et de monter toujours plus en puissance. M. Kong Quan, porte-parole du ministère chinois des affaires étrangères explique clairement que « La Chine veut, avant tout, promouvoir un entourage stable, favorable au développement»[2]. Le gouvernement de Pékin milite pour un monde multipolaire. Ni l'unipolarité, ni la bipolarité ne sont du goût des chinois. Au fil du temps, la nouvelle génération au pouvoir a bâti une doctrine stratégique autour des « quatre non » énoncés par l'ex président Hu Jintao : « Non à l'hégémonisme, non à la politique de la force, non à une politique de blocs, non à la course aux armements » Il s'agit de « construire la confiance, atténuer les difficultés, développer la coopération, et éviter les confrontations »[3].

2.2.2. Une émergence diversement appréciée

Selon Fareed Zakaria, « les grandes puissances arrivent sur la scène internationale comme les grands divas des opéras, commandant et retenant l'attention de tous ceux qui sont dans le théâtre »[4]. L'émergence de la Chine suscite l'attention de toute la communauté internationale. Entre admiration, méfiance, et inquiétude, l'ascension de l'Empire du Milieu est diversement appréciée. Pour les pays africains, de nombreuses leçons

1. Voir: Bertrand ATEBA, *China's Superpowers Policy during the Cold War period.* Master's Degree Thesis submitted to the School of International Studies. Peking University, 1998; et Bertrand ATEBA, »Le Poids de la Chine comme acteur structurateur de la recomposition de l'échiquier international ». *Revue de Droit International, de Sciences Diplomatiques et Politiques.* Genève Suisse. Volume 87, No.2 Mai-Aout 2009.

2. Point de presse du 25 juillet 2005 au Ministère chinois des Affaires Etrangères.

3. Discours d'avril 2004, cité par Joshua Cooper Ramo, *The Beijing Consensus*, The Foreign Policy Centre, Londres, 2005.

4. Fareed Zakaria, rédacteur en chef de « Foreign Affairs ».

peuvent être tirées de l'émergence de la République Populaire de Chine. D'abord, l'esclavage et la colonisation ne sont pas une fatalité qui condamne à jamais ces pays au sous développement et à la misère. En Afrique, on prend souvent très vite de manière honteuse et servile l'esclavage et la colonisation comme raisons ou causes permettant de justifier le retard qu'accuse ce continent par rapport à d'autres.

Depuis les guerres de l'Opium et les Traités Inégaux de Nanking qui ont divisé le pays en zones d'influence étrangères, la Chine a connu elle aussi les ravages et les humiliations de l'occupation et de la colonisation. Entre l'impérialisme européen et le militarisme japonais, la Chine a connu ses moments sombres. Pourtant, elle a su tirer les leçons de son histoire tourmentée et œuvrer pour que les conditions qui ont mené à son occupation ne se reproduisent plus. En fondant le 1er octobre 1949 sur la place Tiananmen à Pékin la République Populaire de Chine, Mao signalait au monde entier, la naissance d'une Chine nouvelle. Cette Chine était affranchie de toute emprise extérieure, et était décidée à développer les armes avec lesquelles elle a été vaincue, à savoir la technologie moderne. En choisissant une voie originale de développement, et en refusant de se faire dicter sa conduite par le monde occidental, la Chine a montré la voie à l'Afrique dont on attend qu'elle marche sur ses foulées et amorce aussi son émergence. Dans ce continent aujourd'hui, où la recherche de l'émergence est l'air que l'on fredonne un peu partout, peut être que le soleil tant attendu se lèvera du côté de Pékin.

L'émergence de la Chine est vue d'un tout autre œil par ses voisins asiatiques et le monde occidental. Il ne s'agit plus ici d'admiration, mais de crainte, de suspicion et de méfiance. En effet, l'émergence de la Chine a fait naitre la psychose d'une menace que représente désormais ce pays en ascension. Les arguments foisonnent et varient d'un pays à l'autre[1]. Entre autres, la Chine représente une menace militaire en raison de la modernisation de ses moyens de défense. La Chine est un Etat rebelle qui refuse de se plier aux normes internationales. La Chine est une dictature qui viole les droits humains de ses citoyens. La Chine se laissera tenter comme toutes les autres grandes puissances par l'impérialisme et l'hégémonisme, lorsqu'elle aura consolidé son statut de grande puissance etc. Tous ces arguments sont discutables, mais nous tenions à les présenter pour prendre la mesure des réactions que l'émergence de la Chine suscite sur la scène internationale. La Chine pose un sérieux problème à l'Occident, en ce qu'elle rame à contre courant des idées et valeurs véhiculées par ce dernier. Comme pour se venger, le monde occidental saisit toute opportunité à lui offerte, pour diaboliser l'Empire du Milieu afin de l'isoler sur la scène internationale. Malgré les critiques, et les dénonciations, la Chine continue sa marche royale vers l'émergence, imperturbable face à un environnement international qui ne lui est pas toujours favorable. Cette émergence de l'Empire du Milieu parle aux africains.

1. Voir: Bertrand Ateba, *The Rise of China and International Security*. Ph.D. dissertation submitted to the School of International Studies, Peking University. June 2003.

Conclusion

La gouvernance mondiale peut servir la cause de l'émergence des pays qui sont encore en proie aux difficultés de toutes sortes, les empêchant de décoller économiquement. A quoi servent donc les principes de solidarité et de coopération internationales si au lieu d'aider les moins nantis, on interfère dans leurs affaires intérieures, leur imposant des orientations et des choix qui ne cadrent pas avec leur contexte ? Les instances de gouvernance mondiale que sont les institutions internationales à vocation régionale ou universelle gagneraient à réajuster leurs politiques si elles veulent résolument être ces appuis au décollage économique des pays tiers-mondistes. Lorsqu'on sait que les institutions internationales sont les arènes d'expression de la puissance des Etats et que ceux-ci n'agissent qu'en fonction de leurs seuls intérêts, il y a lieu d'être peu optimiste par rapport à une émergence des pays pauvres par la vertu de la gouvernance mondiale. Les pays candidats à l'émergence devraient plutôt se focaliser sur les moyens qu'ils peuvent mobiliser au plan national pour que l'émergence vienne affranchir l'humain de l'emprise de la misère et du mal être qui le caractérise dans les Etats qui n'ont pas encore connu un début réel d'industrialisation. A la mauvaise gouvernance mondiale, il faudrait désormais opposer la bonne gouvernance nationale et locale, c'est à ce prix que les pays pauvres atteindront cette émergence à laquelle tous les espoirs sont suspendus.

Bibliographie sélective

Ateba (B), "*The Decline of China's Communist Ideology*". Revue de Droit International, de Sciences Diplomatiques et Politiques. Volume 80, No.3 Août-Décembre 2002.

Aron (R), *Paix et Guerre entre les nations*, Paris Calmann-Lévy, 1962.

Carr (E. H.), *The twenty years crisis 1919-1939*. New York, Harper and Row 1964.

Faure (J), Prost (Y), *Relations Internationales: histoire, questions régionales, grands enjeux*. Ellipses 2008.

Mende (T), *De l'aide à la recolonisation*. Editions du Seuil 1975.

Merle (M), *Bilan des relations internationales contemporaines*. Economica 1995.

Nathan (A.J.) & Ross (R. S.), *The Great Wall and the Empty Fortress: China's Search for Security*. W.W.Norton & company. New York, 1997.

Roche (JJ), *Théories des relations internationales*. Montchrestien 1997.

Samir (A), *La déconnexion*. Editions la découverte 1987.

Senarclens (P), *La mondialisation : théories, enjeux et débats*. 2e édition. Armand Colin 2001.

Shively (P.W.), *Power and Choice: An Introduction to Political Science*. 4th edition, New York McGraw-Hill 1995.

Peyrefitte (A), *Quand la Chine s'éveillera, le monde tremblera*. Editions Fayard 1973.

Thucydide, *Histoire de la guerre du Péloponnèse*, Paris, Folio Classique 2000.

Young (O), *International Governance. Protecting the environment in a stateless society*. Ithaca. Cornell University Press 1994.

République démocratique du Congo aux éditions L'Harmattan

Dernières parutions

LE CONGO-KINSHASA, UNE RÉPUBLIQUE DÉMOCRATIQUE ?
N'Kupa Ntikala E-Benya Didier - Préface d'Edmond Jouve
Depuis son accession à l'indépendance, la République Démocratique du Congo a traversé différentes crises politiques qui laissaient croire à sa partition imminente. Face à toutes les menaces et agressions, le peuple a toujours néanmoins gardé son influence sur les politiques pour la sauvegarde de l'unité de ce majestueux pays dont la construction peine à venir. Voici une vision synthétique retraçant les faits annonciateurs de la naissance d'une forte nation qui s'affranchit des pactes secrets qui l'ont condamnée avant même son indépendance.
(Coll. Études africaines, série Politique, 55.00 euros, 670 p.)
ISBN : 978-2-343-08997-3, ISBN EBOOK : 978-2-14-001648-6

LES ÉLECTIONS EN RÉPUBLIQUE DÉMOCRATIQUE DU CONGO
Contribution à une pratique électorale efficiente et aisée
Kamufuenkete Luvumbu Pascal
Les élections s'imposent, jusqu'à preuve du contraire, comme la voie obligée pour garantir la démocratie. Hélas, en Afrique les élections sont souvent l'occasion de conflits violents et source de grosses dépenses publiques pour lesquelles l'aide financière internationale devient une nécessité. Comment conjurer cette situation qui est présentée comme une fatalité ? Ce livre offre des solutions rationnelles et raisonnables à emprunter en vue de la mise en place d'une législation et d'une pratique électorale efficiente et aisée.
(10.00 euros, 96 p.)
ISBN : 978-2-343-09669-8, ISBN EBOOK : 978-2-14-001596-0

LA JUSTICE TRANSITIONNELLE EN RDC
Quelle place pour la commission vérité et réconciliation ?
Mwamba Matanzi Godefroid
La justice transitionnelle est sans juges ni tribunaux ; mais grâce à elle, les sociétés démocratiques apprennent à affronter la part sombre de leur histoire. Ses objectifs ultimes consistent à faire la vérité sur les sales guerres menées par les princes contre leur population pour se donner une chance de reconstruire une société plus juste et plus équitable. L'idée de mettre en place une Commission Vérité Réconciliation procédait de la nature particulièrement délicate de la gestion de l'après-guerre en RDC en termes de paix. Et ainsi avoir une capacité de panser toutes sortes de blessures et de plaies dues aux affres d'un tel contexte.
(Harmattan RDC, 18.00 euros, 168 p., Illustré en noir et blanc)
ISBN : 978-2-343-09478-6, ISBN EBOOK : 978-2-14-001548-9

L'INVENTION DU CONGO CONTEMPORAIN
Traditions, mémoires, modernités (Tome 1)
Ndaywel E Nziem Isidore - Préface de Martin Kalulambi Pongo
On peut lire l'ouvrage du professeur Ndaywel de deux manières : comme un essai politique offrant une critique démystificatrice des formes contemporaines de gestion politique depuis l'indépendance, ou bien comme une étude d'histoire des procédures de réinvention du Congo dans sa « modernité » postcoloniale. Sites d'affrontement entre l'État et la société, le passé et la

mémoire conservent un pouvoir de construction de la réalité, du pouvoir et de la légitimité. Or parmi les grandes questions qu'affronte la société congolaise d'aujourd'hui figure celle de savoir comment améliorer l'art de gouverner et reconfigurer le rapport de l'individu à l'État.
(Harmattan RDC, 27.00 euros, 264 p.)
ISBN : 978-2-343-09498-4, ISBN EBOOK : 978-2-14-001559-5

L'INVENTION DU CONGO CONTEMPORAIN
Traditions, mémoires, modernités (Tome 2)
Ndaywel E Nziem Isidore
Les séquences de l'Histoire congolaise révélées dans ce livre enseignent à qui sait les interroger ce qu'il convient de faire. Elles sont l'école de l'homme politique qui est assuré d'y rencontrer, s'il le veut bien, le modèle à suivre ou encore l'exemple à éviter. Elles sont, pour tous les Congolais, un répertoire inépuisable, qu'ils ne consulteront jamais en pure perte.
(Harmattan RDC, 31.00 euros, 294 p.)
ISBN : 978-2-336-30583-7, ISBN EBOOK : 978-2-14-001560-1

LA THÉORIE GÉNÉRALE DU DROIT CONSTITUTIONNEL ET LES INSTITUTIONS POLITIQUES
Sous la Ire, IIe et IIIe République de la République démocratique du Congo
Makengo Nkutu Alphonse
Cet ouvrage s'intéresse dans une première partie aux éléments de base du droit constitutionnel, en abordant l'examen des concepts de base et la hiérarchie des règles de droit, l'État, la Constitution et le pouvoir politique, et dans une seconde partie il analyse les institutions politiques sous la Première, Deuxième et Troisième République en RD Congo.
(Coll. Études africaines, 25.50 euros, 250 p.)
ISBN : 978-2-343-09617-9, ISBN EBOOK : 978-2-14-001354-6

L'ÉLECTRIFICATION TOTALE DE LA RDC À L'HORIZON 2060
Mwemena Kamabwe Nestor - Préface du Professeur Ilunga Ilunkamba
L'électrification totale de la RDC est une œuvre de très grande envergure. Elle exige des moyens financiers, techniques et légaux gigantesques. Ni la SNEL, qui a été transformée en société commerciale, ni les privés qui sont des sociétés à but lucratif ne sont en mesure de réaliser cette électrification dont la rentabilité financière n'est pas évidente. Pour répondre aux besoins d'électrification totale du pays, il est indispensable de définir davantage les standards de production, de transport, de distribution et de commercialisation.
(Harmattan RDC, 45.00 euros, 446 p., Illustré en noir et blanc)
ISBN : 978-2-343-08309-4, ISBN EBOOK : 978-2-14-000826-9

LA PROTECTION DES DROITS DE L'HOMME PAR LE JUGE CONSTITUTIONNEL CONGOLAIS
Analyse critique et jurisprudence (2003-2013)
Wetsh'Okonda Koso Marcel - Préface de Jean-Louis Esambo Kangashe
Depuis son institution en 1968, la Cour suprême de justice a exercé les attributions de juge constitutionnel, y compris celles de juge des libertés. L'objet de ce livre consiste à dresser le bilan, à la fois quantitatif et qualitatif, de cette juridiction en matière de protection de ces dernières. La première partie passe en revue les attributions de la Cour ainsi que son organisation et son fonctionnement et la seconde partie s'intéresse à sa jurisprudence en matière de protection des droits de l'Homme.
(Coll. Notes de cours, 30.00 euros, 286 p.)
ISBN : 978-2-343-08677-4, ISBN EBOOK : 978-2-14-001588-5

COMMUNICATION DES ENTREPRISES COMMERCIALES EN RÉPUBLIQUE DÉMOCRATIQUE DU CONGO
Pombo Ngunza Dyna Albert - Préface de Mwayila Tshiyembe
Après un constat de défaillance de la pratique de la communication institutionnelle en RDC, l'auteur a assigné un double objectif à cet ouvrage : plaider et sensibiliser les dirigeants

des institutions commerciales congolaises sur la nécessité de pratiquer la communication institutionnelle afin de créer, soigner et/ou entretenir une bonne image de leur institution. Le deuxième objectif est de venir en aide aux dirigeants qui voudraient la pratiquer, en leur donnant un schéma pratique et clair à suivre.
(Coll. Géopolitique mondiale, 15.00 euros, 136 p.)
ISBN : 978-2-343-07640-9, ISBN EBOOK : 978-2-14-001472-7

LES EXONÉRATIONS FISCALES DES INVESTISSEMENTS EN RDC
Kabanda Matanda Boniface
La concurrence fiscale comme mesure incitative ou attractive des investissements directs étrangers s'est révélée inefficace. Cette leçon a servi d'exemple à l'État Indépendant du Congo et à la Colonie Congo-Belge qui limitèrent la défiscalisation aux seuls grands projets de développement orientés dans la logique de l'économie mixte. Dès lors, nous voilà dans l'institutionnalisation de l'injustice fiscale qui nous fait assister impuissants à la création simultanée de l'enfer fiscal, du purgatoire fiscal et du paradis fiscal en RDC. Au total les investissements directs étrangers en appellent plutôt à la globalité des politiques publiques et privées.
(Harmattan RDC, 55.00 euros, 830 p.)
ISBN : 978-2-343-09469-4, ISBN EBOOK : 978-2-14-001585-4

LE DÉVELOPPEMENT DU KATANGA MÉRIDIONAL
Tambwe Nyumbaiza, Nkulu Kasongo, Kya Ghoanys Kitaba, Mwanachilongwe Kunkuzya, Mpyana Kaimbi, Bukasa Kayiba
Les réflexions contenues dans cet ouvrage nous donnent assez de lumière sur le Katanga méridional, les actions de développement entreprises, les acteurs en présence, mais aussi et surtout le dynamisme de la population locale dans sa quête d'améliorer les conditions d'existence. En dépit de l'augmentation en nombre des entreprises minières dans cette partie de la République Démocratique du Congo, sa population demeure pauvre dans l'ensemble.
(Coll. Études africaines, 20.50 euros, 212 p.)
ISBN : 978-2-343-06314-0, ISBN EBOOK : 978-2-336-39799-3

LE CONGO BELGE DANS LA PREMIÈRE GUERRE MONDIALE (1914-1918)
Ndaywel E Nziem Isidore, Mabiala Mantuba-Ngoma Pamphile
L'histoire congolaise de la Première Guerre mondiale existe. Les contributions, belges et congolaises, qui font l'objet de ce livre l'affirment et le démontrent. Dès que la Belgique, la métropole du Congo, avait vécu la violation de sa neutralité par l'Allemagne, le Congo belge n'est pas resté longtemps dans le doute. La guerre exclusivement européenne devint une guerre mondiale, impliquant en Afrique les colonies allemandes et celles des alliés.
(Coll. Harmattan RDC, 37.00 euros, 358 p.)
ISBN : 978-2-343-07554-9, ISBN EBOOK : 978-2-336-39906-5

GUERRE ET PAIX: LEÇONS DE L'INTERVENTION DE L'ONU EN RÉPUBLIQUE DÉMOCRATIQUE DU CONGO
Olombi Jean-Claude
L'objet principal de cet ouvrage est de mesurer et de comprendre les causes de la crise en RDC, depuis son accession à l'indépendance, le 30 juin 1960, jusqu'à nos jours et le rôle que joue l'ONU dans ce pays, depuis plus d'une décennie. L'auteur analyse les acquis en matière de sécurité et les actions à mener en matière de gouvernance démocratique et de stabilisation du pays.
(Coll. Études africaines, 23.00 euros, 232 p.)
ISBN : 978-2-343-06177-1, ISBN EBOOK : 978-2-336-39790-0

SÉRAPHIN NGONDO A PITSCHANDENGE
Vie et œuvres d'un professeur émérite
Mandjwandju Mabele Odon
Préface de Léon de Saint Moulin, s.j.
Ce livre est une biographie sur Séraphin Ngondo A Pitschandenge, premier démographe congolais, qui a consacré son existence à l'enseignement et à la recherche au sein de l'Université

congolaise. Il présente le modèle d'un professeur d'université qui aura cherché à combiner sa personnalité scientifique avec ses devoirs de citoyen. Comment dès lors rester scientifique tout en étant dans les méandres de la politique ?
(Coll. Harmattan RDC, 16.50 euros, 154 p.)
ISBN : 978-2-343-08037-6, ISBN EBOOK : 978-2-336-39908-9

KABILA ET LE RÉVEIL DU GÉANT
Le regard des uns et des autres
Sous la direction de Lambert Mende Omalanga
Préface de Matata Ponyo Mapon
Produit par un groupe de témoins de l'histoire immédiate de la République démocratique du Congo constitué par le ministère de la Communication et des Médias, ce livre est une compilation de mises au point et de contre-analyses, reflétant la vision de l'exécutif congolais. C'est également l'occasion d'un compte rendu à la nation et au monde de l'action de stabilisation et de normalisation en cours dans ce pays. Il y est montré que la RDC devient de plus en plus une *success story* grâce à Joseph Kabila et son gouvernement.
(29.00 euros, 264 p., Illustré en couleur, Quadrichromie)
ISBN : 978-2-343-07440-5, ISBN EBOOK : 978-2-336-39537-1

LES NOUVELLES PROVINCES EN RÉPUBLIQUE DÉMOCRATIQUE DU CONGO
État de la question
Muzito Adolphe - Tribunes d'Adolphe Muzito
Adolphe Muzito, ancien Premier ministre de la RDC, évoque dans huit tribunes le problème du découpage territorial prôné par la Constitution du 18 février 2006 et le passage de 11 à 26 provinces. Il y sonne l'alarme sur la « provincialisation » à outrance du pays, qui semble se faire dans la précipitation et qui arrive à un mauvais moment, juste quelques mois avant l'organisation d'une multitude d'élections (locales, législatives et présidentielle). L'ouvrage rassemble ces tribunes.
(Coll. Dossiers, Études et Documents, 18.00 euros, 182 p.)
ISBN : 978-2-343-07720-8, ISBN EBOOK : 978-2-336-39502-9

INSTALLATION DE NOUVELLES PROVINCES EN RDC
Défis et contraintes
Muzito Adolphe
Pour lutter contre la centralisation et créer de nouveaux centres d'impulsion, le nombre de provinces est passé de 11 à 26 en RDC L'auteur note que, sur les 26 nouvelles provinces à installer, 20 ne sont pas en mesure de couvrir les dépenses contraignantes liées à leur fonctionnement. Il explore quelques pistes d'installation effective et heureuse de ces provinces, consistant à lever obstacles et difficultés de tout ordre. (Fascicule broché.)
(Coll. Dossiers, Études et Documents, 6.00 euros, 52 p.)
ISBN : 978-2-343-07711-6, ISBN EBOOK : 978-2-336-39495-4

LA RÉPUBLIQUE DÉMOCRATIQUE DU CONGO : UN ÉTAT SANS PROVINCES (1re tribune)
Muzito Adolphe
L'auteur analyse la situation de la RDC 10 ans après le programme de décentralisation qui est pour lui un demi-échec. Faute de volonté et de vision politique, de culture démocratique, les nouvelles provinces sont restées des coquilles vides sans pouvoir et sans ressources. Ce passage de 11 à 26 provinces est-il alors opportun ? (Fascicule broché.)
(Coll. Dossiers, Études et Documents, 4.00 euros, 26 p.)
ISBN : 978-2-343-07712-3, ISBN EBOOK : 978-2-336-39494-7

L'HARMATTAN ITALIA
Via Degli Artisti 15; 10124 Torino
harmattan.italia@gmail.com

L'HARMATTAN HONGRIE
Könyvesbolt ; Kossuth L. u. 14-16
1053 Budapest

L'HARMATTAN KINSHASA
185, avenue Nyangwe
Commune de Lingwala
Kinshasa, R.D. Congo
(00243) 998697603 ou (00243) 999229662

L'HARMATTAN CONGO
67, av. E. P. Lumumba
Bât. – Congo Pharmacie (Bib. Nat.)
BP2874 Brazzaville
harmattan.congo@yahoo.fr

L'HARMATTAN GUINÉE
Almamya Rue KA 028, en face
du restaurant Le Cèdre
OKB agency BP 3470 Conakry
(00224) 657 20 85 08 / 664 28 91 96
harmattanguinee@yahoo.fr

L'HARMATTAN MALI
Rue 73, Porte 536, Niamakoro,
Cité Unicef, Bamako
Tél. 00 (223) 20205724 / +(223) 76378082
poudiougopaul@yahoo.fr
pp.harmattan@gmail.com

L'HARMATTAN CAMEROUN
BP 11486
Face à la SNI, immeuble Don Bosco
Yaoundé
(00237) 99 76 61 66
harmattancam@yahoo.fr

L'HARMATTAN CÔTE D'IVOIRE
Résidence Karl / cité des arts
Abidjan-Cocody 03 BP 1588 Abidjan 03
(00225) 05 77 87 31
etien_nda@yahoo.fr

L'HARMATTAN BURKINA
Penou Achille Some
Ouagadougou
(+226) 70 26 88 27

L'HARMATTAN SÉNÉGAL
10 VDN en face Mermoz, après le pont de Fann
BP 45034 Dakar Fann
33 825 98 58 / 33 860 9858
senharmattan@gmail.com / senlibraire@gmail.com
www.harmattansenegal.com

L'HARMATTAN BÉNIN
ISOR-BENIN
01 BP 359 COTONOU-RP
Quartier Gbèdjromèdé,
Rue Agbélenco, Lot 1247 I
Tél : 00 229 21 32 53 79
christian_dablaka123@yahoo.fr

Achevé d'imprimer par Corlet Numérique - 14110 Condé-sur-Noireau
N° d'Imprimeur : 133596 - Dépôt légal : novembre 2016 - *Imprimé en France*

www.ingramcontent.com/pod-product-compliance
Lightning Source LLC
LaVergne TN
LVHW010023081026
849535LV00016B/2987